Gratuity

Gratuity

A Contextual Understanding of Tipping Norms from the Perspective of Tipped Employees

RICHARD SELTZER
HOLONA LEANNE OCHS

LEXINGTON BOOKS
A division of
ROWMAN & LITTLEFIELD PUBLISHERS, INC.
Lanham • Boulder • New York • Toronto • Plymouth, UK

Published by Lexington Books
A division of Rowman & Littlefield Publishers, Inc.
A wholly owned subsidiary of The Rowman & Littlefield Publishing Group, Inc.
4501 Forbes Boulevard, Suite 200, Lanham, Maryland 20706
http://www.lexingtonbooks.com

Estover Road, Plymouth PL6 7PY, United Kingdom

Copyright © 2010 by Lexington Books

All rights reserved. No part of this book may be reproduced in any form or by any electronic or mechanical means, including information storage and retrieval systems, without written permission from the publisher, except by a reviewer who may quote passages in a review.

British Library Cataloguing in Publication Information Available

Library of Congress Cataloging-in-Publication Data

Seltzer, Richard, Ph. D.
  Gratuity : a contextual understanding of tipping norms from the perspective of tipped employees / Richard Seltzer, Holona LeAnne Ochs.
    p. cm.
  Includes bibliographical references.
  ISBN 978-0-7391-4422-0 (alk. paper) — ISBN 978-0-7391-4423-7 (pbk. : alk. paper) — ISBN 978-0-7391-4424-4 (ebook)
  1. Tipping. I. Ochs, Holona LeAnne. II. Title.
  HD4928.T5S45 2010
  331.2'166—dc22   2010009365

∞™ The paper used in this publication meets the minimum requirements of American National Standard for Information Sciences—Permanence of Paper for Printed Library Materials, ANSI/NISO Z39.48-1992.

Printed in the United States of America

Contents

Preface Richard Seltzer	vii
Acknowledgments	xiii
Introduction	xv

PART 1 **Restaurants** 1

1	Restaurant Chains	5
2	Family Eateries	17
3	Upscale Dining	25
4	Bussers and Runners	33
5	Bartenders, Cocktail Servers, and Bar-Backs	39
6	Multi-Function Staff	49
7	Specialty Jobs	73
8	Tip Jars	81

PART 2 **Services** 87

9	Household Services	89
10	Deliveries	105
11	Loading and Carting	119
12	Cars	127
13	Animals	143

14	Cosmetology	149
15	Teachers	163
16	Blue Collar Workers	169
17	Officiants	179
18	Medical Care	183
19	Miscellaneous	187
PART 3	**Entertainment**	193
20	Family Entertainment	195
21	Adult Entertainment	207
22	Musicians	221
23	Sports	231
24	Ushers and Sports Vendors	243
Conclusions		249
References		269
Index		275
About the Authors		277

Preface

RICHARD SELTZER

The last time I remember making any money from a tip was in 1964, as a 13-year-old golf caddy at a country club. I was paid $4 for lugging two bags for nine holes and occasionally was tipped an extra dollar by the same older women who regularly hired me. A year later, I worked for $1.15 an hour in the tobacco fields of Connecticut where I weeded, picked, and hung tobacco in the barns. After that summer, vacation jobs mostly involved construction work. Later on, I worked full-time for a landscaping company and eventually earned my living at a lawn sprinkler outfit. Installing home systems, sometimes in hot weather, customers would on occasion give me a soda—the closest I ever came to a tip.

Once I started teaching, I was paid a salary instead of an hourly wage. I started consulting several years later and billed by the hour to supplement my teaching salary. All these years, I have never been given one tip as a teacher or consultant, although in teaching we do get (though not often enough) salary increases. These are often retroactive and the retroactive part is considered by some to be a bonus—although it is not. I do sometimes, however, receive gifts from students. As I look around my office, I notice prayer beads, a small wooden head from Africa, a coffee cup, a Pokemon-type fuzzy from Japan, and a variety of other trinkets. When I smoked back in 1981, a student once offered me a carton of Camels. I considered this close to a bribe, and I politely returned the gift.

The first time I seriously thought about tipping was when I spent ten days in Egypt. I was somewhat offended by the practice of baksheesh. It seemed like everyone had a hand out looking for money. I would have been delighted if tips were simply automatically added to every bill. I was very uncomfortable because I didn't know the protocol. Who gets baksheesh and how much do they get? On my seventh day in Egypt, I was somewhat astounded when I offered baksheesh to an interpreter, and he refused to take it. Why did he refuse? The other two interpreters we had used previously had happily taken baksheesh.

So, how did I get interested in tips and commissions? Most of my research is about race relations and jury behavior. I guess I just got curious. One night, my wife and I had dinner at a restaurant with another couple. We asked that the check be evenly divided into two credit cards. When it came time to fill in the tip, I had a discussion with the other person who was paying: "How much should we leave?" He said we only should tip 18% on the food portion of the bill and not to tip on the liquor portion. I had never thought about this before, and it didn't seem right to me. What's the proper tip and how should we figure it out? If we did not tip for liquor then how did the bartender get tipped? Did the server split the tip with the bartender? I didn't have a clue.

Out to dinner another night, we got to talking with our waitress. That's when I first heard about the tip out. I was surprised. I didn't know that most servers give a portion of their tips to the other staff, but I asked myself, "Who's included in the tip out?" Does the tip out involve bussers, runners, bartenders, managers, cooks, and hostesses? Who makes the decision about who shares in the tips, and what is the proper amount of the split? Eventually, I found that I had stumbled upon several interrelated questions:

1. How much money do servers make from tips, and how does this compare with their hourly wage?
2. What is the typical amount that people tip?
3. What factors affect the amount of the tip: the type of restaurant, time of day, characteristics of the server (gender, race, attitude), or characteristics of the customer (gender, race, age, class)?
4. How do servers share their tips with others in the restaurant? With whom do they share the tips? How much do they give each one? How are these decisions made?

PREFACE

ix

Once I began to ask questions about tipping for servers it was an easy jump to other workers. The person who cuts my hair owns the hair salon. The 15 minutes it took to get my hair cut provided ample time to discuss the protocols of tipping and tip outs. Over half-a-dozen haircuts, I learned that the process is not clear-cut.

At same the time that I began to get curious about tips, my family moved to a new home. We sold a house and bought another one. I was aghast that the realtor wanted 6% of the sale price on the old house. Six percent of $400,000 seemed like a lot of money ($24,000). I really had no idea how the commission structure worked in real estate. I learned that if the buyer also had a realtor, the two realtors would split the 6%. If I found a buyer, I would only have to fork over 4%. If the buyer walked in without his or her own realtor during an open house, our realtor could keep the full 6%. Then, I got curious. Does it always work the same way? Everywhere? Everytime? At an open house one day, a colleague substituted for our realtor. How was the stand-in realtor compensated?

Furthermore, if the realtor got 3%, did the realtor I was working with get to keep it all? How much went back to the real estate agency? Did she actually work for the agency, or was she an independent contractor? The house was advertised in at least three different newspapers. Who paid for this? This experience with my house got me thinking about how commissions and bonuses fit together with tips. Like tipping, calculating the amount of commissions and bonuses is not obvious. Who gets commissions and bonuses? How much do they get? And how are they split?

I use the term nonstandard compensation to group together tips, commissions, and bonuses. If you don't get a tip, a commission, or a bonus, you should know how much you will earn hourly or by the pay period. This book deals specifically with tips, and there is a companion volume that takes a similar approach to understanding commissions. Much of this project really arises from my curiosity of how people get paid when the amount of compensation is not straightforward.

My wife says that I am too nosy, but finding out about tips, commissions, and bonuses is important in its own right. However, an added benefit of this research is that people talk a lot about their jobs: the nature of their work; whether they like their job or not; why they have a positive or negative attitude toward their work; what they think of their coworkers, managers, and customers?

Detailed notes were taken during the interviews, and the respondents' stories are essentially presented in their own voice. This approach is intended to provide authenticity. More importantly, narratives tell an interesting story that reveals insights that no other method adequately conveys. A number of the respondents commented on customer characteristics such as race, gender, age, sexual orientation, and so forth. In those cases, the relevant characteristics of the respondent were included in the narrative, as well as when the interviewer knew the demographic characteristics of the respondent, to provide the greatest degree of clarity of context.

This book is divided into 3 broad sections and 22 subsections: (1) restaurants; (2) services; and (3) entertainment. Approximately 450 people across 600 different jobs were interviewed. Obviously, we cannot include all 600 narratives in this book or its companion. Readers who wish to read the archived essays can send an email to rseltzer@howard.edu. There are some situations in which we reference an archived narrative and we note this by stating the essay is not included.

It was somewhat difficult to create a classification scheme and sometimes difficult to decide where some interviews should be placed. Should people who groom animals have their own chapter or should they be placed with personal care workers such as hair stylists? Should a tennis pro at a club, who has a complex commission structure, be placed in the sports section or in the companion volume on commissions? There are many, many examples of these issues. In the end, we did what we thought made the most sense and hope that the reader will enjoy reading the essays regardless of how we classified them.

Approximately 15% of respondents have more than one job. For most of these respondents (when the jobs were very different), information about each job is placed in the relevant chapter. For example, if someone worked in a restaurant and later worked as a ski instructor, their stories appear in two different sections. Many people who work in restaurants have worked in more than one restaurant or have worked in multiple positions within one restaurant. These restaurant workers were included in their own "multi" restaurant chapter. There are a few other situations where disparate narratives were kept together (e.g., a person who received tips from a tip jar at a restaurant and also delivers for the same restaurant and a person who baby sits and also works in a pre-school). The goal is to facilitate the readability.

At the beginning of most chapters, an accounting of the number of people who worked in the relevant occupations according to the U.S. Census Bureau and their average annual earnings[1] based upon working 50 weeks per year. I find it interesting to see how many people work in the kinds of jobs discussed, how much they officially earn, and how the Census Bureau tries to categorize different types of occupations.

NOTE

1. Census 2000, PHC-T-33. Earnings Distribution of U.S. Year-Round Full-Time Workers by Occupation: 1999.

Acknowledgments

We are grateful to many people who helped bring this book to fruition. The 450 people who were interviewed deserve the most thanks. They gave us their time, and they spoke from the heart. Many respondents also helped by referring additional people to be interviewed. Our families and friends gave us a lot of support (as well as names of people to interview). Seltzer's immediate family (Grace, Mike, and Mat) developed tolerance for his conducting interviews at every opportunity: restaurants, parking lots, taxi rides, and so on. The patience and understanding of our family and friends has been invaluable. Ochs would not be able to do her work without the support of her family (Kuroki, Rita, Frank, and Mike). Many friends and extended family were also extraordinarily helpful in finding people to be interviewed. Several colleagues read all or part of the manuscript and gave us many thoughtful suggestions. In particular, we thank Dave Heffernan, Yolanda Curtis, Lisa Brown, Gary Roth, Anne Lopes, and Hillary Watts Bird. The anonymous reviewer from Lexington Books gave us pages of useful feedback, for which we are profoundly grateful. In addition, our editors at Lexington Books, Joseph Parry and Tawnya Zengierski, were very helpful throughout this process.

Introduction

A tip is a price set almost entirely by a customer, less connected to demand than to social code. It is not obligatory, and the amount of the tip is not determined in advance. Tips are provided following the provision of services and supposedly correspond with the customer's satisfaction. Payments made by customers prior to service are inducement tips; otherwise known as a bribe or illicit advance to assure a certain service or level of service (Rose-Ackerman 1998). However, the difference between a tip and an inducement or bribe can be quite minimal, and even when the tip is paid following service, it may still be considered a form of extortion as economic theories recognize only the price as the legitimate value of a given product or service. The conventional wisdom is that tips represent a reward for quality service and may reduce uncomfortable feelings of inequality. Tippers may conform to norms of tipping for any number of reasons or goals, but the act of tipping also provides a mechanism by which tippers may attempt to promote a certain social status or seek approval.

Tips represent a form of work remuneration that varies across time and space. The practice seems arbitrary in many ways. Why do we tip bartenders but not doctors? In this case, we actually tip for a service that we do not need (at least not in the way that we need medical care) and one that may in fact be self-destructive—at least for some. The fact that we do not tip for those services that are integral to our survival might undermine the rational notions that tipping is a self-interested act to facilitate quality service. Moreover, the strictest economic logic indicates that a voluntary payment following the provision of service that extends beyond the service's contracted cost should not exist. Yet, the practice of tipping does indeed exist and varies more in accordance with culture than economics.

In fact, the variation in habits and customs associated with tipping has been the subject of numerous guidebooks for travelers. In the United States, tipping remains one of our most controversial, confusing, and highly variable norms. Americans are apparently the world's most lavish tippers, but 40% report that they in fact loathe the custom (see Lynn and McCall 2000). The tipping institution is estimated to be about a $16 billion dollar industry in the United States. Customers in U.S. restaurants tip between 8–37% for service deemed "excellent"; although the correlations between the tip and quality of service is relatively weak (Lynn and McCall 2000). It is interesting to note the lavish tipping practices of Americans. If indeed tips are a means by which people come to reduce uncomfortable feelings associated with inequality, the vast and growing inequality in the United States might make one consider some intriguing questions. Do tips rise with rising inequality? Are tipping practices more lavish in countries with higher levels of inequality? Do lavish tips in fact decrease uncomfortable feelings associated with inequality? Do tipping customs reinforce inequality by establishing social status or militate against inequality by serving a redistributive function?

A number of noteworthy national differences in tipping exist. U.S. customers tip more than 30 different service professions, but Icelandic customers do not tip service professionals (Star 1988). Alternatively, tipping is insulting in Japan and illegal in Vietnam. Porters may be customarily tipped between 50 cents to one dollar per bag. However, in some countries porters may not be tipped at all, and in other countries, the tip may be as high as two dollars per bag. Tips for taxi drivers may not be customary or may be expected only when a special service is provided. When tips are the standard practice, they may vary from only 50 cents or simply rounding up the amount of the fare to upwards of 15%. Table 1 outlines some of the average variation in tipping norms across countries based on the information for travelers provided by Magellan's Travel Advice.

Some researchers have attributed these differences to what they call national values.[1] This line of research contends that tipping customs may be explained at least in part by differences along four value dimensions: (1) power distance; (2) uncertainty avoidance; (3) individualism; and (4) masculinity. Power distance is a concept that reflects a nation's acceptance of power and status

Table 1. National Tipping Norms

Country	Restaurants	Porters	Taxis
Argentina	No more than 10%	$1	Round up fare or small discretionary tip
Armenia	10%	50 cents–$1 per bag	None
Australia	10% for fine dining only	$2 per bag	Round Up
Austria	5% above service charge	$1–$2 per bag	Round Up
Azerbaijan	10%	50 cents–$1 per bag	None
Bahamas	10%	$1 per bag	10%
Bahrain	10%	$1–$2 per bag	10%
Belgium	10% if no service charge	$1 per bag	Round Up
Bolivia	10%	75 cents per bag	10%
Brazil	10–15%	$1 per bag	10%
Brunei	None	None	None
Bulgaria	10%	$1 per bag	Round Up
Canada	15%	$1–$2 per bag	10%
Cayman Isles	15% unless there is already a service charge	$1 per bag	10%
Chile	10% on top of the service charge	$1 per bag	None
China	3% only in large cities	$1–$2 total	None
Colombia	10%	75 cents per bag	None
Costa Rica	None	$1 per bag	10%
Cuba	$1 for special service	$1 for special service	$1 for special service
Czech Rep	5–10%	$1 per bag	Round Up
Denmark	None	$1 per bag	Round Up
Ecuador	10% unless there is already a service charge	75 cents per bag	None
Egypt	5–10% + service charge	$1 per bag	Round Up
England	10% if no service charge	$1 per bag	15%
Fiji	None	None	Round Up
Finland	10% if no service charge	$1 per bag	Round Up
France	5–10%	$1 per bag	Round Up
Germany	5–10%	$1 per bag	Round Up
Greece	5–10% in addition to service charge	$1 per bag	Round Up
Guatemala	10% in addition to service charge	$1 per bag	10%
Holland	5–10%	$1 per bag	Round Up
Hong Kong	10% in addition to service charge	$1 per bag	Round Up
Hungary	10% unless there is already a service charge	None	Round Up

(continued)

Table 1. (*continued*)

Country	Restaurants	Porters	Taxis
Iceland	10% unless there is already a service charge	$1 per bag	Round Up
India	10% unless there is already a service charge	$1 per bag	Round Up
Indonesia	10%	50 cents total	Round Up
Ireland	10–15%	$1 per bag	Round Up
Israel	12–15% unless there is already a service charge	$1 per bag	12–15%
Italy	10% in addition to service charge	$1 per bag	Round Up
Japan	Tipping is perceived as insulting	None	None
Kenya	5% if no service charge	50 cents per bag	None
Luxembourg	5–10%	$1 per bag	Round Up
Macao	10% in addition to service charge	$1 per bag	Round Up
Madagascar	10%	50 cents per bag	Round Up
Malaysia	None	None	None
Mexico	10–15%	$1	50 cents
Morocco	Leave loose change	50 cents per bag	Round Up
New Zealand	None	None	None
Nicaragua	10% for special service	$1 per bag	10%
Norway	10% if no service charge	$1 per bag	Round Up
Oman	None	None	None
Paraguay	10%	75 cents per bag	10%
Peru	Up to 10% for special service	75 cents per bag	None
Philippines	10%	50 cents–$1 per bag	Round Up
Poland	10%	$1 per bag	Round Up
Portugal	10–15% unless there is already a service charge	$1 per bag	Round Up
Romania	Round Up	$1 per bag	Round Up
Russia	10–15%	$1 per bag	Round Up
Samoa	None	None	None
Saudi Arabia	10–15%	$1–$2 per bag	10%
Scotland	10–15% unless there is already a service charge	$1 per bag	Round Up
Singapore	None	None	None
South Africa	10% unless there is already a service charge	50 cents total	10%
South Korea	None	None	None
Spain	7–10% in addition to service charge	$1 per bag	10%

Country	Restaurants	Porters	Taxis
Sweden	10% unless there is already a service charge	$1 per bag	Round Up
Switzerland	Round up	$1 per bag	Round Up
Taiwan	10% unless there is already a service charge	$1 per bag	None
Tanzania	10%	None	None
Thailand	None	None	None
Turkey	Round Up	$1 per bag	Round Up
Ukraine	10%	$1 per bag	Round Up
United Arab Emirates	None	None	None
United States	15–20%	$1–$2 per bag	10–15%
Venezuela	10%	75 cents per bag	10%
Vietnam	None	None	None
Wales	10% unless there is already a service charge	$1 per bag	10%

SOURCE: Magellan's Travel Advice Worldwide Tipping Guide. Available online at http://www.magellans.com/store/article/367.

inequity. Because tipping gives customers power over servers, it is expected that high power distance is associated with a relatively high acceptance of tipping. The concept of uncertainty avoidance represents the extent to which citizens of a nation are uncomfortable with uncertainty. The emphasis on the individual is negatively associated with the national acceptance of tipping as tipping is considered a contribution to a public good. And, the national commitment to what are defined as the traditionally masculine values of achievement, status, and materialism are inconsistently linked to the national acceptance of tipping. One striking feature of this perspective when applied to the American case is the relationship between inequality and tipping norms. The United States is a highly individualistic society in which inequality is extremely high. Many Americans claim to be outraged by the extent of inequality in the United States. At the same time, Americans are lavish tippers who generally hate the practice. If Americans truly are outraged or uncomfortable with inequality in the United States, why does the actual behavior of Americans reflect a desire to exercise power over servers when tips are a means by which some demonstrate social status? Or, do Americans use tips to redistribute wealth? If tips serve a redistributive function, why would Americans support tips more than living wages (broadly)? Perhaps widespread disagreement on issues of wealth and status over time makes tipping the most feasible of options in the United States. In other words, it is a means by which people can demonstrate social status and redistribute wealth. One has to wonder though, why inequality continues to increase in the country with the most lavish tipping practices if tipping actually serves a redistributive function.

There are a number of arguments both for and against the practice of tipping. Those who oppose tipping cite the following reasons:

- Tipping creates disequilibrium among citizens in a democratic society.
- Tipping distorts economic incentives and denies workers fundamental rights.
- Tipping does not protect customers from poor quality service.
- Tipping interferes with the relations between the employee and employer by creating an alliance between the customer and employer to monitor employees.
- Tips are only weakly associated with the service provided.
- Tips allow for tax evasion.
- Tips are often disbursed by those who are not responsible for payment. For example, business professionals often use corporate accounts to pay for business lunches, including tips, paid for by the firm.
- Tips inhibit genuine social relationships by fostering relationships based on economic concerns rather than humanistic concerns.
- Tipping increases income uncertainty and role conflict for servers.
- Many of the perceived collective benefits of tipping are not empirically supported.
- Some people perceive tipping as demeaning or insulting.
- Tipping is an unwanted custom that puts undue social pressure on people to part with money that they would rather not part with to satisfy or conform to the prevailing norm.

Those in favor of tipping cite the following:

- The server is more likely to be responsive to the customer's needs if the tip is based on the service quality.
- Motivated servers can affect their own wages.
- Tipping may result in a reduction in guilt and anxiety associated with inequality.
- Tipping may result in an increase in the consumer's social status and recognition.

- Tipping may result in an increase in the self-perceived freedom of customers in that customers are free to determine the tip amount.
- Tipping may result in an increase in the self-perceived freedom of servers in that they may believe that they can positively affect their wages directly and immediately.
- Consumers may experience psychological rewards from the feeling that they are contributing to the well-being of servers.

Overall, the theoretical and empirical research gives no consistent indication as to whether or not the benefits of tipping outweigh the costs.[2] Moreover, the proponents, opponents, and researchers have generally excluded the perspective of those who receive tips in their analysis and conclusions regarding the merits of the system of tipping. This study is not an attempt to address the value of tipping norms. This study is intended to contribute to our understanding of people's lived experience with norms broadly and to provide insight regarding a perspective on tipping that has largely been ignored. This book uses the stories told by tipped employees to demonstrate that management has a considerable degree of power to determine the tone of the experiences of tipped employees and set the atmosphere experienced by customers by extending trust to employees. This affords them greater control over the work environment, allowing for more effectual emotion management and more credit to give customers. These narratives unveil the complexities of management quality and provide numerous issues for critical reflection regarding the broader political and socio-economic context.

THEORY

The theory of social norms assumes that norms are fundamental to understanding human behavior (Aronson 2003). Norms construct the social order in a number of ways, including but not limited to determining meaning, reflecting value, defining property rights, and shaping our understanding of the rights, duties, and obligations of human interaction (Hume [1739] 1978). Behavioral norms describe what the majority of people in a social context do or how the majority behaves in a given circumstance; whereas, attitudinal norms describe what the majority of people in a social context believe about how others should act (Bicchieri 2006). Norms affect the expectations of individuals in a social context and set standards that allow people to predict the likely behavior of others in a given circumstance. Once a customary pattern of behavior becomes a rule or standard, conformity to the social norm is "preferred" (to the suboptimal or unpredictable outcome) when the expectation is that others are also likely to conform (Lewis 1969). Norms are maintained through social interaction and enforced through the hierarchy of organizations.

Some degree of conformity is required for the adequate functioning of any society. There are two major types of conformity (Mann 1969): (1) normative and (2) informational. Normative conformity is essentially yielding to group pressure because a person wants to fit in or be perceived of as appropriate. Informational conformity occurs when a person lacks knowledge of a given context and looks to the behavior of others for guidance. Norms are also associated with one's status in a specific situation, and conformity to social norms and role-specific expectations maintain the status quo (Zimbardo and Lieppe 1991). This social hierarchy is reinforced by the relationship between authority and obedience. The Milgram Experiments demonstrate that obedience (or in some cases conformity) is not confined to particular social groups or "types" of people or even to types of situations (Milgram 1965). Individuals of various social groups, even those of arbitrary definition (i.e.; dichotomously defined gender, nationalistic categories, and various racial/ethnic identities), exhibit high levels of obedience, and the overall aggregate levels remain relatively stable over time. Conformity and obedience are relatively stable in societies in which the norms are salient, clear, consistent, assumed by all the participants, and regularly enforced (Asch 1955; Cialdini et al. 1990), but people also tend to defer to or engage in informational conformity when they are in ambiguous situations as well (Sherif 1935).

Additionally, hierarchy is an implicit component of any social regulatory regime because people vary in their readiness to obey and to extend trust. Useful hierarchical relationships require competence of the norms, standards, and system of enforcement (Milgram 1965). For example, spectators in a concert hall do not respond to the instructions of the conductor. The perception and response to the legitimacy of a given norm requires an understanding between those who are incorporated into a system (in this case, an economic system). In the economic context, the institutional standards are set by the system of capitalism and maintained through various mechanisms of norm enforcement.

There are essentially three mechanisms for norm enforcement. The first is a purely social phenomenon in which norms are sustained by the motivation for coordination. In this case, active social enforcement is not especially necessary. People follow the norm because it would be unsafe or a waste of time to ignore the norm. The second mechanism involves the threat of social disapproval or punishment for violations of the norm (Coleman 1990). Evidence suggests that people will incur substantial personal costs to enforce norms in this manner (Fehr, Fishbacher, and Gächter 2002). The third enforcement mechanism is the internalization of the norm, which may lead to uncomfortable emotional experiences when a norm is perceived to have been violated even when there is no third party present to enforce (Coleman 1990).

Tipping norms are enforced through any combination of these mechanisms. For example, a bartender who does not meet the expectations of the patrons can be "pushed out" when he or she fails to receive tips or receives notes regarding poor performance instead of a tip and cannot afford to support himself or herself in that form of employment. Alternatively, bartenders may receive immediate reinforcement for behavior that is consistent with or supports the established standard. The narratives in this study reveal a great deal about how norms are enforced within the formal and informal organizational structure. For example, respondents discuss what they liked or disliked about their jobs and why and how they decided whether or not to remain in a particular job. Respondents also talk about the formal organizational rules and how those rules affected their employment decisions. The narratives demonstrate the role of informal mechanisms of enforcement as well. Informal means of maintaining social norms are difficult to capture but can be reasonably evaluated through narratives.

Conformity can also serve society in important ways (Milgram 1965; Zimbardo and Lieppe 1991). Norms are tremendously advantageous in addressing dangers or threats to security, providing stability and facilitating cooperation. The absence of norms can lead to greater levels of violence. In other words, norms can minimize the likelihood that force will be applied in an economic exchange in which the participants have different expectations regarding optimality.

Economic theories of norms: Although norms are not invariably efficiency-enhancing, norms are generally considered efficient in an economic sense because they minimize transaction costs (Wärneryd 1994; Roth 1985). Norms are also considered a form of social capital in that they reduce the risk of a coordination failure and increase the likelihood of social exchange (Coleman 1990). Complex social rituals (such as tipping) allow people to signal their sensitivity to norms in general and serve as a part of the socialization process (Henrich, Boyd, Bowles, Fehr, and Gintis 2004).

There are essentially three ways in which norms are established and evolve. Top-down influences such as edicts and role models represent the first way in which norms evolve (Samuelson 1997). Local customs and practices coalesce into norms over time through a somewhat mysterious bottom-up process of negotiation (usually among unequal participants) reflected in the second way in which norms evolve. The third way in which norms evolve is through lateral influences on existing norms producing changes through learning (which may or may not be considered progressive, efficient, or optimal). However, some research suggests that norms of fairness may result from the forces that compel people to engage in social interactions over time (Binmore 2005; Young 1998; Fehr, Fischbacher, and Gächter 2002).

It is also important to note that some norms are inherently more stable and durable than others simply because they coordinate people's expectations about how to interact with one another (Samuelson 1997; Kandori, Mailath, and Rob 1993). This is particularly relevant when it comes to understanding how arbitrary patterns of exchange in which socially constructed groups are required to compromise more on a regular, repeated basis (see, e.g.; Shapiro 2004; Bowles, Gintis, and Groves 2005). Tipping can be conceived of as a durable norm, but there is a considerable degree of variation across contexts.

Acts of trust are required when the obligations and rewards for both parties are not clearly defined. Formal and impersonal interactions reduce the likelihood of trust and reciprocity (Merton 1949). Personal interactions contribute to mutual expectations of trust and reciprocity. In settings where tipping may occur, the obligations of the client and the rewards for the employee are often not specified by the rules of the organization. In other words, the tips are essentially wages that are not specified by a formal contract and are usually not negotiated. The employee extends trust, engaging in a personal interaction to foster trust and anticipating reciprocity. Interestingly, employees who are extended greater control over their work environment have more credit to give (Butler and Skipper 1981). In other words, attitudes of resentment, suspicion, and distrust or trust, confidence and reciprocity are determined by the credit extended to the employee by management. People are more likely to trust when they have been extended trust and vice versa. In organizational settings, the organizational climate is set by management and has important implications for service provision as well as client satisfaction.

Although some claim tipping can be traced at least to the Roman Empire (see Hemenway 1993), tipping has a long well-documented history in economic exchange from the sixteenth-century English vails given to servants in private homes (see Segrave 1998) to commercial tips in London coffee houses (see

Brenner 2001). In the United States, tipping was well-established by the end of the 1890s (Segrave 1998). People conform to the social norm of tipping out of convention and to avoid embarrassment (Azar 2005). Tipping remains a durable norm because people derive benefits from tipping by impressing others, improving their self-image, and being (or perceived of as) generous and kind, and the fact that tip percentages tend to increase over time implies that at least some people tip for emotional rather than strictly rational reasons (Azar 2007a).

The literature on tipping is vast and limited at the same time. Early models examined tipping in the context of repetitive customers engaging in self-interested behavior intending to invest in continued quality service (Ben-Zion and Karni 1977). Tips have been understood to serve various functions, including consumer protection (Sisk and Gallick 1985), to increase profits (Schwartz 1997), and for employee monitoring (Jacob and Page 1980). Most of the empirical research on tipping examines variables that affect tip size (such as bill size, previous tips, service quality, and group size) and evaluates the extent to which tips affect service quality.[3] Alternatively, Azar (2004) examines the costs of disobeying the tipping norm. Innovative research has also recently begun to examine how tipping affects workers and firms (Azar 2008), but curiously, there is a gap in literature in which the perspective of the people who receive tips is not addressed.

While the functions that norms serve are well understood, several aspects of norms remain unclear. Where or with whom do norms originate? What are the specific processes by which norms evolve? What impact does the social or economic context have on the development of norms? How does the individual perceive and experience social norms? How is the authority to establish and maintain a norm understood? Under what conditions are norms called into question? How are other-regarding or mutually-beneficial norms facilitated? It is also widely understood that there is a tremendous gap between perception and reality in the experience of norms (Berkowitz 2004; Perkins 2003; Borsari and Carey 2003), making experiential evidence highly valuable in understanding the pieces of the puzzle that remain with respect to norms.

Interestingly, when norms are not well understood or are inconsistent, individuals assert preferences by engaging in rituals that are believed to impact behavior. This may be based on bias, theory, trial-and-error, and experience. In other words, people develop standard practices that are usually considered to be within the organizational rules to facilitate tipping in a given circumstance. The narratives in this study show how tipped employees engage in regularized behaviors to encourage or pressure people to tip. For example, a ski instructor describes putting money on his clipboard to facilitate tipping.

This exploration is an exercise in the understanding of norms in economic exchange. Specifically, we are interested in exploring the experiences of people who receive tips with the norms related to their respective work environments. We utilize a series of narratives regarding tips and commissions in numerous job contexts. We identify the common elements across cases and provide experiential evidence of the individual understanding of the social norms and institutional standards. In many cases, the evidence describes behavior and attitudinal norms as well as the institutional standards as they are understood by the respondent.

METHODOLOGY

Although convincing evidence regarding the cause and effect relationships between norms and behavior are evident in extant experimental research (see, e.g.; Fehr, Fishbacher, and Gächter 2002), the primary source of knowledge regarding variations in norms is experiential (Schram and Caterino 2006). Our interest is in the variation in norms across work environments and understanding the experiences people have in the context of the norms specific to their various job categories. Therefore, the semi-structured interview is the most viable means of understanding the variation in socio-economic norms and outlining the interplay between the people and the norms within which people operate in different work environments.

The semi-structured interview is a widely used social science method for understanding contextual data. It is a qualitative method comparable to the structured or standardized interview employed in survey research. The researcher-administered, structured interview is a quantitative survey method intended to control for the context so that data can be aggregated and compared across groups; whereas, the semi-structured interview is designed to explore contextual variations.

The goal of this project is to understand the experiences of people in different contexts of the tipping culture. The semi-structured interview is the best tool for capturing the experiential elements of a particular domain. The method combines a degree of faith in what the participant says with a degree of skepticism about what (s)he is saying. It is an effort to capture the meaning, which requires that the interviewer continue questioning the participant to fully test the hypothesis without affecting the responses (Honey 1987). This approach allows us to deepen, discriminate, and clarify conceptualizations relevant to the experiences of the participant. The general script of the interview guarantees uniformity of topics across the whole sample, each particular interview may vary with respect to the specific follow-up questions intended to clarify the responses of the interviewee. This technique offers feedback about how well our theories hold up in the beliefs and experiences of people and offers the interviewer the opportunity to explore an issue. It allows the interviewee to express opinions, attitudes, concerns, and feelings that provide us with a general impression of tipping norms from the perspective of the participants when taken together.

There are some general guidelines regarding conduct during a semi-structured interview that minimize bias and maximize the yield from two-way communication (Shea 1998). Of course, proper care in the interaction with human participants must be evaluated and approved in accordance with the Nuremberg Code[4] (which forms the basis for the evaluations that Institutional Review Boards conduct when assessing whether or not a research project meets the approval of a university sponsoring research that involves human participants) and institutional standards before any interviews are conducted. Once approval is formally granted preparation for the actual interviews follow these commonly accepted guidelines:

1. Develop and memorize a checklist so that each item is covered without constantly referring to the checklist.
2. Take extensive, detailed, and accurate notes and maintain a permanent file of all responses.
3. Dress in an appropriate, respectable manner that minimizes the psychological distance between the interviewer and interviewee.

The following guidelines are upheld in conducting the interviews:

1. Ask the participant if (s)he is willing to talk and explain the ways in which the information will be used.
2. Be certain that permission is granted before proceeding.
3. Let the participant know that (s)he can refuse any question or discontinue the interview at any time.
4. Consider the responses that people give in comparison with other respondents and with respect to theory, and seek more information when there appear to be contradictions.

When asking questions during a semi-structured interview, the following guidelines are commonly accepted:

1. Ask clear and direct questions.
2. Keep asking why.
3. Ask one question at a time.
4. Only ask questions to which the respondents can be expected to know the answers.
5. Be clear about the time period in reference.
6. Avoid phrasing questions in a way that assumes or implies that the respondent should follow (or that others have followed) a specific course of action.
7. Avoid leading questions.
8. Avoid value-laden language in the phrasing of questions.
9. Do not induce particular answers by helping the participant to respond.

GETTING THE INTERVIEWS

A variety of mechanisms were employed to find the respondents interviewed in this book and the companion volume that takes a similar approach to understanding the commission system from the perspective of those who receive commissions.

1. People were approached in streets, airports, parking lots, and other public spaces working in relevant jobs: parking lot attendants, red caps, baggers, and so on. It is very difficult to talk to people while they are working. Most people do not have the luxury of taking ten minutes off to be interviewed while at work. In those cases, the interviewer tried to get their phone numbers to follow up. Approximately half of those who were too busy at the time allowed the interviewer to follow up, and only about ten interviews were conducted as a result of this approach.
2. Students in Professor Seltzer's classes at Howard University who had relevant employment were given the opportunity to receive extra credit (or cash) if they were interviewed, or if they could refer me to someone who could be interviewed. Twenty-five interviews resulted from this technique, and another 40 people were referred.
3. Whenever the interviewer came into contact with people who provided a service involving a tip, a commission, or a bonus, an interview was requested. This included servers in restaurants, parking valets, hair stylists, cab drivers,

store clerks, repair people, and so on. This technique produced about 50 interviews.
4. The interviewer utilized over 200 personal contacts and interviewed those who were appropriate to the project. In addition, those people were asked for their help identifying more people to interview. Approximately 20 personal contacts were interviewed, and about 150 interviews were the result of referrals by personal contacts.
5. Almost everyone interviewed was asked if they could refer anyone else to interview. Approximately 150 interviews were generated by this type of "snowball." There were several people who were interviewed in the fifth generation of a snowball.

With a few exceptions, only one person per location with the same job description was interviewed. For example, only one server from a specific restaurant was interviewed for that specific job. However, a runner from the same restaurant or a server for the same restaurant chain who worked at another location was interviewed with their consent. There are a few situations where this protocol was accidentally violated and often the difference in answers was instructive.[5]

There were several factors that were integral to obtaining the interviews.

1. *Money*: Everyone interviewed (except students enrolled in one of the methodology courses taught by Seltzer who had the option of participating in an interview to receive extra credit) was offered $10 for the interview and $5 if they could successfully refer someone else to interview. Money clearly talks. People were paid on the spot. If the interview was by telephone, the money (in cash) was sent within 24 hours. Each person interviewed received a letter with the cash, thanking them and asking for help in finding additional people to interview. Sometimes respondents requested that the money be donated, and the interviewer provided those donations in accordance with their request within the same 24 hour period.
2. *University Affiliation*: A number of people agreed to talk simply because the research was being conducted by university professors.
3. *Personal Referral*: By far the most important factor in obtaining the interview was referral. The person who had been referred was contacted, and the interviewer would state: "Jane Doe said I should call you." In the typical telephone survey conducted by Gallup or Harris, the response rates are about 25%. In this study, there were less than five refusals in the 300 or so people

referred and interviewed using this introduction. An additional ten people never picked up their telephone or returned my message. This response rate is extraordinarily high.[6]

The response rate was over 95%. Even though the response rate was exceptionally high, ironclad conclusions about people who receive tips cannot be drawn from this sample. The sample in this study is not a random or representative sample. This study is based on a convenience sample combined with a snowball sample. Most of the respondents live in the D.C. area, and most are only two or three stages of separation away from the interviewer. Although the sample is not random, it is very diverse. Respondents came from 37 states and are very heterogeneous by race, class, and gender. The sample represents a broad range of jobs: restaurant servers, bartenders, strippers, car valets, pizza delivery drivers, ski instructors, nannies, concierges, musicians, cab drivers, (and in the companion volume) clothing salespeople, realtors, tire salesmen, telemarketers, travel agents, employment agents, loan officers, membership directors, etc.

Respondents were promised confidentiality. In some situations, the name of the business where the respondent worked is referenced. Chains such as Home Depot and Ruby Tuesday are identified. There are also some situations in which the names of some well-known firms are not mentioned at the request of the respondent. In some cases, the location of the respondent (e.g., Northeast instead of Connecticut) is intentionally vague to ensure confidentiality.

There was a standard set of questions used in most of the interviews. For example, servers in restaurants were asked the following questions:

1. Do you like your job and why?
2. What is your hourly wage?
3. What is the average tip percent?
4. How much do you make in a typical weekday and weekend shift?
5. How do you split your tips?
6. What type of people are more likely to be generous in their tips?
7. What haven't I asked about that I should I know about tipping?

Other questions that were sometimes asked included:

1. What was your biggest tip?
2. How often were you stiffed?

3. Was there competition with other servers?
4. How much do you tip when you go to restaurants?
5. How were tips dealt with when people paid by credit cards?

There was very little specific prompting in the questions. For example, although respondents were asked who was more likely to be generous about tips, they were not asked whether tipping was affected by age, race, gender, and so on unless the person asked for clarification (which rarely occurred). Avoiding this type of prompting reduces the likelihood that the interviewer might be "putting ideas into respondent's mouths." The respondents were not asked about taxes (although a number of respondents refer to taxes) because the lore is that most people who receive tips do not report them all. If questions about taxes had been included in the interview structure, it is likely that some people would refuse to be interviewed. More importantly, taxes are not the subject of this investigation. With a few exceptions, only one person per location with the same job description was interviewed. Detailed notes were taken during the interviews, and the respondents' stories are essentially presented in their own voice. The interviewers followed a checklist for the interviews, but the primary advantage of the semi-structured interview (and in some ways it's weakness as well) is that the interviews often play out more like a conversation.

There are a number of advantages to using semi-structured interviews. First, the response rate tends to be higher in comparison with other interview methods, and the research can almost invariably obtain data to account for non-response bias. Second, the ability to explain or clarify the content of a question or the meaning of specific word(s) in a given question achieves a few worthwhile goals. It allows the experience of people who might otherwise be excluded from the data to communicate their experiences. It also provides uniformity in the interpretation of questions without unnecessarily limiting the responses of the participants. Ultimately, this leads to a great deal more information. Third, allowing the respondent to elaborate on answers both minimizes biases in interpretation and maximizes our understanding of the meaning of experiences of people. Fourth, a skillful interviewer can implement a semi-structured interview like a conversation, which tends to produce open, honest dialog that cannot be obtained using any other research method. Fifth, the wealth of information that can be obtained in a semi-structured interview adds depth to our understanding. Perhaps more importantly, this depth has a degree of validity (although not broadly generalizable) that quantitative analyses attempt to reflect. In other words, this approach captures the meaning of the experience in the participants' own words rather than simply providing a numerical reflection of an aggregated value. Although both authors are statistically inclined, the data collected in this study are not readily quantifiable. There is such a degree of variation in the tip amounts and percentages reported by the respondents that it renders quantitative measures uninterruptable if not altogether meaningless.

There are some limitations to this approach. First, the data collection and analysis is extremely time-consuming and costly. Second, there are at least two possible interviewer interaction effects that require a skillful interviewer to avoid: (1) the suggestion of answers and (2) failing to exhaust a line of questioning sufficient for capturing the meaning. Third, there is the universal problem of perception. All data requires interpretation, and such translation requires that the researcher perceive the relevant data in a manner consistent with the participants intended meaning and that is also reliable and coherent in the scheme of common perceptions of reality (Shannon 1949). Fourth, because data collected from semi-structured interviews cannot be easily aggregated and compared across groups, we can only speculate on the extent to which the analysis can be generalized across contexts. Furthermore, the causal relationships under study are based on the beliefs of the participants and allow us to understand what it is that people tend to believe but do not necessarily tell us much about the validity of those beliefs.

NOTES

1. See Lynn and Lynn (2004) for an extensive review of this literature.
2. See Altman (2006) for a review of the economic literature.
3. See Azar (2007b) for a review of the literature on tipping.
4. The Nuremberg Code is a set of principles intended to provide an ethical code of conduct guiding research involving human participants. The code based on what was learned about the atrocities of human experimentation by the Nazis and from the subsequent Nuremberg Trials.
5. For example, our interviews include two people with the same job for the same company greeting people when they arrived for cruises. Don reports receiving a lot of tips, and Danele claims very few tips. Don presents himself or is likely to be perceived as the "all-American boy," and Danele is from another country.
6. See Seltzer (2005) for an analysis of response rates and minimizing non-response bias.

Part 1
RESTAURANTS

Restaurant tips are the most common type of tip. When people were asked if they could refer friends or family who worked for tips or commissions, restaurant workers were mentioned so frequently that a disclaimer eventually had to follow, "Except people who work in restaurants."

Tipping in restaurants is almost universal. A December 2006 Gallup survey found that 85% of respondents said 15% or higher was an appropriate tip and 36% said 20% or higher was an appropriate tip. However, 46% of respondents reported not leaving a tip at one point because of bad service. There has been a fair amount of research examining what influences the size of the tip. Tips are generally higher when alcohol is served, the quality of service is high (Bodvarrsson and Gibson 1997; Conlin, Lynn, and O'Donoghue 2003), when women are servers (Lynn & Simons, 2000), and outside of the Midwest (Lynn 2006). Research on more subtle aspects of tipping norms found that tips are higher when servers wrote *thank you* on the bill (Rind and Bordia 1995), wrote patriotic messages on the check (Seiter and Gass, 2005), or when the server leaned over at the table (Leodoro and Lynn 2007).

Most restaurant workers are paid below the standard minimum wage because of the expectation of receiving tips.[1] Government intervention into the compensation structure among those who receive tips goes beyond setting a minimum wage. In particular, there is extensive controversy about taxing tips. The IRS believes that tips were underreported by over $2 billion in 1990.[2] They set up a variety of different mechanisms by which employers had to withhold income taxes, FICA, and Medicare for those receiving tips equally to at least 8% of total receipts.[3]

The U.S. Census Bureau reports the following occupational categories for restaurant workers who receive tips:

- bartenders (136,840 workers; earning on average $21,000)
- waiters and waitresses (442,390; $19,000)
- dining room and cafeteria attendants and bartender helpers (53,100; $18,000)
- hosts and hostesses, restaurant lounge, and coffee shop (26,850; $20,000)
- food servers, non-restaurant (50,870; $21,000)
- dishwashers (59,420; $16,000).

The last two categories encompass runners and bussers, respectively. This section is an attempt to understand tipping from the experiences of restaurant workers. It is organized by subsections that explore in greater detail different contexts based on the different job functions defined by the U.S. Census and different work environments based on common differences between restaurants.

Due to the significance of gratuities in the restaurant industry, we attempted to re-interview as many of the restaurant workers as possible in 2008 regarding the effect of the economic downturn on their restaurant tips. Telephone numbers for 45 of the 111 restaurant workers initially interviewed were still valid. Seven of the 45 valid telephone numbers were no longer the phone numbers of the original respondents, and 6 of those original 45 respondents no longer work in restaurants; three of whom graduated college and started other careers. A voice message and one additional call-back were attempted, but 21 calls failed to produce a follow-up interview. However, 13 servers were available for a follow-up interview. These interviews are also incorporated into the essays in this book. The 13 follow-up interviews come from a convenience sample but are nevertheless crucial for understanding the interplay between tipping norms and economic conditions as perceived by tipped employees in the restaurant industry. According to the 13 respondents in this study, the effect of economic conditions on tipping norms may vary considerably by context. Five of the respondents reported that there was no change in either business or tipping. Four of the respondents indicated that tips were down, but business was the same. Two respondents perceived business to be down but that tips were the same. And, two other respondents perceived both tips and business to be down.

NOTES

1. For minimum wages of tipped employees broken down by states, refer to the following: http://www.dol.gov/esa/programs/whd/state/tipped.htm.

2. See testimony of William Conlon, Director Reporting Compliance, Internal Revenue Service in front of the House Committee on Ways and Means, Subcommittee on Oversight, July 15, 2004.

3. These procedures are complicated. However, in 2002 the Supreme Court ruled that the IRS has the authority to assess taxes based upon aggregate estimates of tip income. *United States v. Fior d'Italica.*

1

Restaurant Chains

Chain restaurants include fast food and casual dining establishments that are generally franchised and in which servers wait on customers. In the United States, they include but are not limited to Applebee's, Ruby Tuesday, T.G.I. Friday's, IHOP, Cheesecake Factory, and so on. The stories told by wait staff at restaurant chains revealed several themes. Interestingly, restaurant workers often make broad generalizations about customers that are used to explain the tips. In many cases, demographic characteristics of customers are regularly used by wait staff to predict and explain the tip outcome. There are no scientific theories to support these notions. Some of the servers in this chapter believe they can predict who will give better tips when the customer walks in while others claim that there is no way to predict this. In fact, most logic dictates that customers determine tips in accordance with their knowledge of the custom, the extent to which they are motivated by the emotional or rational elements of the tipping norm, and the quality of the service. However, the perspectives of a number of the wait staff in chain restaurants appear to be guided by the assumption that there is a considerable degree of consistency in their own behavior and the quality of the service. When there is consideration of their own role in the work, the focus tends to be on attitude and "personality." There is not much indication that customers are really providing feedback to the servers on the service, either through the tip percentage, by leaving a note, or by speaking to the manager.

$ $ $

Denise works as a waitress at the Cheesecake Factory. Here is what she had to say in her own words.

I am working my way through college. I like working there. The restaurant has a great atmosphere.

I earn $3 per hour plus tips. The average tips are 14–15%. Over the last four months, three tables stiffed me. One stiffed me because they did not like the service, and the others probably forgot. The biggest tip was 30%.

The morning shifts are six hours, and the evening shifts are eight hours. I earn about $50 in tips in the morning and $100–$150 in the evening. I give 2.2% of total sales to the buses, 1.1% to the bartender, and 0.8% to the food runner. This is determined by a cash-out report at the end of the night. I give these three people cash, and all of us sign the cash-out report. If I have more than one bus, I give the cash to the main bus; who then splits it up.

Some buses want more and will tell you if their minimum (set in their own mind) is not met. So, sometimes I will give them an extra $1 or $2. If someone is working real hard, I sometimes will voluntarily give them a few extra dollars.

The hostess is paid salary and does not receive tips from the staff. He or she is not allowed to take tips from customers.

In an eight hour shift I bring in about $1,000–$1,200 in sales, so the bus would get about $20 from me. I think the bus might also work for other waits as well. I once gave a bus $32.

The bartenders make the most as they are getting percentages from many waits. They are usually former servers.

I do not like the system because not everyone is working hard. If I don't receive good tips, I get screwed. I should tip out of my tips. The problem with that would be that people would have to trust me.

At cash out, the management takes all credit card slips, and I might get some cash if all my sales are credit cards. Usually, I give them cash.

Taxes are determined at the end of the night when I declare them. The management gets suspicious when I state they are under 10%.

The biggest tips occur at lunch hour from business people. There is a somewhat true stereotype that blacks tip 10% and whites 20%.

$ $ $

Scott works at TGI Friday's in central New Jersey. The following narrative details his experiences receiving tips.

I hate working there. The customers are yuppies who don't tip well. They are rich and spoiled and only go out so they don't have to cook.

I earn $2.15 an hour plus tips. The typical tip is 15%. I've been stiffed only a few times. My biggest tip was $140 for a funeral party. Eighteen percent was automatically added to the bill, and they doubled it.

Shifts are eight hours each. In a typical day shift, I earn $80 in tips, and for a night shift, I earn $100.

At the end of my shift, I tip out. Three percent of my sales go to others: 1% to the buses, 1% to the bartender, and 1% to the host. I give the 3% to the manager who pro-rates the tips according to hours worked. I give the manager at the end of my shift all the money I collected for sales plus the 3% tip out. I keep the rest.

I don't like the system because sometimes the bus does not help, and the host is unavailable. I never give extra tips.

I used to be a food runner. Food runners were paid directly by the wait person, and I could earn $140 a night running food. Now the runners are paid salary without tips. There are stereotypes about who tips better or worse. It is said that blacks and young people tip the worst. I found this not to be true, and it is difficult to predict how much a person will tip. The stereotypes don't work.

People come in expecting to tip a certain percent and will tip that regardless of good or bad service. Sometimes I don't do a good job, and I still get a good tip. And other times I really hustle, and the tip is lousy.

$ $ $

Thomas works at a Mongolian Barbecue in the Washington, D.C. area. He was also interviewed a few days before this interview at his other job selling Christmas trees (essay not included). Here is what Thomas had to say about receiving tips at a restaurant chain.

I have worked at this restaurant for 14 months and earn $2.65 an hour.

People don't tip as much at this restaurant because the food is served semi-buffet style. The typical tip is 13–14%. In a typical night, I work six hours and make $150 on the weekend and $65–$70 on other days. My biggest tip was $50 for a $24 bill. I don't know why they gave me this tip.

I get stiffed for a tip every three–four shifts.

At the end of each shift, I tip out 3% of my total sales. This is divided between four types of people: the kitchen, the grillers, the host, and the bartenders. I don't know the percentage breakdown among these four groups. I never give extra tip outs.

I hold my cash all night and turn it in at the end of the night. The computer tells me how much to give to the manager.

The tip system is fair, but I guess it would be nice to know how the tip outs get distributed. I never talk to customers about tips, but the staff sometimes talk among themselves.

Black people don't tip as much. In general, rich people tip the most. I can read a person in a minute and figure out how much they will tip. You can get a bigger tip by being nice. But for some people, it does not matter how good the service is. They will tip the same amount.

$ $ $

Elizabeth has been a waitress at a Ruby Tuesday in New Jersey for the last seven months. She is currently in college and works hard on the cheerleading team. This is her story.

I like my job because I like the people that I work with, and I like to have money in my pocket without having to wait for my paycheck. I am also a people person.

I get paid $2.60 an hour, I think. The average tip is 15–20%—probably closer to 20%. There was only one time that I did not get a tip. I don't know why. The service was good. I think they were just in a bad mood. My biggest tip came from a friend. He gave me $25 for a small bill.

The night shifts are five hours long, and I make between $40 and $70 in tips. The average is probably $50. The lunch shifts are three hours long, and I average $30 to $35.

I share tips in the following way. The hostess gets $2 on a busy night. The person who fixes the salad bar gets 75 cents, and the bartender gets a couple bucks. If there is no one drinking, the bartender would get nothing.

The computer figures out how much each person should get. I don't do the math, and I don't understand the exact percentages. I give the money to the manager. We don't have a busser or runner. Sometimes the hostess will help if things are really busy. I don't give more than required. I don't want to give my money away.

When I go to a restaurant, I give 15% even if the service is bad. With really good service, I will give over 20%.

Elizabeth was re-interviewed in 2008 when the recession began. She said she had not noticed a difference in tipping or business. People who have money still go out, and good tippers still tip well.

$ $ $

Wanda worked at a Clyde's restaurant in downtown D.C. She shared the following story.

I love working there. The environment is nice, and the managers and the staff make the job fun.

I get paid $2.77 an hour. People tip 17%–20% if they are getting good service. I work seven–eight hours in a shift and will typically get $100–$150 in tips. On a Saturday night, I can get $150–$200. The larger the group the more they tip. We don't automatically add on a gratuity.

My biggest tip was $150. Personality will help. You need to connect with the people and read them. You need to be there when they want you and leave them alone when they want to be left alone.

We share tips at the end of the night. I give the tip outs in cash. The busser gets 10% of the tips and the back waiter (runner) gets 20%. This is done on the honor system. If they think you are cheating, they can look at the sales sheet. This has occurred a few times. Not everyone is honest, and it can get ugly.

I give the busser more than the 10%. I will give him an extra $5 or $10. You need to make sure they are taken care of. I don't give extra to the back waiter. There is not that much more that they can do to help me.

On who tips the most—everyone is different. Corporate types (those in suits) tip the most. The smallest tips come from those who eat late at night. They don't care. Some people don't know how to tip. They will just leave $5.

When I go to a restaurant, I always leave 20% if the service is especially good.

$ $ $

Roberto has been a server at T.G.I. Fridays in Northern Virginia since it opened eight months ago. This is his story in his own words.

I like working there. The manager is cool. I have some good friends. Few of the staff complains, and I like serving tables. I'm now going to culinary school.

I get paid $2.13 an hour. The average tip should be 18%. I actually average 15%. Some people will tip me 12% and even 10%. Maybe I screwed up, or maybe they don't know how to tip.

On a weekend morning, I work from 10 am to 4 pm and average $100–$110 in tips. On a weekday night, I get $60–$70 for working 8 hours, and on a weekend night, I get $100–$110. The mornings do well as a lot of people come with kids, and then the kids go to the movies. Holidays are real good.

My best night ever was last Saturday night when I got $160. When I first started, there were some nights I only got $30. The restaurant was new, and things were screwed up.

At the end of my shift, I tip out 3% of my sales. The bartender, hostess, and busser each get 1%. When my shift is over, I roll silverware, clean up my station, and print out my service financial. This is a long piece of paper. It says how much I owe in cash or how much they owe me, the amount of drinks, and so on—and the amount of tip out.

The tips are all placed in a pool and shared by all the appropriate staff. About 40% of the time, I will give the busser a few extra bucks if I had a really good night and if he worked really hard. I don't give any extra to the hostess who gets paid $9 an hour or to the bartender.

Business people tip the most. They are easy. They are more laid back. You don't have to kiss butt, and you just need to leave them alone while they discuss business. The worst are foreigners, African-Americans, and teenagers. The foreigners don't know how to tip. Most of our foreigners are from Asia or Europe.

When we have groups of eight or larger, we automatically add on 18%. Last week we had a group, and I added on 18% or $25. They also left $15 on the table. Occasionally, someone might not realize that 18% is added on and give me a tip I did not deserve. It is not my fault.

If I do my job, I am recognized by the tips.

$ $ $

Manuel has been a server at an Uno's in the Washington, D.C. area for over a year. The following narrative details his experiences receiving tips.

I really like my job. I like the people I work with. Most of them are college students.

I'm paid $2.75 an hour. My average tip is 18–19%. During the 5 pm to midnight week night shift, I get about $100 in tips. During the 4:30 pm to 2:00 am weeknight shift, I average $150–$200.

My biggest tip was $50 on a $100 bill. It was a group of girls, and they were celebrating one of their birthdays. I don't know why they tipped so well.

I occasionally get shafted. A couple of times a customer told me they had no more money. Foreigners will sometimes shaft you as they don't understand tipping.

[It took me a while to understand the tip out system.] If I have $600 in sales I tip out the bartender $600/60 ($10), and the bus would get half of that ($5). I often give the busboy an extra $3–$5. I don't give extra to the bartender because he does not really earn it. At the end of the night, I cash out with the manager and then give cash to the bartender and the busboy. I don't tip out the hostess unless there is no runner, and the hostess is helping to bus the tables.

There is sometimes conflict over the tip out. We usually round up or down. One server would owe the bartender $6.40 and give him $6. But, the server would also give $6 if the amount was $6.60. The bartender said he would no longer make drinks for that server. He was a bartender for six years and had more seniority than the manager. What he said went. Another server was slow tipping out the bartender. He also stopped making drinks for her, but they made up.

When I eat at restaurants, I always tip at least 20%.

There is competition among servers. The competition is for sections—not tables. I am the senior server, so it is not a problem for me. Who gets what section is up to the manager. There is sometimes conflict, but the manager decides.

Whites tip the most. I am African-American. Two white females would usually tip 20%. A white male and white female will tip a little less than that. Two white dudes will tip 15%. African-Americans tip half of what whites tip. Last week I had two African-American men with an African-American female. She had me running all over. I had other tables. I got $3 on an $80 bill. The servers are all blacks and will sometimes tell the manager—no more black tables. We will share the black tables.

[Manuel would not take the $10. He said that he wanted to share the information.]

$ $ $

Sabrina has been a server at an IHOP for a year and a half in a town in Virginia about 60 miles from D.C. She was incredibly upbeat, and this is what she had to say about tips at chain restaurants.

I love working here. I've been serving for 25 years. The bosses are great. They are awesome. I also make good money.

I get paid $2.13 an hour. My average tip is 20–30%. On a typical day, I have $500 in sales that I can see from the print-out that I make $100–$140 in tips. I am very good. I love working with the public. I love what I do. I treat customers like I would like to be treated. I treat kids like they were my own kids. Today, some kids came in and left no tip. That's OK. I'll make it up at the next table. I have a positive attitude toward everything.

We do not share our tips with each other. I tip out the busboy 1% of sales. We usually have one busboy for the entire restaurant. I give the 1% to the manager. If it is really busy, I will give him an extra $5 or $10. I give it to him directly. He is Hispanic and has a lot of pride. He says, "no-no-no." But, I insist that he takes it.

We do our own running and do not tip out the hostess.

You never know who will tip more. There was this one gypsy [homeless] family that lived in their car. The first time they came in we almost had a fight. By the end of the meal, we were hugging. Now, they come in twice a month and always leave a $20 tip. Most people tip well.

People usually leave the tip on the table if they pay in cash. There has never been a problem here. At other restaurants, there have been issues with the busboy, hostess, or manager. It stopped.

Over half the people pay with credit cards. Ninety percent of them put the tip on the credit card. The rest will give us cash.

We have to declare our tips. Sometimes our paychecks are zero. I tell the other servers, "You get $500 a week for a service job. Don't complain."

$ $ $

Fred worked at a Friendly's for three months that was located in suburban Maryland. This is what he had to say about tipping norms in chain restaurants.

I did not like my boss, but I liked the money that I made. It was much better than working for a wage. I liked working for tips.

I earned $2.50 an hour. The average tip was $5. This was about 15%. In an eight hour shift, I made $75–$80 on average. On my biggest night, I made $170. I was really good that night. I refilled drinks without being asked, and I was quick. I did my section and part of another section.

When someone simply bought a cup of coffee for $2.50, they usually tipped a dollar. They usually left $3.50 or $5 if they got some refills.

Very few gave nothing. Some people tipped really well. The people who did not tip well did not know how important it was to a waiter. They don't know how little we are paid.

We did not share our tips with anyone. We bused our own tables. The competition among servers was sometimes ugly. Some would complain to some of the other servers and call them greedy and selfish. It wasn't really mean. We understood that the person was like that, and we just wouldn't speak to them.

The biggest tippers were black women between the ages of 25 and 40. Young white women between 20 and 30 also tipped well. The best tippers were my friends who ate at the restaurant. Single old white women did not tip well. Some of them tipped well, so it really varied.

When I go to restaurants I always tip more than I should. I tip 20%.

$ $ $

David has worked for the last year at an ESPN Zone in the Washington, D.C. area. This is what he had to say.

The job is very stressful. ESPN Zone is owned by Disney, and we are seen as cast members. The management sucks. There are arguments every day. Most of the arguments are between the front and the back. The people who prepare the food [the back] are paid a real wage ($18 an hour), and they don't see the need to bust their butt. The servers [the front] live on their tips, and if the food does not come out in time, we don't get tipped.

I get paid $2.77 an hour. My tip totals have ranged from $20 to $150. This is for a five hour shift. I average $120–$150 per shift. We are a sports bar. If people are coming to watch a game, we don't make much money. If the Redskins are playing, people will try to stay at their tables the entire game. We tell them that they have to order at least $10 an hour per person. No matter, we lose on tips. The bartenders do well on game day.

Tipping really depends upon race. Whites and the black middle class tip 18%. Ghetto blacks [respondent is black] tip $5 no matter what the bill is. Sometimes they give nothing. We see certain people coming and say, "Please don't sit them in my section." Older celebrities tip 20–25%; whereas newer celebrities are horrible tippers. The new celebrities tip only 10%. The newer celebrities [sports and entertainment figures] are real problems. They will complain that their lemonade is watered down, or they really wanted a Sprite instead of lemonade. They are not all like that, but most are pretty bad.

We are supposed to tip out the busser 2% of sales, the bartender 1%, and the runner 1%. We get a "complete financial" print-out at the end of the shift, and everyone is supposed to sign it. We give the tip outs directly to the people. However, if the person is not working hard, I won't give them the full amount. The bartender is supposed to have drinks ready in three minutes. If it takes him seven minutes, I am not giving him the full 1%. I will let them know how they messed up.

If they are working real hard, I give them more. If I owe $5, I will give $8. There is one busser who I always give $25. He hustles and turns over the tables quickly.

The hosts have real wages, and I don't give them any tip out.

I also get bribes. People will give me $20 to sit in a booth, or in a special section, or to stay beyond their time limit. The basketball players and the drug dealers are big on this. I use to take weed as a bribe when I smoked. I would not take cocaine. I average $100 a week in bribes.

We lie a lot. If the food is late, I will tell the diner that there was a fire in the back instead of saying that I forgot. I am happy to blame the back. All we are thinking about is the money.

Most of us live extravagant lives. I will spend $200 on a pair of jeans knowing that I will make it back the next day.

When I go out, I tip over 20% if the service is good. If it is real good, I tip 25%.

$ $ $

The narratives offered by the wait staff working in chain restaurants show over and over again that people tip more with other people's money. It also appears that the management plays a strong role in the experience of the workers of chain restaurants, as does the perception of the clientele. Interestingly, it is the culture of the workplace that impacts the attitudes of managers and vice versa (see Billing and Alvesson 1994). Consistent with theories of trust and reciprocity in social and economic exchange, these narratives suggest that service workers in restaurants extend more credit to clients when they themselves are trusted by management and allowed a greater degree of control over their work environment. When the organizational climate is characterized by suspicion and mistrust, stereotypes dominate the perceptions of clients, and animosity typifies the relationships among employees.

The tip amount does not seem to be a strong signal to the server, but oftentimes people take leaps in logic when tips are determined to be reflexive of some aspect of the customer's character. In those cases in which workers interpret the tip to reflect their performance, there is not much specific information as to what exactly can be improved upon (except maybe "hustling" more). It is also interesting that the narratives indicate that people who liked their jobs tended to describe the customers more positively, and whether or not a server in a chain restaurant liked his/her job seems to be less associated with the tips than the management. The evidence indicates that management has an important impact on the experience of norms from the perspective of tipped employees. Management exercises a good deal of authority over tipping norms and the distribution system (the tip out). Perhaps more importantly, the tone set by management acts as a thermostat for the climate experience by the staff and the credit available to customers. In other words, people who are happier with their job feel like management extends some control over the work environment to employees, and those people tend to describe customers in more positive terms. Managers who attempt to induce heavy controls on employees and use tips as monitoring mechanisms appear likely to fail in at least two respects. First, restrictive management practices impair emotion management, increasing the potential harm of the emotional aspects of work and decreasing the likelihood that employees approach customers in a manner that facilitates reciprocity (Hochschild 1983). Second, tips are a weak signal regarding the quality of service and are unlikely to provide useful feedback to management or push out employees who are not well suited to service work.

2

Family Eateries

Family eateries are defined as family-run establishments that generally cater to families and often serve meals "family style." In comparison with the other work environments included in this study, restaurant workers in family eateries tend to describe their experiences in gendered terms. The respondents who worked in family eateries did not often relate their experiences to the demographic characteristics of the customers as much by comparison to the wait staff in chain restaurants. It also appears to be more common in family eateries than chain restaurants that salaried employees are not tipped out by the wait staff. Moreover, the relationship with management seems to be understood differently. The restaurant workers in family eateries tended to describe their experiences in accordance with their process of socialization at work. In other words, those who work in family eateries tended to talk about how they were trained, the "tip system," and often use "we" in reference to all those they work with at the restaurant. For example, several of the narratives in this section describe their work in terms of the competition or cooperation.

$ $ $

Linda worked for two years in a steakhouse that had peanut shells on the floor, located outside of Blacksburg, Virginia. This is Linda's story.
 I was paid $2.13 an hour—way below minimum wage.
 During a typical weeknight shift of four–six hours, I would earn $30 a night in tips. During a nine–ten hour weekend shift, I would earn $125 a night in

tips. I got the most tips on Saturday. I also got a small bonus at the end of the year—about $25.

I held all the money until the end of the night. The amount that I gave the manager went according to the following formula: (total sales + 3% of the sales) minus (amounts charged to the credit cards). I would keep the rest of the cash. This system ensured there was no cheating on reported tips.

The 3% of the sales went for tips to the busboys and hostess. They got their tips in a cash envelope when they received their paychecks. Their division of tips was pro-rated according to number of hours worked.

The bar staff also got a percentage of the bar totals since they made all the drinks. There were no tips for those on real salaries—the manager, dishwashers, and the cooks. I never gave the dishwashers or cooks extra tips. They were on salary.

I never gave additional money to the busboys, etc. The only person we gave other money to was the person who rolled the silverware. She was also paid $2.13 an hour but received no tips. Therefore, we each gave her $4 per shift. We had the choice of rolling our own silverware or paying her.

About 60% of the tips were via credit cards, and the rest came in from cash. College students tipped the best, especially if they were with their parents. The average tip was 12%. Many regulars tipped only 10%. One customer said, "Why should I tip you? You earn the same as I do—minimum wage." She did not realize that I only earned $2.13 an hour. I never raised the issue of a tip with a customer.

I liked the tip system. It was fair. Everyone worked hard.

$ $ $

Edgar has worked for the last five or six months at a family restaurant in Bethesda, Maryland. This is what Edgar had to say.

I like working there as the coworkers are really nice, and I like the atmosphere.

I earn $2.38 an hour. If all goes well—the food is on time, and I don't make any mistakes—I get 20% tips. If the timing is off, my tips will be 15% or lower. The morning shifts, which are for lunch, are four–five hours, and if it is busy, I will earn $30–$40 in tips. This is mostly a business crowd, they are in a rush and don't order drinks. The evening shifts are about six hours, and I can earn $100 on a good shift but average $60–$70.

I've never been stiffed for a tip. I sometimes (rarely) am given a tip of $1. This is usually from foreign people who don't know how much to tip.

At the end of the shift, I tip out the bus people for 2–3% of the total sales. This is not a company policy but is expected. There is no formal policy on this. I tip out according to how hard they worked and if I had a good shift. The bartender is also tipped out for either 1–2% of total sales or 5% of the bar total. If there are a lot of people at the bar and less at the tables, I tip out the bartender less. Alternately, if the bar is not crowded and more people are eating, I tip more. I don't tip out the hostess.

We don't talk about our tips. The system is not set in stone. If you get few tips, you still tip out the standard amount.

At one restaurant where I worked, we split all tips. I didn't like that as much. I like working for my tips. I'm in control.

With credit cards, the computer knows how much is for meals and how much is for tips. I hold all the cash and credit card receipts till the end of my shift, and then we settle up. If they owe me money for tips (a lot of credit card sales), I get cash out of the drawer. About 10% of the people who pay in credit card will leave a cash tip.

People tip the most when they are happy to go out. When they are expecting to have a good time, they will pay for it. Some people look for reasons not to leave a good tip such as the food being slow. In turn, they penalize the waiter even though it is not the worker's fault. You know they can round up or round down. Not getting that extra dollar means a lot psychologically. Sometimes I scratch my head.

$ $ $

Olivia is a waitress at a family restaurant in Watertown, Massachusetts. Here is her story.

The restaurant serves Mediterranean food at a medium price. There are a lot of regular customers. I've been working there for 16 years.

The restaurant fits into my life. I am an artist, and I have a lot of flexibility to paint during the day and still bring money into the family. When I go home, I leave the job at work.

We want 20% tips but probably average 18%. The tips are our bread and butter. Our typical shift is from 4:00 pm to 11:30. On a weeknight, I average $100 in tips, and on a Saturday night, I average $160 but hope for $200.

I rarely get small tips. The biggest tip I got was last Christmas when a businessman had 30 people in the restaurant for his office party. We tack on 18% for parties larger than eight. He paid the 18% which amounted to about $400, and then he added an additional $700 because we worked really hard. It was really nice.

We pool our tips. We started this about ten years ago. It used to be too confusing with our outdoor patio. The server who worked there was making all the money. Now we pool the tips, and we help each other out. It eliminated the competition and levels the playing field. We all work hard. If someone is late or has to leave early, we usually still give her the same amount. They need the money as much as I do, and it will even its way out.

The money goes into a kitty, and one person figures out the split at the end of the night. It takes 30–45 minutes to figure this out. When we take the tips we fill out a chart. We take the money in cash unless too much money came in from credit cards. Then, we get a check from the restaurant.

There was one holdout on pooling—the bartender. On busy nights, she would make a lot of money. We used to have to tip out 15% of the bar total to her. We sometimes got so mad we wanted to sell wine instead of cocktails, but on slow bar nights she also lost. She eventually realized that it all evens out. It took her a year to give in on pooling. There was a lot of tension.

It is hard with new people. They have to be team players. We have a lot of trust among us.

We tip out the bus person 15% of total tips. On the night we got the huge tip, we also gave some money to the cooks. When we are really busy, we have a food runner who gets 5% of the tips or a minimum of $30.

We get the smallest tips from foreigners. They don't understand the tipping culture. If we get a tip of less than 10%, sometimes the manager will ask if anything was wrong with the service. I've never done that. There is a stereotype that groups of women yak away and don't tip well. They do yak away, but they tip OK. You get surprised all the time at who will tip well. People who work in restaurants tip well. When you get a good tip, you feel understood.

$ $ $

Kelly was a server for two months at a waterfront sit-down crab restaurant near Annapolis, Maryland. This is what she had to say about receiving tips in a family eatery.

I hated working as a waitress. The pay was not good, and it was a lot of work. I got $2.35 an hour. Tips ranged but averaged out at 20%. It was really busy in the summer, and because of that, we were slow serving. When we were slow serving, our average tip was 15% or below.

I also ran food. I had a six hour shift as a runner.

My shift as a waitress was five–eight hours. On a good night, I could make $150. The beginning of the season was rainy, and on one night, I only made $15. There were no tables.

My biggest night was $250 on a weekend night. My biggest individual tip was $50 from a group that ordered a lot of crabs and a lot of other seafood.

I gave 1% of my sales to the bartender and 2% to the food runner. This occurred when I cashed out at night. If they were real good, I might give them an additional $5 or $10.

One night when I was a runner, the server did not tip me out properly. I talked to the manager, and I got my money.

When I became a server, I did not feel it was right to tip out the runner when I brought out most of the food. When there were two runners, I would split the tip out among them.

The hostess did not get a tip out. Once, I gave her 1% of my sales on a really good night. That happened just once.

There was a lot of competition among the servers. You wanted people who would order crabs. There were cliques at the restaurant. It was a very catty place. There was no cooperation. Other servers would let food get cold rather than help someone else who was busy. If you were friends with the hostess, she would help you out. I was friends with her but did not push for especially good tables.

I used to tip 15–20%. Now, I give 20% because I realize how hard it is.

You never know who is going to give you a good tip. You are often surprised. Older people tipped the most (40–60 years old). People I know tipped well. Younger people did not tip well, and the locals did not tip very well either. People who got off of a boat tipped the most.

$ $ $

Rick was a server for two summers and during winter vacations at a small Italian restaurant in Annapolis, Maryland. He was also interviewed for two of his other jobs: a food vendor at Redskin's games (essay not included) and working for commission selling executive education packages (essay in the companion volume). This is what Rick had to say about working in a restaurant.

The job was easy and fun and young. The restaurant was very family-oriented, and the work was not very hard. You did not have to memorize the menu.

I got paid $2.38 an hour. The average tip was 15–20%. The night shift was six hours, and I would get $60–$80 on a weeknight and $80–$120 on a weekend night. Lunch was not that great—$30–$50.

During lunch, we bused our own tables. At night, we tipped out 1% of food sales to the bus, and 10% of all alcohol to the bartender. If they did well, we gave them more. The bartender was often bad. I had to pour my own wine. The busser was good, so I usually gave him a few extra dollars. At cash-out, the manager would look at the computer and say, "you owe—say $15." I would usually give $20 to the manager who would give the extra money to the busser. If you treated them nicely, they treated you nicely.

There was not much competition among the servers.

On who tips the most—these are vague stereotypes. Middle-aged whites tipped well. Families tipped well. Older people were bad. Europeans were terrible. Asians and Indians were horrible. I sometimes got stiffed from Asians and Indians, or they would give you a dollar. The stereotype is that whites are better than blacks. This is only somewhat true.

When we had groups, we would add on 16% and tell them. About 25% of the time, they would not realize the gratuity was added on, and we would end up getting double tipped.

$ $ $

Cory worked for four months last summer at an Italian restaurant ten miles outside of St. Louis. The following narrative details his experiences receiving tips in a family restaurant.

The restaurant sold mostly pastas. It was high-paced some days and slow-paced at other times. The job was OK. I needed the money, so it worked out.

I was paid $3.10 an hour. The average tips were between 15% and 20%. I worked eight hour shifts. On a weekday shift, I took in only about $40 in tips. Over the weekend, I would take in $200.

I only had to tip out the busboy if we had five or more people at a table. If this was the case, I gave him one-third of my tip. I would occasionally slip him a few dollars on other tables. I would tip him out directly. We had a runner on the weekend, but I did not tip him out. I also did not tip out the bartender.

I got bigger tips from people who were friendlier. Middle-aged people tipped the most. High school kids did not tip well.

There was no real competition among the servers. There were a few who were competitive, but we were mostly team players.

Almost everyone paid with plastic—over 90%. If they paid in cash, the tips were put in the little black books. I had no problem with honesty.

$ $ $

Paul worked for seven months at a family restaurant serving Mexican food in Tennessee. Paul is also discussed elsewhere in this book where he worked the parking lots of Wal-Mart and Home Depot and as a worker at Chipotle. This is what Paul had to say about restaurant work.

I earned $2.13 an hour and lived off my tips. I liked the job. I like talking to people. I like the food industry, and I got to prepare food.

The tips went down when gas went up to $3 a gallon. Five percent did not tip at all. These were younger people and seemed to be angry in general.

The average tip was 10–15%. Mondays–Wednesdays were slow, and I would average $30 in a six hour shift. On Thursday and Friday, I would get $50–$70, and on Saturday nights, I could get up to $150.

We tipped out the cook 1% of our tips, the food runner 2% (they also made $5.15 an hour), and the bartender 1%. I did not tip the host as she got $7–$8 an hour.

The biggest tips came from older couples and those having business meetings. We had no minimum gratuity. There could be 50 people at a table, and there was no automatic gratuity added.

We all got along pretty well, and the host pretty much rotated the customers to the servers. Some of us were more skilled and might get a few more tables.

Fifty percent paid by credit card and 20% of those left a cash tip. We never had an honesty problem.

$ $ $

Theresa worked as a server in a soul food restaurant in Washington, D.C. for four months. Her job as a telemarketer is discussed in the companion volume. Here is what Theresa said about her work as a server in a family restaurant.

I liked the job at first. I liked the customers. My regular customers said I brought light into the restaurant. I needed the money since my scholarship had not yet come through. I quit because my tips were stolen by a woman who worked there as a server and a cashier. The food was very unhealthy in how it was prepared. The inspectors really need to check this place out.

I made $3 an hour. We did not sell liquor. The average bill was $15, and the average tip was $3. Thirty percent of the customers left no tip at all. In a typical three hour shift, I made $100 in tips.

Older men and families tipped the most. College students tipped the least. I learned to dress provocatively in order to get better tips from the older men. I also would drop the line that I was a student. Regulars also tipped more than other diners.

The cashier stole from my credit card tips. You could not tell the amounts of the tip from the receipt. I was given the tip from the credit card as soon as the person left. However, sometimes the tip was for $5, and I only got $2. I knew this from what some of my regular customers said. This happened a lot. I never told the manager because he would not have cared. I told some of my regulars who began to leave me cash tips.

$ $ $

Respondents working in family restaurants regularly mention the psychological and/or emotional elements of their experiences with tipping. "The emotional style of offering the service is part of the service itself" (Hochschild 1983, 5). They tend to describe the work environment or "atmosphere" rather than referring to the job, management, or customers as was more common among chain restaurant employees. The performance of emotional labor is exhausting for some and a source of satisfaction for others (see also Macdonald and Sirianni 1996). Research shows that a greater sense of control reduces the harm of emotional work (Hochschild 1983), and these narratives highlight that relationship as well. The respondents who describe work relationships as trusting also tend to express positive emotions about their work and often hold positive attitudes about their jobs.

Trust is necessary when uncertainty and risk are possible (Webster 1975). Many of the narratives describe the relative level of cooperation or competition, and in some cases, the perception of cooperation versus competition affects the experience of "trust" and "honesty" in the work environment. Cooperation, trust, and honesty appear to be correlated in these accounts. In fact, there are a number of examples of social pressure to cooperate, sometimes against the economic interests of an individual. This leveling is captured in statements like, "It all evens out."

3

Upscale Dining

Upscale dining is defined as those establishments serving entrees that are minimally priced at around $20. Upscale dining establishments are very often family-owned and not franchised but are not considered family eateries. Upscale dining includes high-end restaurants that may specialize in ethnic food or may have a menu determined by the chef.

$ $ $

Todd is a waiter at a high-end restaurant in Rehoboth Beach, Delaware. His work as a chambermaid is discussed in another chapter. This is Todd's story in his own words.

The typical entree is $25. I've been working at this restaurant for seven months. I love the restaurant. It is not corporate. It is individually owned, and I can wear whatever I want. Everyone is unique.

I make $2.13 an hour. The typical tip is 20%. I only get stiffed by mistake. Someone might take the credit card slip by mistake. In other situations, a party might split a bill, and half is paid by cash and half by credit card. They might assume the other person is leaving the tip. Sometimes the person will put half the bill on a credit card and pay the other half by cash. They mistakenly calculate the tip on just half the bill.

My biggest tip was from my friends who left $150 tip on a $400 bill. I do the same for my friends when I go to their restaurants.

At the end of the night, the bartender gets 13% of my tips, and the food runner gets 7%. If there is no food runner, I will give the bartender the full 20%. Sometimes there are few people sitting at the bar, and I will split my tips 50–50 with the bartender if he is acting as the food runner. We don't tip out the cooks because they get an hourly wage. We bus our own tables. Sometimes there is a backup waiter for me. I will give him the "host" salary of $50.

I calculate the tip outs myself and give the people cash at the end of the night. If everyone is paying by credit card (a rare occurrence), I will write them a note for the next night.

My typical shift is from 4 pm to 11 pm. I make $200 in tips on a Saturday night and $150 on a Friday night. In the middle of the week—off season—I sometimes make only $50, and on some nights, no one walks in. During the season, I make $150–$200 every night. After Labor Day, there is less business. But, there are also less servers, so I can still do well.

[Spontaneously] Tipping is a great study of demographics. People from Pittsburg tip 5%. They are brought up that way. Lesbians are horrible tippers. I sometimes get $6 on a $150 bill. I don't know why they tip so poorly. Some blacks, teachers, and some who are retired don't tip as well. The best tippers are gay men; perhaps that is because I am gay as well. Young heterosexuals on dates are pretty good tippers. Europeans tip 10%.

Families with kids will order the one kid-friendly item we have on the menu (pasta with butter sauce or a red sauce). They don't compensate for the cheaper items that the kids are ordering. I like kids, but this is a business. They are not optimal from a tipping perspective.

$ $ $

Indira works at a waitress at a moderately expensive Indian restaurant in Washington, D.C. She has worked there for three years. During the daytime, she works as an accountant. This is what Indira had to say about her experience working in an upscale dining establishment.

I like working there. The food and environment are authentic, and the people are nice. I like customer service a lot. There are a lot of different people from many different cultures.

I make $2.77 an hour. The average tip from Americans is 20%. Europeans do not tip very well. They average 10%. Arabs and Indians also tip around 10%. The best tip I ever got was 40% for a table of four. I was so happy.

We pool all of our tips. The tips are distributed by the manager at the end of the night based upon a point system. We get cash. Servers and runners have the same share. Bussers make less. For every $100 I make in tips, the bussers make $55–$60. On the other hand, the bussers get paid $5 an hour, while I get $2.77. The bartenders are not part of this system. They get their own tips, and they make the most money. The hostesses are also not part of this system. They sometimes get their own direct tips.

I like the pooling of tips. If we kept our own tips, we would concentrate on our own tables. By pooling tips, we all help out. If you are free in your section, you help in another section. We know each other very well. We have worked together in this restaurant since it opened. We change sections every night, so the amount of work evens out over time.

On a good night, I will make $200 in tips. On a bad night such as the night after Thanksgiving, I will make about $100.

When I go to a restaurant, I tip 20–30%. I know how much a tip means to a server. Servers always tip well at other places.

[Indira refused to take the $10, saying that she was just happy to help.]

$ $ $

Jenny has been a waitress at two upscale restaurants. The following narrative details her experiences receiving tips at upscale restaurants.

The first restaurant was an upscale restaurant in Eastern Pennsylvania on the Delaware River. They served seafood and fillets. The average entree was pricey, about $28–$42. I liked how the restaurant looked. It had a waterfall going through it, but I did not like my boss.

I was paid $2 an hour. The tips were always 20%. People who went there did not go on a regular basis. They went on special occasions and were expecting to spend a lot of money. I don't ever remember getting a bad tip.

The evening shift was from 5 pm to midnight. On the weekends, I would earn $150–$250 in tips. During weeknights, the tips averaged $50–$150. We also had a lunch shift from 12:00 to 2:00. I could make $30 on a bad day and $100 on a good day.

I gave 10% of my tips to the bartender. This was on the honor system. We bused our own tables, and the hostess was the owner. So, she did not get a tip out. We declared our tips at the end of the night, and we always took out our tips in cash at the end of the night. That was nice.

For large groups, an 18% gratuity was automatically tacked on to their bill. They usually gave more. The larger the party, the larger the tip percent over 18%. My biggest tip was $300 for a holiday party of 25 that I handled all on my own.

The second restaurant where I worked is a nicer restaurant. Entrees range from $18 to $25. There is also a pub where they serve sandwiches and salads. I get paid $5 an hour for working days and $3 an hour for working nights. On a Saturday night, I can make $120–$200—sometimes $250. During the week, I make $120–$150 at night and $110 during the day.

I give 10% of my tips to the busser. This is done on the honor system. The bartender is given $5 per shift for nights only. The bartender collects the tips for the busser as well. Although the hostess is not the owner, we do not tip her.

Women are much worse tippers—especially older women. Businessmen tip the most.

There is no competition among the servers. We are assigned sections.

When I go to restaurants, I always tip 20% or more. If the service is good, you should give a good tip even if the meal is bad. Being in the industry, I know when the server deserves a good tip.

[Jenny was interviewed again in 2008 when the recession began. She said that tips have gone down a fair amount.] You used to be able to depend upon 20%, but not anymore. People tip more with credit cards, and lately people have been paying more with cash.

$ $ $

Cam has worked as a server for the last six months at a restaurant in Washington, D.C. The following narrative details Cam's experiences receiving tips.

The restaurant is laid-back but upscale. I like working there. I have control over how much money I make. My tips (which is how I make money) depend upon the quality of my work.

I get $2.77 per hour. The tips are almost always 18%. For a four hour lunch period, I get $50–$70 in tips, and for a four hour night shift, I get $100–$120. My biggest night was $300. That night I worked in the cocktail area, and people ordered a lot of food and drinks.

I share tips in the following way. The food runners get 2% of food sales. There are two runners, and one of them is my favorite. I will usually give them more than the 2%.

The busboys—there are six—collectively split 2% of total sales (not just food).

I don't have to give the hostess money, but I usually give her $2 for the lunch shift and $5 for the dinner shift.

There is no set fee for the bartender. I usually give him $3 for lunch, and out of courtesy, I will give him $5 for a good night shift.

At the end of the shift, we cash-out with the manager. I then give tip outs in cash to the people I mentioned.

Drinkers tip the most. Whites who are just out of professional school (young doctors, lawyers, etc.) also tip well. Europeans and foreigners don't tip well. They are not used to tipping at home.

African-Americans don't tip well to a degree [Note: the respondent is African-American]. But, this depends upon how your treat your tables. If you treat everyone well, there are no real racial differences.

There are also verbal tippers. They compliment you a lot and are very nice to you, but they are horrible tippers.

I leave 18% when I go to restaurants.

A serving job is great when you are in school and you need some extra quick cash. The hours are flexible, and it's great if you're a people person. However, it sucks as a career. There are no retirement or health benefits. You got to be cool under pressure to get tips. If you maintain control over your table and don't let people see that you are sweating, you will do OK.

$ $ $

Samuel is also discussed in the companion volume where he worked as a telemarketer and sold ads on his own website. This is what he had to say about tipping norms.

I worked for a year as a server at the Capitol City Brewing Company. This was a restaurant near Union Station and Capitol Hill in Washington, D.C. I liked the job initially because the money was good, and I did not have to work very hard. I eventually disliked the job because people talked down to you. The customers did not respect me. I got written up a lot because when they were rude to me, I was rude back to them. I got paid $2.15 an hour. The average tip was 15%. I would make about $10 an hour in tips. In a typical six hour shift, I would get $60–$80. This really varied. Some days were $30, and others were $200. The season had a lot to do with it. Winter was slow and so was August when Congress was on vacation. Tourist season in the spring was good and so was fall when Congress came back from vacation.

I tipped out 3% of my sales to the busboy, 1.5% to the runner, and 1% to the bartender. We got print-outs of sales at the end of each shift, and I gave them their money directly. I occasionally gave the busboy extra, especially when there was a big party. For parties of eight or more, they would automatically add 20%. Very rarely did people in these large parties give you more.

Women tipped poorly, were very demanding, and most likely to complain. Blacks [respondent is black] tipped a lot or very little. In general, they tipped poorly. Foreigners, especially Europeans, were horrible tippers. The elderly were tight with their money. Interns on the hill were bad. They had inflated egos, looked down on you, tipped poorly, and had the attitude that I was there simply to serve them.

The section you were in made the biggest difference. You did not want the smoking section. The best section was where people stayed late. You would get an extra two hours in and could double your tips. Cute server girls seemed to get the preferred sections. In general, the manager tried to be fair on rotating you in and out of sections, but it could have been done better.

You really wanted the big parties in the back room. They would have huge checks with 20% tacked on, and you would be done in a couple of hours. After you served, the busboys would clean up.

Half the people paid with credit cards. Of those who paid with credit cards, 10% left their tip in cash. Almost everyone left the credit card statement and/or cash in the little black book we gave them when they got their bill. There was no problem with dishonesty from the other staff.

Tips rarely depended upon how well you did. Some people don't have it in them to tip.

$ $ $

Mary has been a waitress at a fancy ocean beach hotel on the Delmarva Peninsula. She works in the restaurant and also delivers room service. This is what she had to say.

I've been at this hotel for five years. I like it a lot because I interact with people. I am a big talker as you can tell. I've been a server for 19 years. It is easy money, and no one tells me what to do. I'm a real fireball. I get paid $3 an hour.

The average gratuity in the restaurant is 15–18%. Our slow day is Friday when people are checking out. On slow days, I average $100–$125 in tips. On good days, I get $250–$300.

Winter is not bad. A lot of the locals come as they try to avoid the crowds in the summer. The hotel also has different plans to bring people in using fashion shows, package plans, etc. One of the package plans includes hotel stay, meals, and gratuities. When the gratuities are included, I get 18% from the hotel when I ring up the free bill, and about 75% of the customers will still give a tip. The average tip they give is $5 cash per meal.

The best tippers are gays, and they are also very easy going. A lot of the tip depends on the server. You have to talk to people and be upbeat.

Each server tips out the bussers. It is 15% times 25% times the total bill, so if my shift total is $400, we give $400 x .15 x .25 = $15. I don't know why they do it in such a complicated way [Note: this comes out to 3.75% of sales]. We don't tip out the bartender or runner. If the busser is working extra hard, I will give him a few extra bucks. Sometimes I will give him an extra $20.

When I do room service, 18% is automatically added on to the bill. About half will give me more. They usually add an extra 5–10% to the bill, so instead of an 18% tip, I might get 23–28%.

We sometimes use runners to take the food to the rooms. We do this when it is really busy. The 18% will appear as my tip, and I just give it to the runner.

There are some other sources of tips. Some VIPs will sometimes give me $5 just for clearing a table when it is not my table. Because I take food orders over the phone, sometimes a guest will come down and slip me a few bucks just to say thanks.

$ $ $

Perhaps the most notable theme among the responses provided by those who work in upscale restaurants is that so many inferences seem to be made about the customers. The inferences about customers made by the servers in upscale restaurants are quite inconsistent. Race, gender, sexual orientation, geographical frame of reference, and assumptions about the economic status of customers are regularly employed to explain tips. Although, it is important to point out that Cam did note that the tipping behavior of black clients is most likely related to how they are treated by the server. Surprisingly few of the respondents provide much information about the quality or consistency of the service they provide. There also appears to be variation within this context regarding the experience of social status. Some of the respondents describe interactions with customers that are demeaning, and other servers describe a sense of control that they attribute to the tipping system. However, many of the respondents do point out that the lack of benefits and the assumption that people in service occupations should be working toward careers in higher status occupations make the work an OK job but terrible career.

Several of the respondents discuss the emotional value of their labor. Of particular note are the responses that reflect how servers are expected to react to perceived rudeness by customers and the emotional costs associated with that type of interaction. For example, Samuel reports that he "got written up a lot because when customers were rude, [he] was rude back to them." This exemplifies how tipping norms are used to monitor employees but also demonstrates how this form of control can undermine a person's sense of self. In other words, the extent to which workers must subtract themselves from the emotional machinery of their experiences impacts their ability to access their "real selves" (Hochschild 1983). Consequently, workers who are subject to interactions that are demeaning on a regular basis have to choose between the cost of suppressing their emotions to make money (see also Macdonald and Sirianni 1996) or not concealing their true emotions and risking serious financial consequences. As Cam states, "You got to be cool under pressure to get tips."

4

Bussers and Runners

Bussers are responsible for clearing and cleaning tables so that they can be turned around as quickly as possible. Often, bussers are required to do the bulk of the cleanup at the end of the night as well. Runners are responsible for helping ensure that the food reaches the tables hot and fast. There is a considerable degree of variation. Some restaurants do not have bussers or runners. In some restaurants, bussers and runners make at least minimum wage, and may be tipped at the discretion of the wait staff. In other restaurants, bussers and runners make less than minimum wage and rely on tips from the wait staff or tips that are divided among the staff. The following narratives describe the experiences of bussers and runners.

$ $ $

Carla works as a busser/runner at a French restaurant in Northern Virginia. This is her second job. Her other job as an office cleaner is discussed elsewhere and her previous job as a babysitter is also discussed in another chapter. She speaks very little English, and an interpreter was used in this interview.

    I get paid $5 an hour. The waiters decide how much to give me from their tips. I don't think there is a formula. On Thursday, there is one bus and two waiters, and I usually get $96 for myself. On Saturdays, there are two bussers, and we both split the $96. Yes, even though it is busier on Saturday, I make less money.

The waiters make more on Saturday, but they have it in their head to give the busser (or busses) no more than $96. On a slow day, we might only split $30.

Sometimes a customer will slip me a few bucks. One lady often gives me $10 or $12. Every once in a while, the owner will slip me $50 and tell me to keep quiet about it. This occurs when I am doing extra work. Or it is a slow day, and the waiters are not giving me much of their tips.

I like the waiters. However, only one shows me the cash receipts at the end of the night.

$ $ $

Miles was a busboy for a summer at a fine dining restaurant in the D.C. area. The next summer he moved up in that organization's hierarchy to a runner. Here is what Miles had to say about his experiences in his own words.

Next year I will be a server. I loved working there. The staff was really nice.

I got paid $5 an hour. All the servers put 10% of their tips into a pot for the busboys, and they put another 10% of their tips into a pot for the runners. There were two–four busboys and one–two runners; depending upon how busy was the restaurant. The runners made more money as there were less of them to split up the tips.

The opening shift was from 10 am to 4 pm. You usually only received $25–$40 in tips for that shift. The closing shift was from 4 pm to 9 pm, and sometimes it could last till 1 am. The average tip the busboy received was $50–$100. Runners would get more.

You did best with parties. I once got $220 for a party. It was a wedding, and I think the person who paid us was really drunk.

Tip outs are given by the servers on the honor system. I had my doubts about one server. I think he under-tipped. Someone else had an argument with him about this. The managers were not brought into this.

The bartender did not have to tip out, but he would occasionally slip me $20 if I was really helpful to him. Every once in a while a server would give you an extra $10 or $20 if you did a particularly good job. He would slip it directly to you, and it did not go into the pool.

[When Miles was re-interviewed after the beginning of the recession, he had become a server at an upscale restaurant.] The tip percentage has stayed the same. However, there are fewer people in the restaurant. "Business is slow."

$ $ $

Tony was a food runner for three and a half years at an Italian restaurant in Pottstown, Pennsylvania. He has since returned to college. Tony shared the following.

I liked working at the restaurant. It was family owned. The pace was fast and because of this, it was not a drag. You were exhausted but well paid at the end of the night.

I was paid $4.50 an hour. I got 10% of the server's tips and 5% of the tips of the bartender. This was done at the end of the evening. It was on the honor system. Sometimes you know a server cheated, but you didn't argue about it. You might occasionally say something, and they made it up the next night.

We pooled our tips among the bussers. The servers and bartender would give our tips to the manager, and we would split it up at the end of the night. My shifts were from 5 pm to 11 pm. I would leave with $50–$70 on average. The best night was New Years and Mother's Day. I would get $120 in tips. I never got a direct tip from a customer. Sometimes the server or bartender gave an extra tip out. They would say good job and put an extra $10 into the pot.

When I go to a restaurant, I give at least 20% unless the service was horrible. I understand what it is like to work in a restaurant.

$ $ $

Brian was a busboy for two years at a steakhouse in Cincinnati. After being a busboy, he became a banker. His experience as a banker is discussed in the companion volume. This is what Brian had to say about working as a busboy.

It was a very upscale steakhouse with a high-class atmosphere. I liked working there.

I earned $2.15 an hour. I also got 18–20% of the servers' total tips. This was done on the honor system. I trusted them. I worked for them, and they worked for me. Eighteen percent was the minimum. If I did a good job, I got 20% or more.

I got to the restaurant at 3 pm to set up, and the restaurant opened at 5 pm. I would often be there till midnight cleaning up. On a good weeknight, I would get $80 in tips. On a good weekend, I usually earned between $100 and $120.

About three–four times a month, I got a direct tip. A customer would love my attitude and give me $5 or $10. I also got occasional tip outs from a bartender. He might ask me to get a case of beer. Therefore, I got a $5 bill five or so times a month.

Business people were most likely to tip well. People tipped well if they saw what you were doing, and they appreciated it. Hillbillies didn't appreciate what you were doing and didn't leave crap.

The high rollers would get the best tables. They would be known, or they might call in advance and say put a $1,000 bottle of wine on the table. They got the best servers, and the servers got the best bussers. I was one of the best bussers.

About 8 months after I started working at the restaurant, a team of three bussers got together and took over the bussing as a team. We worked as a team and shared our tips. At first, the servers gave us our tip outs individually, and we split it up. There was some shafting in that process. Someone would keep an extra $5 or so. Some would not put all their money into the kitty. To remedy this, we had the servers give the tips to a bartender, and then we would split it up.

That generally worked well. However, we had some arguments because not everyone worked as hard. Why should we share when our tables were bringing in higher tips? We stopped sharing. It wasn't fair. We went back to keeping our own tips. That required the restaurant to hire more bussers because we were no longer a team.

Each server has three tables, and each busser has about three servers. I stopped helping other bussers. There was a lot of animosity. We were out to make our own money.

$ $ $

The narratives of the bussers and runners interviewed show a different perspective of the restaurant business. Bussers and runners appear to view the tips as more often a reflection of the quality of their work. However, they also tend to imply a consistency in their work effort and explain withholding of tips by wait staff as a matter of selfishness on the part of an individual. These stories reveal a more vulnerable workforce that depends a great deal on other people who have more interaction with the customers. They have to trust that others give them their fair share or work out a way to instill credibility in the system (e.g.; having the bartender distribute the tips to the bussers rather than one of the bussers divide the tips). In some cases, bussers and runners rely on the generosity of other restaurant workers to level their pay. "Slipping" bussers and runners additional money may also serve the interests of those providing the bonus by incentivizing certain behaviors, facilitating loyalty, and minimizing animosity in addition to possibly being perceived of as generous, kind, or a "good boss."

Conformity to norms and norm enforcement are evident in these narratives. Sharing and "working as a team" is perceived as valuable and respondents report that this behavior tends to result in higher wages. Additionally, those who do not conform or when compliance is not sustained, the situation is often described as "unfair," or the person who does not cooperate is referred to as "selfish." The narratives also illustrate a number of different mechanisms for enforcing conformity and facilitating trust in the tipping system, including relying on a third party to distribute tips. Perhaps most notably, the respondents tend to report more consistent and trusted evaluations of their work performance from those who have first-hand knowledge of the demands of the job.

5

Bartenders, Cocktail Servers, and Bar-Backs

Bartenders make and serve drinks behind the bar and made the drinks for the wait staff to serve to customers who do not go to the bar. Cocktail wait staff are most often women (although not always) and usually referred to as cocktail waitresses. Bar-backs are sometimes referred to as bar porters and are primarily responsible for ensuring that the bar is clean and fully stocked at all times with ice, glasses, beer, coffee, and so on. These servers rarely handle food themselves, usually work afternoon/evening or night shifts, and are often more likely to deal with customers with impaired judgment. Bartenders, cocktail servers, and bar-backs often work closely, may divide tips among themselves in a number of ways, and usually depend on volume sales. Consequently, there is a good deal of variation in their experiences, particularly when compared to food-service staff.

$ $ $

Jean has been a bartender for the last nine months at a casino in Connecticut. This is her story in her own words.

I love it. I am in the bar with the high rollers. There are good conversations and good money. High rollers are people who bet a minimum of $100 at the tables; very often they are betting $1,000 or $10,000.

I get paid $8 an hour. I am a bartender, and I also bring drinks to the tables. The drinks are free and are of high quality. Ninety-five percent of the people I serve tip me. The average tip is $5 to $25 per drink. I was once tipped $500. On my best night, I earned $900 in tips. Most people give me chips instead of cash. I cash in my chips once a week.

There are only four betting tables in the area that I work, and there are not many people. On average, I bring home $200 to $300 per night.

Some high rollers offered me trips to Florida or Boston. I've been offered cars. There is a price for this, and I have not taken any of these offers up.

Regulars tip the most. They know me and want to keep up their reputation with everyone. You are not going to use my name—right. Asians tip the least. Some tip well, but the majority tip a dollar or not at all.

When I am at the bar, usually one person leaves a tip for the couple or the group. Twenty dollars is the average tip for two drinks. The bar is rarely full. I go back and forth between the bar and the floor. I get an extra $50 just for tending the bar because it is slow.

We do not share our tips. I am supposed to give my bar-back 5% of my tips. I actually give him 20%.

We don't talk among ourselves about how much we make. I don't want to lose my bar to someone with more seniority. I tell them that I only earned $10 last night.

You have to be personable. Personality is important as well as having a professional look. I wear a tuxedo shirt, bowtie, and a black vest. I am always clean, and my makeup is perfect.

Most of the customers are nice. They are cocky and expect a lot.

[Jean was also re-interviewed in 2008 after the beginning of the economic downturn.] Tips are way down. I used to get $5 tips, and now it is only $2 or $3. Most people are tipping less. The price of gas is up, and the economy is not doing as well.

$ $ $

Hugh is a bar porter at a casino in Connecticut. Here is what he had to say.

A bar porter is also called a bar-back. I clean up around the bar, make sure the beer is tapped, sodas are flowing, and that there is plenty of ice. I've been doing this for four years. I like the job because of the money. There is a lot of potential to make money.

I start out at $6.75 an hour. Both the bartender and the servers tip me out at 5% of their tips. You have to trust them. Some don't tip you what they should. They will make up reasons like "you didn't have the coffee ready." Others will just walk out without tipping you. Others give you large tips. They might have made $50 in tips and will give you $10. They say, "You did such a fantastic job. I just have to reward you."

I work an eight hour shift. My tips range from $10 to $200. The average is $30–$40 a night. My biggest night was $200—I really had to run. Sweat was running down my head, and the bartender said, "You really busted butt tonight."

One Japanese businessman gave a bartender $15,000 as a tip. It was not my bartender. I wish it was. One high roller almost gave me a black chip ($100). He was just kidding with me.

I have a tough job. I can't do anything else without going to college. I am not physically well enough to work construction.

You get good tips when you keep everyone happy. It is the same as when I used to work at McDonalds. You want to keep the customer happy. I have a tip bucket. Some servers will put money in throughout the night. Others will wait till the end of their shift. Some estimate how much they owe me, while others will count up their tips and pay me exactly.

$ $ $

Dorothy was a bartender throughout her undergraduate and graduate education at a college bar in Bethlehem, Pennsylvania. This is what Dorothy had to say about her experience as a bartender.

I loved working there. I interacted with people. It was fast paced, and I made good money. The bar was in a historic restaurant and had food during the day. It was mostly a bar scene at night.

I was paid $5.50 an hour. The average tip was not percentage based. College students gave $1 per drink, and even if they ordered two drinks, they would give a dollar. Business people would tip much more. They would tip $1 to $2 (average $1.50) for a beer and $2.50 for a more complicated drink like a Cosmo.

A lot of the tipping depended on how well they knew you and if you could connect with them. I would compliment a person in some way or remember a detail about what they like to drink (for example, no fruit or a brand of vodka). You needed to connect with the customer. Touch them on a personal basis. If someone was from the Midwest, I would say, "so is my dad." I would joke around a lot. Little items made a big difference.

On the Saturday night shift of four hours, I would get $250–$300 in tips. During the summer, there was an outdoor bar on the patio and—with working some tables—I could get $200–$250 on a good night. It was a very long night—ten hours.

I did real well with parties. If there was an open bar, they would add 20% for my tip. About 70% of the people would also give me a tip per drink for the open bar. I would get $200 in three–four hours.

I also got tips from the hostess and servers who dealt with drinks. There was no set policy. They gave me what they felt like. I would get $5–$10 per server for a total of $20–$30 per night.

I tipped out the bar-back 20% of my tips. I sometimes gave him more. We never argued about tips.

$ $ $

Leslie is a bartender in Cincinnati and a personal trainer (essay not included). This is what Leslie had to say about her experience as a bartender in her own words.

I love bartending. I like to talk to people. I can't stand sitting around. I am social, and I can make more money. Our bar does not serve much food. We have DJs, karaoke, and several bar areas.

I get $2.50 an hour. The average tip is 20%. It depends more on the person than the drink. Two people can order the same thing and tip very differently. Some might tip higher because I'm a cute girl.

Some people don't tip at all. You remember them. You don't serve them quickly. I also remember those who tip well.

A beer costs $3.25. A person usually leaves a dollar tip or rounds up to $5 and leaves $1.75 in a tip. Usually, a person will order several drinks that average out to $12. They will leave $2 or $3. Usually, they leave $3 as it rounds up to $15.

My shift is 9 pm to 3 am. On Fridays, I usually make $100 in tips, and on Saturday night, I can make $200 if I am extra social. I don't work many weekdays. My best night was New Year's when I got $500 in tips.

I share tips with a bar-back. I tip him out depending upon how hard he is working. He gets 20% of my tips if he is good. Last night he was not good. I put away a lot of my own liquor, did a lot of my own cleaning and got a lot of ice. He got 10%. He didn't really care because I was at one of the little bars.

If two of us are working a bar, we split the cash 50–50. We put the cash in a bucket next to the register. However, we keep our own credit card tips. The system is pretty honest. If a friend comes and leaves $20, we might not put that in the common pot. There are some people on the job with whom I would not like to work. However, we are mostly girls and are pretty close.

There are no real stereotypes on who tips well. A guy could be hitting on you and leave no tip, and a girl might leave you a good tip. You never know.

$ $ $

Jonathan has had several jobs where he took in tips: a bartender and bar manager, a manager of a spa, and a house cleaning service. He is the bar manager and bartender in an upscale restaurant in Rehoboth Beach, Delaware. Jonathan shared the following about his experience as a bartender and bar manager.

The bar has four stools and five small tables. I've been the bartender for a year, and I really like the job. It is a lot of fun. The staff is sweet. They have great food, and the restaurant is very popular. I receive an hourly wage of $6 or $7.

People tip at two ends of the scale. Some will leave a buck a drink. Others will leave a percentage. My drinks average $10. Half will give me a buck, and half will give me 20% ($2). When there is a large group waiting for a table, they might order six drinks for $65. On average, they will leave $10. Very few people leave almost nothing.

One time, a person that I knew from another job came to the bar. He asked for a club soda which I gave him for free. He left no tip. It was galling. I would have left $10—or the cost of the drink. If you get a free drink, you should always leave the cost of the drink.

I remember big tippers. They get better service. Some people repel you on a molecular level. They are simply obnoxious, but a good tip makes up for a lot. If someone in a group is being obnoxious, someone in that group should leave a larger tip.

I also get tipped out by the waiters at the end of the night. If a server makes $200 in tips, 20% ($40) goes to the floor. I get 75% of the $40, and the rest would go to the food runner.

On my busiest night, I made $350 in tips. My average is $150. On a bad night, I might only make $20 or $30. I have no bar-back, so I don't usually share tips. I once gave the dishwasher $20 as a thank you when she voluntarily cleaned the restroom.

It is hard to predict who will tip well. It is often surprising. People do not understand the importance and impact of their tipping. Generous tipping can make the experience more memorable than you will ever know. I would rather cut off my hand than be considered cheap. Some people (like my parents) are tightwads.

[We re-interviewed Jonathan when the economic-downturn began. He reported that tips had not changed for him.]

$ $ $

Gary was a bartender for years at a casual dining restaurant outside of Nashville, Tennessee. He is discussed in the companion volume in his job as a tire salesman. Here is Gary's story.

I was paid $2.13 an hour. My shifts were from 4 pm to 1 am. On a weekday, I would make $80 in tips, and on weekends, I would get $110–$150. At the bar, the average tip was a buck a beer and $2 for a mixed drink or a glass of wine.

If we had a busy night and had two bartenders, we would put our tips in a jar and split it at the end of the night. Sometimes a customer would say this tip was for you. I would put that in my pocket. We caught one bartender putting tips in his pocket. He was fired.

I got my biggest tips from white males in their mid 20s and my smallest tips from African-American females. I know the likes and dislikes of the regulars, and hence I got bigger tips from them. A regular would usually tip 20–30%.

The servers put 1% of their sales into a common pool which was split between the hostess and bartenders. I would get somewhat more if the liquor sales were high that night. The manager would give me this. The average that I received from the servers was an additional $35 per night.

We only occasionally had a bar-back. If he worked really hard, I would give him $10. If he also helped clean up, I might give him $20.

Seventy-five percent of the bills were paid by credit card and 10% of these people would leave a cash tip. Blacks were more likely than whites to pay in cash.

$ $ $

Stacey has been a cocktail waitress at a casino outside of St. Louis for the last seven months. This is what she had to say about receiving tips as a cocktail waitress at a casino.

I don't like the clientele. They are not very smart. There is not that much sexual harassment, but they are not that nice. However, I like the people I work with.

I get paid $4.50 an hour. We used to give out free drinks. Now we charge. We still give out free soda, juice, and water. Tips have gotten worse lately—maybe because we now charge for drinks. I only work Saturdays and Sundays. I used to get $200 for two days. Now, I get $150.

About 25% of the people at the slot machines will tip me. The average tip is a quarter or 50 cents—sometimes a dollar. About 75% will tip me at the tables—usually 50 cents or a dollar. I don't know why the slots are different than the tables.

The average tip for both is 50 cents. We charge $2.50–$3.25 for a beer. People who order martinis are at the tables, and they tip better.

My biggest tip was $65. This guy had one drink and a couple of waters. I guess he just liked me.

We do not pool our tips. We are supposed to tip out the bartender between 15% and 20% of our tips. Fifteen percent is the minimum. I always give 20%. I don't think that gives me better service. The bartenders make more from the people that order from the bar, and they get first priority.

There is no competition among the waitresses.

Middle-aged white men tip the best [the respondent is black]. Middle-aged black women tip the least.

[Stacey was re-interviewed after the beginning of the recession. She had changed jobs and now works as a server at an upscale restaurant.] Business is down. Everything is so expensive. I used to get 20% tips. Now, I only get 10%. I have to do a whole lot more flirting than I used to.

$ $ $

Desta works for a catering company and is also a bartender. She is from Ethiopia. She was interviewed serving drinks at a fundraiser in Washington, D.C. This is what Desta had to say about bartending for a catering company.

I work for the catering company every two or three weeks. I bar tend for them at events. I like working for them. It is fun, the job is easy, and the pay is good.

I get $18–$20 per hour. I usually work an eight–nine hour shift. At some functions, I am not allowed to take tips. At other functions, the person putting the function on will sometimes give us a tip at the end. At the last function, I got $100 that way. At other functions, I have a tip jar. Last night I was at an out-of-the-way table, and I only got $9 in the tip jar. I gave half to the girl helping me. Usually, I get $40–$50 in the tip jar.

[Desta also works as a bartender at a fancy hotel in downtown Washington, D.C. Here is what she had to say about her work as a bartender.]

I like the job because it is a good crowd.

I get paid $11.49 an hour. The average tip is $15–20%. It depends on the person. Europeans don't tip well, and Arabs don't tip. I get 15–18% for all the drinks—from beer to martinis.

I usually work the morning shift, and it is slower. I get $40–$50 in tips, and I spend a lot of my time helping to set up for the evening shift. If there is a big function at the hotel, I can get $300 in tips by bartending. The tips at night are usually $100–$200. I also get tipped by the servers. That averages $50–$60 a night from all of them. There is no fixed amount of what they should tip me. They pay what they think is right.

I don't share my tips. There is no bar-back or busser.

[We re-interviewed Desta after the economic downturn. She said that the tip amount is the same, but business is way down.] "The bar is basically empty."

$ $ $

Dwight worked as a bar-back at a nice bar in Pittsburg. He also worked there as security. This is Dwight's story in his own words.

I was paid $7 an hour. A bar-back gets ice and bottles and cleans the bar area. As the night gets older, I would take out enormous amounts of trash.

Each waitress gave me $3–$4 an hour, and the two bartenders I worked with would give me $5 an hour. If the bartender had a bad night, he would give me the minimum. With a good night, I got a larger amount. I averaged between $65 and $120 in tips. At the end of the night the bartenders and waitresses counted what they made and then gave me my share. I trusted them. We had a good rapport.

I was tipped only a few times by a customer. This happened when I helped them find something or for some other special service.

I also worked as a security guard (bouncer) at the bar. I would ID people and act as doorman. Some people would want to skip the line. They would say, "What would it cost me to get in?" I'd ask how much were they thinking. Whatever they said I would ask for more. They would say, "$10." I would say, "How 'bout $20." This did not happen a lot. I averaged $10 a night for these under the table tips.

$ $ $

The narratives of cocktail waitresses, bartenders, and bar-backs reveal a number of trends that are consistent with existing research on socialization, gender, and role-specific behavior. "The cultural rules and rituals of bar life reaffirm the definitions and status attached to masculinity and feminity" (Spradley and Mann 1975, 3). Male and female roles often represent an extension of the traditional view of women as passive, sexual objects, low in status, peripheral to male social life, and as persons who serve others (for less). "People learn the values and attitudes of their sexual identities, not from philosophical statements or even serious formal discussion, but as they interact with members of the opposite sex in routine activities" (Spradley and Mann 1975, 145). In the gendered workplace, sexuality is a double-edged sword because it can increase earnings while simultaneously decreasing status. For example, Leslie pointed out that "[s]ome might tip me higher because I'm a cute girl."

Higher status male coworkers and employers, as well as customers, tend to interact with female employees in ways that attempt to increase the social distance and reinforce the sexual division of labor and the correspondingly unequal value of that labor to sustain power (see also, LaPointe 1992). The norms of tipping within the system exemplify this to some extent as well. For example, cocktail waitresses are most often women. They are also expected to conform to tipping norms that require them to tip out bartenders and bar-backs who are more often than not male and almost always make more than the waitresses. In addition, "They [the bartenders] get first priority." The highly gendered aspect of this type of work is also evident in their lived experiences. Jean's narrative provides a fairly clear illustration of how women in "traditionally female jobs" are less likely to perceive and report sexual harassment because it is often perceived as "part of the job" (Gutek 1985). Jean states, "Some high roller offered me trips to Florida or Boston. I've been offered cars. There is a price for this, and I have not taken any of these offers up." The implication is that she has been solicited and that "high rollers" who subtly request services well beyond her job description are not described as sexually harassing her.

6

Multi-Function Staff

Multi-function staff are classified as those restaurant employees who work several jobs in the same restaurant and/or in several restaurants. Some people gravitate toward restaurant jobs, and some of their stories allow us to compare and contrast different types of restaurant jobs or different roles in the restaurant. The responses of multi-function staff also provide an understanding of the work environment from several perspectives as described by the same individual. The value added by this approach is that people who have experience in various positions in an organization may describe a more comprehensive understanding of the tipping system and evaluate the experience differently.

$ $ $

Steve has worked at Houston's restaurant in Bethesda for the last four months. He also worked as a runner and as a busser in Delaware. Previously, he was employed as a lifeguard (essay not included). This is Steve's story.

   Business has been slow lately. When business is good, the job is very worthwhile. I get $2.30 an hour plus tips. The average tip is between 15 and 20%. The bill automatically prints out what a tip would be based upon 15%, 18%, and 20%.

   I get stiffed on tips once or twice a week when someone forgets to sign the credit card slip or leaves with the restaurant's copy. In these cases, I receive no tip. I would like to think that people do this by accident.

My biggest tip was 40%. Another time, someone just gave me an extra $20 bill just to say thanks for good service. The average tips for a night are around $100. A really good night is $160.

We bus our own tables. There is a tip out of 2% of total sales that covers the cooks, hostess, and the person at the expo station. The expo station is a type of quality control. The person makes sure that the orders are correct and that they look nice and so on. No one ever gives extra tip outs.

At the end of the shift, we have the "service financial." This computes all credit cards, cash, and so on. If we owe the restaurant money (a lot of cash sales), we give them the cash. If most of the sales were by credit card, I get cash from the manager.

We have a team atmosphere. Everyone helps each other, and we all have input. If someone helps someone else clear a table, etc.—you don't ever give them any money for helping you because later you will be helping them. The problem is that sometimes the other waiters don't really reciprocate.

[Steve also worked at a crab house in Bethany Beach, Delaware.]

The restaurant was a sit-down restaurant. I got paid $8 an hour. I did three kinds of jobs at the restaurant: helping with carryout, running food, and bussing. I sometimes got direct tips for helping with carryout. About 20% of the people I helped gave me a tip. The average tip was a buck or two. I once got $50. If it was really busy, I could get $30 from tips in a night.

When I was running food or bussing, I got a 2% share. This came to about $35 for a night. I was given my tip out in cash the next day, and I received my salary check every two weeks.

I did not really care if I was tipped because the restaurant was so much fun. I loved working there and thought the owner was a great guy.

$ $ $

Jack has been a food runner at a fine dining restaurant in Wayne, Pennsylvania. He also spoke of his experience working a summer job as a server in a Mexican restaurant in New Jersey. This is what Jack had to say about his work as a food runner at a fine dining establishment.

I like my job. The money is good. The restaurant is privately owned and is not corporate. I like that.

I get $3.50 per hour. When I am the only runner, I get 15% of the servers' tips. On the weekends when there are two runners, we each get 10% from each server. Everyone is pretty nice, so you trust them to give you the right amount.

The typical shift is from 5 pm to 9:30 pm. On a weeknight, I average $70 in tips, and on a weekend, I get about $100. One runner will stay till 3 am and get $180. The tip outs are given directly to me. If I am doing really well, I can get an extra $5 or $10. We are all pretty good friends. We all bus the tables.

The bartender also gives us a tip out. If a server gives me $15, the bartender will usually give me $20. I've gotten direct tips from a customer on two occasions. I once got $5.

I also worked at a Mexican restaurant in New Jersey. I was a server during a summer. I make more money as a runner in my current job. Mexican food is cheap, so the total bill was not very high.

I got paid $2.75 an hour. I often had to work a double shift. During a lunch shift from 11 am to 2 pm, I would get $50 in tips. Night shifts were from 5 pm to 11 pm, and I get about $100. I never got stiffed. My biggest tip came from my family when they ate there. Another time, two priests gave me $100 on a $45 bill.

There was no tip out of the busser. They got paid hourly, and we ran our own food.

The people who tipped the most were guys out together. Senior citizens tipped the least. You've got to pay attention to customers to get a good tip.

There was no competition for better tables. The restaurant had some contests like whoever sold the most food would get a free meal. We all got along OK.

When I go to a restaurant, I always give over 25% unless the service is really bad. I did not tip as well before working in this industry. Now, I realize how hard the work is.

$ $ $

Jonathan was a server for three years and then a bartender for three years at a restaurant in Seattle, Washington. Here is his story.

The restaurant served nouvelle soul food. It was located in an affluent area near an area that was undergoing gentrification. About 7% of our clientele was African-American. I absolutely loved working there. The owner was very flexible, and he was very loyal to the employees. He helped us a lot. There was a lot of diversity in the staff.

As a server, I got $2.50 an hour. The average tip was 18–20%. Shifts were one hour of preparation and four hours of serving. I usually got $180 in tips during the weekend. I didn't work often during the week as I had senior status.

At the end of the shift, I would tip out the bar 10–12% of my tips, and in the last couple years as a server, they added a hostess who would get 5% of my tips.

Once a month, I would give them more than the required amount if we had a lot of tables. I would give them a few extra bucks.

Couples tipped the most, especially if I knew them. I knew them if they were regulars. Blacks tipped the least [Jonathan is black]. The average among blacks was 7%. Single black females were the worst. I think they tipped low because they were expecting something more traditional—not "nouvelle" soul food. Regulars tipped well. We all had regulars. If a lot of regulars came in, I knew I would get 10–15% more in that night. For me, a really big tip was $40.

There was no competition among the servers.

As a bartender, I earned $6 an hour. I had different sources of income. The servers on the floor would give me 10–12% of their tips. This averaged $120 per night. I also got $170 on average from people leaving tips at the bar. A person who ordered two drinks for $10 would leave $2.50 on average. A beer cost $3.00, and the average tip was 50 cents. A martini would cost $6.50, and the average tip was $3.00. People would also order a $35 bottle of wine and generally leave $5.

I also served food at the bar. The average meal costs $30 at the bar, and people would generally leave 10–12% tips.

I was the only bartender, so there was no pooling of the tips. I would sometimes tip out the hostess $5 if she sent people to the bar. If she did not sit my bar, she was on her own. In the last six months, we hired a bar-back. I started tipping him $40 per night.

When I go out to a restaurant, I leave 20% if the service was good. I define good service as checking on me. If they don't check on me to make sure everything is OK, I leave 10%.

$ $ $

Zack is also discussed in his job working on a parasail boat. Here he discusses two jobs in the restaurant industry in Pennsylvania and one in Maryland.

I first worked at an Outback Steakhouse as a busboy. I hated this job. No one respected me. The servers, hostess, and manager would yell at me. There was no "please." They did not take the time to get to know you.

I was paid $3.50 an hour. I got 1% of total sales for my tip. I would split it with the other busser, so I really got one-half of 1%. I would average $40–$45 in tips per day. My best night was $75 when I bused by myself. The servers never gave more than the minimum. They would give it to the manager who would give it to me the next day in cash.

I was never given a direct tip by a customer. They never talked to me.

MULTI-FUNCTION STAFF

I had a summer job working as a short-order cook at a pool bar in Ocean City, Maryland. People would eat around the pool. I made hotdogs, pizzas, and so on. I also acted as a bar-back. It was not a bad job. People were nice.

I was paid $7 an hour. There were three–four bartenders who gave us 5% of their tips, and five–six servers who gave us 15% of their tips. I shared the tips with the other short-order cook. I got $100 a day in tips for working from 11 am to 5 pm. Sometimes they would give me more than the minimum. When they gave more, they would give it to me personally. I don't think the other short-order cook did as well.

I only once got a direct tip from a customer. A guy gave me $10 when he saw how hard I was working. There was little interaction with the customers. I now work as a runner in a family restaurant. I am also going to college. I grab food and give it to people. We all bus.

I love this job. The money is good. The people are nice, and I am friends with a lot of them. It really helps to be friends with your coworkers. We can all do favors for each other.

I get $8.50 an hour. There are three–five servers and one–two bartenders. They each give me 15% of their tips. On Monday thru Friday, there is only one runner. On the weekend, there are two runners. One of us leaves after the dinner rush, and the other stays till 11 pm to help clean up. The person who stays late gets 60% of the tips. The servers and bartenders at this restaurant don't give extra tips. On a weekend night, I average $180–$190 if I am closing and $100 if I am not closing. On a weeknight, I average $70. People who have jobs involving tips are go-getters. I don't like an hourly wage. There is no incentive to work hard without the tips.

$ $ $

Stevie worked at a small Italian restaurant in Connecticut for a summer as both a server and a runner. He shared the following story.

I was a food runner for three weeks and then a server for seven weeks. It was really tough work, but it paid off because I like working with people. The waitress part was fun, but the food runner part was hell.

As a food runner, I got paid $7.10 an hour. I never received a tip out as a food runner.

As a waitress, I got paid $5.05 an hour which was the minimum wage in Connecticut for restaurant work. The average tip was 10–12% during the day and 18–20% at night. The night shifts were four hours, and I could make $150 in tips. During the day shifts, my tips were only a total of $10 for a four hour shift. During the day, people did not drink. There were less tables, and the average percentage tip was less. Sometimes there would only be two tables. You would make crap.

Once for a Baptism party we each got an extra $50 in addition to the 18% ($40) that was added on. They didn't even serve liquor. That was really nice.

People in Connecticut tip nice. I never got less than 10%.

At night, I tipped out 15% to the bartender and 10% to the bus. During the day, I just gave 10% to the bus. On a really good night, I would round up. I gave in cash at the end of the night. It was all on the honor system. It really sucked when people put their tips on a credit card as that would get taxed. The host was not tipped out because he was the boss. When the boss was not there, one of us would host.

There was some competition among the servers. We were divided into rooms. When I first started, a bartender took five of my tables. I had to complain to the manager. It did not happen again. During the day, we alternated tables. If one of us messed up and took a table out of turn, it would get made up with the next table.

Runners should get tipped out. They get paid the same as the bus ($7.10 an hour), so they should also get a tip out. Running is really hard work. When I became a server, I did not tip out the runner. We didn't have to. However, I ran a lot of my own food.

When I eat out, I always tip 20%. I know how much it stinks. Everyone should be a waitress at some point in their life, so they can see how hard it is.

People should tip in cash, so servers don't have to pay so much in taxes. If you put your tip on a credit card, you should leave a larger tip.

$ $ $

Torrie had two jobs as a server. This is what she had to say in her own words.

I worked at a country club in Connecticut for a summer. The job was nice. I did not like my boss. He was awkward and favored the Spanish staff as he was Spanish.

I worked private parties. We had weddings, birthday parties, and Communions. I got $9.50 an hour plus tips. We could not take tips from people during the event. After the event, the person who sponsored the event would tip us individually. They were all rich people, and it was pretty bizarre. Everyone gave us a tip. It was not required or added to the bill. The average tip was $20–$50.

Men tipped better than women, and birthday parties tipped better than other events.

I also worked at a Mexican restaurant in Brewster, New York for two years. I LOVED it. The people were good. It was a lot of fun, and I looked forward to going to work. As a server, I got $15 an hour. I know that is high. The average tip was 18% or more. Shifts were from 4 pm to 2 am. I would get $50–$100 in tips.

All the tips were put in a box and split with the other three–four servers and the bussers and runner. I don't know the exact splits for the bussers and runner. I trusted everyone. We were all pretty close, and I don't think anyone cheated. It was hard to get away with cheating because one girl was the money person and did it all.

Men definitely tipped the most. It helped being a girl. Teens tipped the least. My biggest tip came from a guy who came almost every night. He gave me $50.

I was also a bartender at the Mexican restaurant. During the night, I would go back and forth to being a server and a bartender. I would get tipped a dollar or two for a beer and $3 to $4 for a martini. I could make $100 an hour as a bartender on some days. It is good to be a girl. Everyone tipped. I've had people give me $20. This would usually come from people you know—the regulars.

Tipping is all about your attitude. If you're mean, people are not going to leave a good tip.

When I go out, I leave 20% and more if they are nice. A lot of tipping depends on the waiter or waitress. Nice servers get better tips.

$ $ $

Betsy worked at three different restaurants over four years. The first was a countertop restaurant in Fells Point, Baltimore. This is Betsy's story.

I worked there for two years. I loved it. The people who owned it were family friends. It was very laid back, fun, and busy.

I was paid $7 an hour. The average tip was $2. A burger, fries, and soda cost $5.30. People would leave a dollar or two. Some people would tip me $5 and even $10. Some people came in regularly and really came in to talk. They were real friendly. There was a real mix of people. The attorneys tipped the most. There were a lot of homeless people. They stiffed me a few times a day. I didn't mind as they didn't order very much, and other people tipped well.

There was a lot of in and out. People came and left quickly. There were two of us who were waitresses. We put the tips in a jar and shared them. My share was $80 to $110 in a five hour shift. There were no bussers or runners to share the tips with.

I worked for a year in a steakhouse in College Park, Maryland. I was paid $2.30 an hour. I liked working there. It was harder and more formal than the countertop restaurant. We had to wear uniforms, and the hours were longer.

The average tip was 18–22%. A shift lasted from 4 pm till midnight. I would make $100 to $140 in that time frame. Days were more popular for servers. We were in a hotel, and a lot of business travelers would eat there during the week. Mondays through Thursdays were the busiest days.

I only had to tip out the bartender. I gave him $3 to $4. He never did a good job. The hostess was not tipped out. She was paid a good hourly wage. There was also no tip out to the runner or busser. They also had a real hourly wage.

There were a lot of retirees, and they did not tip well. Businessmen tipped the best. I'm a young college girl and that helped. My biggest tip was $60. The other waitress knew the family. The customers liked me because I'm a good waitress. I was never stiffed at this restaurant. There was never any competition among the servers.

When I go out I tip 20% if the service is good. If it sucks, I give 15%.

I was a hostess at a sports bar in Atlanta. This was in an athletic club. I was paid $6 an hour. The job was OK. There was no tip out even though I did a lot of the servers' work. It was frustrating. I did more than they did.

Customers sometimes tipped me directly. About every fourth shift, someone would give me $5 or $10. This was because I did a really good job. For example, helping them with their kids was above and beyond the call of duty. I knew 80% of the customers because I also worked out there. If there was a 30–40 minute wait, I would seat them early, and sometimes I would get a tip from that.

I hate to say it, but looks have a lot to do with tipping. If a waitress is pretty she will make more. A smile is also important. Once the customer found out I was going to school, I got a higher tip. It was good to be cute, young, and a college kid.

I liked the countertop restaurant the best. Everyone was friendly. The hours were flexible, and five hours is easy.

$ $ $

Monica has been a waitress at two different restaurants in the Washington, D.C. area. The following narrative details her experiences as a waitress.

I worked for a year at a Mexican restaurant. I liked the job. It was my first server job, and I learned a lot. The restaurant had a good atmosphere. Our main job was to sell drinks.

I earned $2.13 an hour. During the lunch hour, the tips were only 10–15%. For dinner, the tips were a bit higher—15%. On a typical weekday, I would get $20–$30 in a five hour shift. On weekends, the tips ranged from $50–$100. People buy more on Saturday dinners.

My biggest tip was $90 from a party of five businessmen. They ordered a lot of appetizers and drank a lot of good bottles of wine. The biggest tippers were businessmen. They know how much to tip. Regulars tipped less unless they were with a large family. People who sit in groups of two or four don't tip very well.

At the end of the night, we tipped out the bartender 1% of total sales, and the busser got 2%. We gave them cash at the end of every day. I usually gave more than that. I wanted a good busser. If I owed him $8, I would usually give him $10–$13. A good busser made for fast turn around, and I would make more money.

I worked for two years at the Olive Garden restaurant. I worked in one in the D.C. area and one near home in Michigan.

I earned $2.15 an hour (two cents more than the Mexican restaurant). I loved working at the Olive Garden. It had a great atmosphere. We tried to make everyone feel at home.

People tipped more than the Mexican restaurant. The average tip was 15–20%. For a weekday, I would make $40 in tips for a four–five hour shift. On weekends, I averaged $90–$100. My biggest day was $250 on a double shift on a Saturday.

I tipped out the busser 2%. I always tipped out more; like I did at the Mexican restaurant. I would usually give $10–$13. The bartender was supposed to get 1% of sales if people were drinking. If people were only having sodas and water, we did not have to tip him out. I usually gave him more, especially on Saturday. If I owed him $9, I would give him $13–$15.

Business people and parties tipped the most. For large groups, they automatically tacked on 18%. They would usually give more. I once got $50 above the 18% gratuity for a $200 bill. They know that 18% is being tacked on. We make a point of reminding them.

I tip more than 20% when I go to restaurants. I know how hard it is. Most people don't realize how hard it is to get orders out on time. You are working several tables, and it can be hard to manage. Servers should get more than 15%.

I now sell clothes without commissions. I like it better. I know how much I will be getting, and during hard times—like now—you don't want to depend on tips.

$ $ $

Katrina has worked in two different restaurants. This is what she had to say about her work in the restaurant industry.

The first was as a server in a pub in a nice suburb of St. Louis. We served bar food like burgers, salads, and pizzas. I liked the job a lot. It was easy, and there were nice families who frequented the restaurant. I worked there for nine months. I was paid $2.75 an hour.

The average tip was 20%. I only worked weekends from 4 pm to 1 am. I averaged $130 in tips. My biggest night was $220 and my biggest tip was $50.

I was supposed to tip out the bartender 10% of my tips, and the busboy got 5%. I gave them more. If I owed the bartender $13, I would give him $20. We were all real close. I did not tip the hostess. The vast majority of people paid with credit cards, and very rarely did we get tips in cash.

There was no competition for tables. I had five designated tables.

The people who tipped the most had little kids. They felt sorry for us. Retired people tipped the least.

You made better tips if you were friendly. You needed to pay attention. If someone ordered iced tea, you needed to keep refilling the glass. It was a very straightforward job.

I now tip at least 20% when I go out.

My husband is in the Marines, and we move around a lot. I was a clerk at a kitchen in a golf club in Orange County, California. I was paid $10 an hour. We had hot dogs, hamburgers, and beer. People paid when they ordered. I could put the food on the counter, but I soon learned that I got better tips if I brought it to their table.

Sandwiches cost $6, and people usually left a dollar. Seventy-five percent of the people left a tip. For the 6 am to noon shift, I averaged $60 a day in tips. It was fairly busy in the morning. We also sold breakfast stuff. For the 10 am to 5 pm shift, I averaged $35 in tips.

People also tipped when they bought beer to bring onto the course. One guy bought a $30 12-pack. It was expensive. And, he gave me a $5 tip.

We also had banquets. The boss would often tip me out $100 in addition to my usual $10 an hour. The person putting on the banquet would also sometimes tip me out $50. The boss once gave me $300!

People who tipped the most just had a good golf day. Regulars also tipped well. Sometimes a regular would just come up and give me a tip for nothing!

We had a beer pitcher where most people left their tips. I had some overlap with another person. For the time we worked together, we split what came in for tips.

$ $ $

Paula worked at an upscale Bistro near American University while she was a student there. She also worked as a tipped employee at a very upscale bowling alley. This is what Paula had to say about tipping norms.

I had three different jobs at the restaurant. I earned $2 an hour as a waitress. The average tip was 20%. It was a high-class restaurant, and some people got snooty and occasionally did not tip at all. My biggest tip was $50 on a $50 bill.

I easily made $200 on an average night, and on my best nights, I made $500. This was especially true with big parties in the back room.

For big parties, they automatically added on 18%. About 10% of the time, people would give more than the 18% for big parties.

You could sometimes tell who was going to tip well when they walked in the door. Even though we were expensive, we got some high school and college kids. They did not tip well. Families tipped well. They did not want to stiff you. When friends came in, you gave them a discount, and they usually made it up with a tip. People who drank a lot were feeling good, and they tipped well. And, their bottles of wine were often expensive.

At the end of the night, we tipped out. We gave 15–20% of our total tips. This was on the honor system, and sometimes servers would lie. The bartender got about half of the tip out, and the remainder went to the runner and the hostess. The runner got more than the hostess. I occasionally gave more money into the pool if it was a good night. Nothing went to the cooks.

I also worked as a food runner. I hated it. I don't have big hands. It was grunt work, and I don't speak Spanish. I did a lot of the fine work—putting sour cream on a plate in shape of a star. The shifts were five hours long, and I averaged $50 from the tip outs in addition to my hourly wage of $6.

As a hostess, I was paid $7 or $8 per hour. I would get $10 or $15 from the tip outs. I was not supposed to take direct tips from customers, but sometimes they would insist on giving $5 for a better table. These tips were rare. I liked being the hostess the best. I made less money. But, the people were nice, and it was a steady paycheck.

If I went to this restaurant, I would tip 16% for the worst waitress and give 20% for better service.

$ $ $

Paula also worked as a waitress at an upscale bowling alley with good food, big TV screens, and a big singles scene. This is how she describes that experience.

I earned $2.97 an hour. I made so much money in tips. I wonder why I left there. I worked weeknights, and I never made less than $180 in tips. I averaged $250. On weekends, I could make $1,000 a night. The average tip was 20%. I did really well with large parties in the backroom. Sometimes members of the Wizards came, and they would tip the 20% that was automatically added onto large parties and then give additional tips.

Guys tipped the most if they were with other guys. We wore cocktail outfits (black boots and a red dress), and I am sure that helped. The guys were out to have a good time. Anytime you are with a lot of guys who are drinking, you will make a lot of money. Girls tipped the least. When kids came for birthday parties, they rented a couple of lanes. The percentage tip was a little lower, and the total tip would be lower because they ordered only sodas.

My best tip was a $180 tip on an $80 bill. These were people from a radio station. The tip process was a little shady. The process was computerized. Some people entered only $15 or $20 in tips for the night (because of tax reasons) and then gave extra tip out in cash. At the end of the night, we tipped out 15% of our total tips to the kitchen and 10% to the bartender.

I made a lot of money at the bowling alley.

$ $ $

Jacques has worked in six or seven restaurants. This is his story in his own words.

I now work at a "gay" restaurant in Rehoboth Beach, Delaware. I love working there because it is the local place to hang out. You get to know the customers, and they are really friendly.

I get paid $2.50 an hour. In season, I work six–seven hour shifts and get $120–$150 in tips on a weekend night and $80–$100 on a week night. Out of season, I get $80–$90 on a weekend night and $50–$60 on other nights. I never got stiffed. However, a woman once left $1.

Ten percent of my tips go to the busser and 10% to the bartender. This is done on the honor system at the end of the night. If they did a really good job, I would give them more; perhaps an extra $10. They are very appreciative when you give them more than the required amount.

Gay men are the best tippers on the planet. They tip 20% because they have more disposable income, and a lot of gay men have experience working in the service industry. They know what a butt job it is. Most other customers tip 18%. Women tip less than men, and blacks tip poorly. My biggest tip at this restaurant was $100.

Once at a "fine-dining" restaurant in Boulder, Colorado, the customers had seven–eight bottles of wine that cost $2,000–$3,000 per bottle. They left me a gratuity of $3,000!

I worked at a nightclub in Boston. They served no food. I was in charge of promotions, but when they were really busy, I would help out behind the bar. They would pay me $1 a minute. If I helped for 15 minutes, I would get $15.

I worked from the ages of 12 to 18 at a Mexican restaurant in Urea, Colorado. This was mostly a tourist town. People usually tipped 15–18%. Some families and some young people did not tip very well. We had a policy that if the tip was below 10% we had to ask them what was wrong with the service. Ninety percent of the time the significant other of the person who paid the bill would be shocked at the low tip and express a lot of anger at his or her partner. I would then get a huge tip. Ten percent of the time they would give me a long list of complaints even if the service was adequate.

At this restaurant, single people with dates tipped the most. I really hated when people came in with high chairs. Even with a good tip, it was a huge mess to clean up.

On a typical night, I would get $100 in tips. This was summer work only.

At this Mexican restaurant, I gave 10% of total tips to the busser and 10% to the bartender. I also sometimes gave $1 or $2 to each of the kitchen staff.

I worked as a bartender in the French Quarter of New Orleans. The typical tip was 30–40% of sales. The tips were insane. Bars don't close. There was a group of coke-heads and coke-dealers who would come in at 4:30 am. They tipped a lot because they were happy. I told them I didn't care what they did outside of the bar, but they couldn't deal or use in my bar. They liked me, and in two hours, I would make $300. It was really busy from 4:30 am to 6:30 am and then dead till later. During the night shifts, I would also earn $300–$500 in tips.

Mardi Gras was crazy. It would take an hour just to count the tips. We literally would fill a milk crate with the money. I could make $800–$900 in a night. It is amazing how much money you could make when you push drinks. Speed is the issue.

At this bar draft beer was $1.50, bottled beer–$2.50, rail liquor–$4.00, calls–$5.50, and premium drinks–$6.00. It is a lot of work to put drinks like cosmos into martini glasses. The customers would often give you $10 for a $6 drink and tell you to keep the change. The usual tip was $2 to $3 for martini glass drinks and $1 for high balls. However, even if I got a $1 for a Cosmo, I was happy.

I did not share tips in the morning as I was the only one working at that time. In the evening, there was a bar-back. He was like a busboy. He would get glasses and ice. I would give him 10% of my tips.

When there were festivals, there would be four bartenders. We would each stake out a section of the bar and keep all our tips from that section. Sometimes it got crazy, and you might grab $2–$3 from their section by accident. But, it would be worked out later. There was no controversy. When you are making $600 a night, it doesn't make any difference.

In general, Europeans tip horribly. It is said that they don't know better. This is not true. They know better but just don't want to give. They are often rude on purpose.

A lot of waiters or waitresses will flirt with you. This is a practiced move to get tips. People who have worked in the service industry tip well because they know how hard it is.

Some business people who tip high let you know that, or they let the person they are taking out know that they tipped high. They are jerks. It makes them look like idiots.

Most people who work in restaurants are really honest. There is an honor code. You don't steal tips. I once thought a busboy had taken a tip, but we found it in the heating grate on the floor. It is the most emotionally intense industry on the planet. You are dealing with 200+ people that you are trying to please. It is always best to give cash to the waiter directly in his hand. If someone does this and says they are taking care of you, you know you will get less.

$ $ $

Helen has been a waitress at four different restaurants. She is presently attending law school, and this is how she described her experience in the service industry in her own words.

I liked working at an Applebee's in Massachusetts. I worked there full-time while I was going to school full-time. I was paid $2.65 an hour plus tips. My average tip was 15% and 20% if I was really lucky. In a typical night, I received $80 in tips.

At the end of the night, I tipped out 10% of my total sales. This was split between the bartender and the hostess.

I also worked at a seafood restaurant in Massachusetts where the typical bill was $200. This was almost always paid on a credit card.

I also received $2.65 an hour at this restaurant. The average tip was 20%, and on a good Friday night, I would clear $250–$300 in tips.

The tip out occurred at the end of the night. This tip out was with the bartender and the busboy, and I don't remember the percentage. I often gave more than the required tip out when the service was really good. Sometimes I gave the busboy an extra $10. He was very thankful and worked harder because of it.

I also worked at a breakfast diner in Massachusetts. I was paid $3 an hour. People paid their bill in cash. A breakfast might cost $10, and people would tip 15–20% on average. Sometimes they would leave $3–$4, and other times a person would leave 50 cents. Tips were often in quarters. There was fast turnaround, and I could earn $60 in tips in a five hour shift.

The restaurant was family owned, and you were told what section to work in. There was an older guy who bused the tables. We never gave him any tips. I think he was mentally retarded. Nobody ever had a conversation with him.

Legal Sea Foods in Washington, D.C. also paid $2.65 an hour. Tips are small after 10 pm when the crowd is younger. They tip 5–10%. Other times, the typical tip was 15%. On a Friday night, I could clear $200 in tips; while on a typical weekday night, the tips would average $100.

At the end of the night, I would tip out the bartender 2.2% of my total sales, and the busser would get 1.8%. The manager printed out the total sales, and I calculated the percentages. We all had to sign the statement. I sometimes gave them more. I would round up an extra $2 or $3. Sometimes I gave an extra $5. I usually gave more to the bartender because he was really good and really fast. He also helped with the appetizers—shucking the oysters and the clams. The hostess was not tipped out because she received a real hourly wage. Although the total tips were high, I did not like the tipping system at Legal Sea Food's because the tip out percentages were too high.

I once gave the chef an extra $20 because of very large party. However, this was very unusual.

Not everyone reported all their tips because of tax reasons. However, I liked working at Applebee's the most because I never owed money on taxes. I had a real problem saving money, and it was good to have the taxes taken out each week.

In general, I found that overseas tourists do not tip well. At a restaurant on Cape Cod, we put out a card in four languages explaining the protocol of tipping and that didn't help either. Sometimes I would get 5% from foreign tourists.

I always tip 20% when I go to a restaurant regardless of the service.

$ $ $

Mary was a waitress at two restaurants in Washington, D.C. She shared the following story about her experiences receiving tips as a waitress.

I first worked at Uno's for six months. I had real problems with the manager. The first manager only wanted black people as servers. The second manager was very inappropriate in his dealings with women both in his touching and in his comments.

I was paid $2.33 an hour. The tips averaged a little under 15%. It was across the street from a movie theatre, and the customers were always rushing. If the food came out 20 minutes after they ordered, they would stiff you. I got completely stiffed only once. More frequently, I would get just a few bucks on a $30 bill.

Once, the silverware was not out when some customers sat down. The guy said, "I have a tip for you. If you want a tip, you should have the silverware out before we sit down." Hey, it wasn't even my job to roll the silverware.

The shifts lasted six–eight hours. On a weekday night, I would sometimes get $40 and other times $20. It was really random. On weekends, I could get $100–$150. I was the senior server after six months, and I would then get the good sections. On a Saturday night, I would get $200 sometimes.

There was no competition among the servers for tables.

Tip outs were not mandatory. I tipped the hostess as she was generally helpful. I would give her $5 to $10 on weekends. I never knew their policy. We bused our own tables. The bartender was heinous. He was eventually fired. I never tipped him although I feel bad about it now that I think about it.

When I go to a restaurant, I always tip 20% no matter how terrible the service is.

At Uno's, there were a few generalities on who tipped the most. Those who flirted with you tipped well. I know that is a terrible thing to say.

I worked a year at a high-end restaurant that served American-style French food. I liked working there at first, but then the owner opened a second restaurant. And, he sort of lost it. He threw food at the waitresses and put salt in our sodas and water.

I got paid $2.77 an hour. The average tip was 18%. The food was more expensive than Uno's, and the tips were higher in percentage and amount. These were people accustomed to spending money.

Shifts were seven hours, and I would earn $50–$70 on Mondays, $150–$200 on Thursdays, and about $250 on Fridays and Saturdays. Some of the more senior servers got as much as $500. My highest was $360.

I tipped out the bartender 4% of my tips and the hostess 2%. On weekends when we had runners and busboys, I would give then 2% collectively. If it was really busy, I would give the bartender an extra $5 or $10 and sometimes $20. I never gave extra to the hostess. I did not give the runners extra as I wanted to run my own tables. I would give the busboys an extra $5.

The manager put these required percentages in a common pool, but if you liked someone, you would give them their extra yourself. This is how my trainer taught me. Older servers got the best tables, and the rest of us rotated. We all got along until one of the servers, who was very young, was promoted to manager. There was a lot of animosity toward him. He was not well liked.

Middle-aged couples tipped the most. Those who fit into the scene tipped well. These were people who were snooty and thought they were better than other people. Younger students who were bringing their date to an expensive restaurant did not tip well. VIPs had the best tables and best servers. I did not wait on them, but they were reportedly good tippers. I'm told that the Clintons did not tip well.

Back room parties were amazing. We got the mandatory 18% tip, but many would tip us throughout the party. People would tip us when we brought appetizers and served the food. In a two hour party, I could make $200 in tips. I only did four of these. More experienced servers got the parties.

$ $ $

Sharon worked as a server in two restaurants. This is her story in her words.

I now work at Ruby Tuesday near the Verizon Center in Washington, D.C. I've been there four–five months. I like working there because it is lively. I get paid $2.30 an hour. The average tip is 20%.

In the morning shift (10:30–4 pm), I get about $50 in tips. During a weekday evening shift (4 pm to 11 pm), I get around $80, and on the weekends, I average $150 a night.

Families tip the best at night. During the day, those in business attire tip the best. High school students are bad tippers.

I tip out the bartender 10% of the bar bill. Therefore, if $60 in drinks was ordered he would get $6. I also tip out the hostess. [Note: She could not figure out the formula for this]. Last night she got $3, and I had about $400 in sales. There is no busboy or runner.

Seventy percent of the people pay by credit card. Of those who pay by credit card, about half leave a cash tip. Twenty percent of the time I am given the cash directly. Once, another server took my tip. He was fired.

The servers all cooperate together. We are like a big family. There are two servers in a section of seven tables. You choose with whom you want to work. There is a lot of turnover of tables.

When I eat out, I tip well. I leave $5 even if the bill is $17. If it is above $40, I leave $10.

There have been problems lately with management. There has been a lot of turnover. There was a recent immigration rally and a lot of the cooks went to it. Some of them were fired. Since then, the ordering has been messed up.

I worked at an Applebee's in Raleigh, North Carolina for two years. It was harder work than the Ruby Tuesday because we had to make the salads. The tables did not turn quickly. In the first year, the tips were better than the second year. In the first year, I averaged 17%. In the second year, there was a new manager, and he hired a lot of cooks who could not speak English. The orders got messed up, sales dropped, and customers blamed the servers for the mess ups. My average tip went down to 9 or 10%.

The restaurant was more suburban. We had a big lunch crowd. I would make $45 per night and $65 per day.

We tipped out the bartender based upon the drinks sold. The host did really well at 7% of sales and the bus got 5% of sales. [Note: She tried to work out this math during the interview, and she realized she did not know how it worked.]

At Applebee's, people on dates tipped the most at night, and corporate types tipped the most for lunch.

We automatically added 17% on for groups of eight or more. Often (about half of the time), a person would give us an extra $5. About 7% did not know that the gratuity was automatically added on, and we would get a double tip.

$ $ $

Mark has worked for the past 14 months at a moderately priced restaurant near the Verizon Center in Washington, D.C. The following narrative details his experiences with tipping norms.

We have American cuisine with an Asian influence: burgers, pastas, steaks, stir fries, etc. We also sell our own beer. I like working there for the most part. I like my coworkers a lot. The money is good, and the management doesn't hassle you.

I get $2.30 an hour. The average tip is 19–21%. We get a weekly print of all our sales, so I pretty much know what the tipping amount is. Our shifts are from 5 pm to 11 pm and sometimes longer. On a typical weekday shift, I get $70–$100 in tips, and on the weekend, I get $150–$200.

We cash out at the end of each night. One percent of the food sales go to the runner, 3–4% (not sure the exact percent) of liquor sales goes to the bartender, and 3–4% of the food sales go to the busser. On really big nights, the tip out has been as much as $100. I give to each person individually, and only rarely do I give them more than the exact amount. Sometimes the bussers have been lousy, and the manager tells me to give them less than the required amount; which I sometimes do.

People from the big city tip the most. The theatre crowd also tips well. Tourists from the Midwest don't tip well. I know that if they ask whether they should leave the money up front or with me—the tip will be low.

There is definitely competition among the servers for the best sections. You want to be a closing server. They make extra money. The competition is not that serious, but some people develop a reputation for stealing tables. And, sometimes words are exchanged. If you are near a closed section, you can sometimes take over part of the closed section as it fills up, and that sometimes creates tension. Other people are the reverse. They want to leave early and are happy not to get extra customers.

Eighty percent of the bills are paid with credit cards. Between 15–20% of those people leave the tips with cash. I had one incident when the tip money I saw on the table was stolen. I am not sure whether it was the busser or the people who next sat down at the table.

I also worked for one year at a new restaurant in Silver Spring. They sold a lot of egg dishes (omelets, eggs Benedict, etc.) as well as steaks and sandwiches. I liked working there at first. Then the manager changed, and the new manager said he did not like people he did not hire. I did not feel respected. I also did not like the clientele. Many of the clients were African-Americans, and many did not tip well [Mark is white]. Six of us left about the same time a few months after the manager came in.

The average tip was 15%. In a five hour shift, I averaged $50 during the week and $100–$150 on the weekend.

We got a cash report at the end of the night, and I added the tip out to the cash I would give the restaurant. The manager distributed the tip out to the busser and host. The tip out was 3%, and I always gave the exact amount. There was no tip out to the bartender. Once, he was having a really slow day and complained that he was only working for the servers. He put out a tip jar, and I put $10 in. That was the only time that happened.

Whites tipped the most. People coming from Bethesda to try out the new Silver Spring restaurant tipped well. Some African-Americans left $5 no matter what the bill was. The bill could be a $100, and they left $5. Some don't try to work out the math.

Both restaurants automatically added 18% gratuity for parties of eight or more. However, the restaurant I work for now does not have space on the credit card to put an additional tip. Only about 5% of large parties will give me an additional tip. The first restaurant had a space for tips even when the gratuity was automatically added on. About 25% double tipped me, and another 25% gave me a tip above the 18%.

[Mark was also re-interviewed after the beginning of the recession. He had transitioned to a bartender position at a moderately priced restaurant in downtown D.C.] I've noticed very few differences. Tourists continue to pinch every penny, and regulars treat us the same. Business was down on Fourth of July weekend, which is normally our busiest weekend. Other than that, business has been the same.

$ $ $

People who serve multiple functions and those who hold multiple positions in the restaurant business share numerous and varied experiences. However, these narratives do show some telling patterns. It is important to note the extent to which restaurant workers place a value on the perception that the customers have of them. In particular, many of the stories reveal a perceptual bias that favors those who are young, attractive, and working toward a higher educational status. If this perceived bias plays out economically, those who have careers in the service industry are likely to be more economically and socially vulnerable. Several narratives highlight these disparities. As Betsy said, "Looks have a lot to do with tipping. It was good to be cute, young, and a college kid." Even some of the male respondents, like Samuel, recognized that among wait staff "cute server girls seemed to get the preferred sections." However, these potential rewards appear to also be contingent upon meeting all the gender and class expectations, particularly being "nice." The gender and class-based differences in the experiences of service workers in the restaurant industry are also exemplified by the early advancement and promotion of men compared to experienced, career waitresses. The narratives in this section also highlight a finding consistent with the management literature that while there are no noticeable differences in management style between men and women and no serious problems for women in management positions, women have a more difficult time obtaining positions of higher and middle management (see also Billing and Alvesson 1994). Mary, for example, provided evidence of this when she talked about the young man promoted to a management position above several more experienced waitresses. Consequently, women who make a career in the restaurant industry may find themselves unable to move up on the organizational hierarchy, managed by men with less experience, and subject to diminishing returns on their wages as they grow away from the gendered expectations of the cute college girl.

The socially constructed process of "doing gender" occurs in interactions between people in situated contexts in which the physical, social, ideological/cultural, and psychological boundaries may be coerced or negotiated, resulting in domination or cooperation (see West and Zimmerman 1987; Gerson and Peiss 1985). Pressures toward degradation and devaluation are inherent in many of the jobs traditionally held by women, and degrading uniforms, stereotyped distinctions of craft-based skills that favor "masculinity," derogatory terms of address, and sexual harassment are social distancing techniques used to reaffirm masculine identities and gain power (LaPointe 1992; Spradley and Mann 1975). The potential for the gendered work environment to impose on the sexual identities of the workers is also evident in these narratives. For example, the cocktail outfits worn at the upscale bowling alley, are a part of the cultural rituals that reaffirm the definitions and status attached to masculinity and femininity, and the wages of the cocktail waitress are dependent upon her compliance with gendered expectations. In some settings, the lessons about the values and attitudes regarding sexual identities may be routinized by poor management. Several of the waitresses reported harassment from managers and owners that included throwing food, contaminating drinks, and "inappropriate touching and comments." The impact of poor management can also extend to men in the organization. A few of the men interviewed spoke of interactions with management that made them feel as though they were "not respected." However, there are two important differences that deserve further examination in future research: (1) The levels and extent of harassment reported by women were much greater than the perceived disrespect reported by men, and (2) men appear to be more likely than women to find other work in those circumstances.

The narratives of multi-function staff also reveal a great deal about the role that the organizational hierarchy plays in not only dividing labor based on task and function, but in maintaining power and status as well. Several of the interviews were conducted during a time in which the issue of immigration and the legal status of migrant workers was a prevalent part of the political discourse, which was also substantially shaded in black and brown discrimination. Because politics is not separate from lived experience,[1] it is likely that some of the responses reflect the broader social context. Sometimes the views that the respondents have on the broader social issues are evident in the language of their story. For example, Sharon notes that when several of the cooks were fired for attending the recent immigration rally, the daily operations were "messed up." The language of the narratives also reveals a subtle, yet pervasive, discrimination against Spanish-speaking people; some of which is tied to the organizational hierarchy. For example, the assumption that the work of bussers and runners is "grunt work" believed to be most often done (or implies that it should be done) by people who speak Spanish; as Paula says, "It was grunt work, and I don't speak Spanish."

These stories also depict tremendous differences in the economic advantages for tipped employees. In some settings, it appears that restaurant workers are making substantially more than many of their counterparts in the so-called low-skilled labor industries; while in other cases, the restaurant workers require supplementary income (either assistance from family or other employment) to meet their basic needs. At the same time, the issue of taxes is a recurring theme that respondents regularly discussed despite the fact that there was no prompting for the topic in the interviews. When respondents brought up the issue of taxes, the narratives indicate that there is somewhat of an expectation on the part of service workers in the restaurant industry that their wages are not taxed in full. This belief is implicit in Stevie's statement, "People should tip in cash, so servers don't have to pay so much in taxes. If you put your tip on a credit card, you should leave a larger tip." With only one exception, this behavior is not perceived by the restaurant workers as dishonest. Paula refers to the underreporting of tips as "shady," but it is somewhat unclear if the suspicion is about the tip out or the taxes. In general, respondents tend to describe the process as fair and people as honest when they themselves are making more money than they expect. Then, they perceive themselves as having control over the choices about who to be more generous to within the hierarchy, and animosity is lower because people seem to believe that "it all evens out." The cooperation and evaluations of fairness are not absolute though. They are integrally linked to the organizational hierarchy.

NOTES

1. See Kelley (1994) for an excellent examination of how infra-politics informs organized political movements.

7

Specialty Jobs

There are a number of specialty jobs in the restaurant industry. These jobs also vary quite a bit depending upon the work environment. Specialty jobs include caterers, the host or hostess positions, poolside servers, cooks, hookah lounge attendants, and the sommelier or wine steward. People hired to work in these positions may be specially trained or have developed a particular knowledge or skill through their experience that qualifies them for the job. In general, customers have a unique set of expectations regarding their performance. For example, the host or hostess is responsible for regulating the flow of customers through the restaurant and providing an adequate division of labor among the staff without imposing on the clients' experience at the restaurant. Poolside servers are often responsible for maintaining a safe, clean environment while serving people who are eating, drinking, swimming, and engaging in general recreation. Alternatively, cooks usually have very little interaction with the customers, but they most often do have a considerable degree of training and experience. Hookah lounge attendants are expected to have a specialized knowledge of the product line and an understanding of the cultural context in which hookah is customary. Some very fine restaurants have a sommelier, which is a certified wine steward. The sommelier is trained in the art and craft of wine making and is tested on his/her knowledge of wines and wine traditions. The job of the sommelier is to provide useful advice to the clients regarding wine choices based on the taste and budget of the clients. In some establishments, these positions are held by employees making minimum wage or even a salary and are not tipped employees, but there are restaurants in which specialty positions require or expect tips.

$ $ $

Kay is a host at a Chinese restaurant in the Washington, D.C. area. This is Kay's story.

I am a senior at a college in the Northeast, and I am a host during the winter and summer breaks. It is a nice place to work, and I like the people who work here.

I get paid $8 an hour. I rarely get tips. Last month I got tips from maybe ten people. A lot of people call for carryout. I almost never get a tip from people who call from their car and ask for the food to be brought out to the car. It seems that most of my tips come from new customers who pay with a credit card and add a dollar or two to the credit card bill. The average tip from those who get takeout is $2.

I get more around the holidays. Some of the regular customers give me a few bucks. One gave me $10. My total over the holidays was maybe $50. When it is really busy, we have a host and a receptionist. The host brings people to their tables, and the receptionist takes the take-out orders. We split tips when we are both working.

I very rarely get a tip out from a server.

$ $ $

Abigail is a hostess at a famous restaurant. She is also a college student. This is what Abigail had to say about being a hostess.

This is a restaurant that a lot of businessmen and politicians frequent. I've been working here for seven months. I love it. The people are nice, and the work is not that hard to do.

I am paid $9 an hour. I only receive tips from people who want to be seated right away. The average tip is $10. Once I was given $100. Out of the 400 people I seat on an average night, two or three will tip me. I share tips with the other hostess. We split up the tips at the end of the night. On an average night, there is $20 to be split between the two of us.

The seaters are also sometimes tipped to get ahead of the line. They don't split those tips with us. I am also never given a tip out from the waiters or servers.

There is no corporate policy on whether or not we should take tips for allowing people to get seated earlier. Some managers are OK with it while others are opposed. No one has ever been disciplined for it.

No one ever sees these tips. I always seat them no matter what the amount of the tip is. I don't know what the amount is until after they've been seated.

The morning host makes a lot from this type of tip. He gets $40 a day in tips and does not share them. He knows everyone and has been there for 13 years. The business people who come for breakfast want better tables. Business people tip the most.

$ $ $

Nancy, who also used to work at an ice cream parlor (essay not included), worked as a waitress at a country club in the Northeast that catered special events such as weddings, reunions, and birthday parties. This is what Nancy had to say about her work in catered events.

I was paid $7 an hour. There was a 15% (maybe 20%) gratuity that was automatically added onto the event bill. This was split evenly among all the wait staff. I usually got an $80 check at the end of the night. For six hours, I would get $42 in salary and about the same amount in tips. I never got money directly from a diner.

Tips are good when you are the one receiving them.

$ $ $

Donald has been a poolside server at a Beverly Hills hotel for the past three months. This is his story in his own words.

It is a pretty good job. I get to work outside next to the pool. I get paid $9.83 an hour. I am also trying to become an actor.

The average tip is 15–18%. My shifts are from 9 am to 6 pm. On Monday thru Wednesday, I average $40–$70 in tips, $100 on Thursday thru Friday, and $100 to $190 on the weekend.

This might be sexist, but the biggest tippers are men. Big groups of women don't tip well, and they are very demanding. Kids are also bad tippers.

We pool our tips. Servers and the bartenders get 100%, the busboy gets 50%, and we give a few bucks to the dishwasher [It is unclear how this math works out so that 150% of the tips are divided among the servers, bartenders, bussers, and dishwasher]. So, last Saturday the five servers and the one bartender each received $190. The busboy got $100, and the dishwasher got $10.

The system would be good if we all worked the same, but some of the servers are freeloaders. I run around like crazy. I hustle. Others don't work as hard.

About 20% of the customers pay in cash. The other customers pay the bill with their credit card or charge it to their room. About 5% of those who pay with credit card or charge it to their room will leave their tip in cash. I trust the other servers with the cash.

We serve drinks at poolside, food and drinks to the cabanas, and we have a main restaurant. People at poolside seem to give us $1 a drink no matter what the cost. People in the cabanas tip more, are more demanding, and have more money.

Sometimes we get a huge tip. One guy gave us a $500 tip on a $13 bill. Pooling tips was nice that day.

When I go out to a restaurant, I tip depending upon the service. If it is adequate, I give 20–25%. If it is outstanding, I give up to 50%. I know how demanding a job it is.

$ $ $

Amber has worked as a server catering to parties and special events for the last two months at an upscale bowling alley. One other interview in this book comes from someone who worked at this restaurant/bowling alley, and they have very different experiences.[1] This is what Amber had to say about her experience catering parties.

The job is OK. The manager gets on your nerves, and you never know whether you are going to have a good tip day or not. The tip outs are not fair.

I get $2.38 an hour. If the bill is over $25 during the day or $100 at night, I can automatically add an 18% gratuity. The average tip is only 8% during the day. There are a lot of families with kids. At night, the average is 15%. There is a lot more alcohol, and it is a younger couples' crowd.

From 11 am to 5 pm, I will usually make $100, and from 5 pm to midnight, I will get $220. My biggest tip was for a corporation that was having a birthday party for one of its employees. They left $100 for a $600 bill.

I tip out the bartender 10% of my tips. That is fair because he is helping you. If he is doing a bad job, I will tip him less than I should. If the service is not good, you have to wait 25 minutes for the drinks. I am not going to give him a full tip. If he is doing a good job, I will sometimes give him more than 10%.

The food runner gets 5% of total food sales. That is not fair. He is already making above minimum wage, and if I don't get tipped well, most of my tip has to go to him. It is not fair. I give the bartender and the runner their tip out in cash at the end of the night.

There is competition among the servers. We have sections but some will not adhere to it. Some will brag and ask, "How much money did you make today?" We don't exchange words, and it works out OK. There are only a few gung-ho types.

You never know who will tip the most. Those in groups between the ages of 25 and 30 tip the best. Teenagers tip the least. You can't assume you won't get a tip. Sometimes you give bad service and get a good tip. And other times you kiss ass and get a bad tip.

The stereotype of blacks not tipping well is sometimes true. I'm African-American, and I am really happy when the stereotype is defied. Older blacks tip well, and younger blacks do not tip well.

When the place is so busy you can hardly move, the tips are not very good. You want it to be busy and organized.

Kids who are having birthdays are not good for tips. They don't have alcohol. Sometimes a parent will give you an extra $25 or $40. We do really well with adult parties.

Before I was a waitress, it is possible that I never left a tip. Now, I always leave 18% or more.

$ $ $

Thomas worked in a hookah lounge in Brooklyn, New York. This is what he had to say about his specialty job in the restaurant business.

I worked one year in a hookah lounge in Brooklyn. I liked it and am trying to open one of my own. It has a good social atmosphere and is very relaxed. I am mostly with people my age. Most are very cultural—a lot of Middle Eastern Jews. You get to know your neighbors.

We have both food and hookah. I am a hookah preparer. There is also a waitress. It takes me about six minutes to prepare the hookah. A hookah lasts about 40 minutes, and people are charged about $8 for their hookah. I am paid $60 for a shift. The shifts are eight–ten hours. We automatically include a 17% gratuity on every bill. This is split equally among all the hookah preparers and servers for that shift. We split this equally. People will also give us direct tips that we do not share.

On a typical weekday, I get $40 from the 17% gratuity and $20–$30 in direct tips. During the weekend, I get $100 a day from the 17% gratuity and $70 in direct tips. About 30% will give me a direct tip. The average direct tip is $5 to $10.

The biggest tips come from those who are not regulars. I get good tips if I can recommend a good flavor. The other day I got $8 for recommending fruit punch. Friends who come in will also give you a direct tip.

$ $ $

Carol has been a galley assistant for the last two years for a cruise line that operates between Portland, Oregon and Alaska. The galley assistant is a position that requires training in the culinary arts. Galley assistants perform any number of tasks to assist the preparation and service of food on a sailing vessel. In addition, the galley assistant is likely to be trained to handle emergencies if anything should occur during a tour. This is Carol's experience with tipping in the culinary arts specialty.

I work for a small cruise line (84 passengers). We only have a crew of 22, and only four of us work in the galley. It is a good job. I get to spend all summer in Alaska, and I keep very busy. I get paid $7.40 an hour, and I work 80 hours a week. I get time and a half. I work for six weeks, and then I take two weeks off. The work is close, casual, and comfortable. Small is the way to go. The cruises are eight nights.

Tipping for the galley staff and crew is totally erratic. We only meet the passengers on the first day of the cruise and the last day. Sometimes I only get a few bucks for the entire cruise. This time one passenger gave every crew member $20, and another passenger gave me and three others $60. The money was in an envelope, and I don't know who the passenger was. This $80 was the best I ever did. It will pay for my personal needs such as shampoo, etc. I won't have to use my debit card. It was totally random.

I probably average $100 in tips over six weeks. I get $10 here and $20 there. There is no way to gauge. The trip is expensive, about $3,000–$5,000.

If I finish the season, I get a $1,000 bonus, and every year I get a raise. Last year I got $6.40 an hour, and this year I get $7.40.

$ $ $

Cherl worked for the summer at a Cold Stone Creamery in California. Her responses are included among the specialty positions because the job included elements that required talents in entertainment. Servers at Cold Stone Creamery are expected to sing and dance when they are tipped. The following narrative details Cherl's experiences receiving tips in this capacity.

I loved my job. It was a lot of fun, and I got free ice cream. I got to sing and talk to customers. I was paid $6.50 an hour for the first two months and $8 an hour after that. When I auditioned for the job, I had to show them that I could sing. I sang an individual song, and then I sang a song with a group. You sing a song depending upon how much you get tipped. Seventy-five percent of customers tipped something. The usual tip was their change. When someone gave a tip, one of us would yell out, "We got a tip." If it was a small tip, we would give a ten-second chant, "tip, tip, hooray." For bigger tips, we would sing a short song. One song used the song, "I've Been Working on the Railroad." We would sing, "I've been working in the Cold Stone, thank you for your dollar."

Some people would tip and ask us not to sing. The biggest tip we got was $40. For that we did a song and a dance.

Sometimes we would throw the ice cream and have another server catch it. People would give tips for this as well.

We split up the tips evenly at the end of each shift. Typically, we would split up $10 for a three hour shift.

Parents tipped the most. They wanted us to sing for their kids.

$ $ $

The narratives of specialty workers in the restaurant business demonstrate how the pervasiveness of the tipping norm affects tips. Specialty jobs are the most likely to be affected by the interaction of the company's policy with the customers' adherence to the norm. Because there is so much variation across restaurants, customers often do not know how their tip is distributed. Moreover, specialty workers have considerably less contact with the customers; yet, their tips appear to be contingent upon the customer's knowledge and respect for their expertise. One striking exception to this is the narrative from Cheryl who worked at Cold Stone Creamery. In that particular case, the specialty is the contact with the customers. Her story does however reinforce the notion that some people tip for specialty services that they have an appreciation for and/or like the recognition of their tip; while some people prefer more anonymity in their practice of the social norm of tipping.

NOTES

1. See Paula's narrative in the section on multi-function jobs.

8
Tip Jars

According to the Census Bureau, baristas and deli-slicers fall under the category of food preparation workers (135,840; $19,000). However, deli-clerks are considered "combined food preparation and serving workers, including fast food" (84,530; $19,000); although in many cases, clerks and slicers trade off during their shift. Coffee bar attendants (those who clean up the tables) are classified as dining room and cafeteria attendants and bartender helpers (53,100; $18,000). To further complicate matters, ice cream servers fall under the category of counter attendants, cafeteria, food concession, and coffee shops (23,740; $18,000). No matter how the occupation is labeled the annual pay of those who work in settings in which a tip jar might be employed to supplement the wages of food service employees is low relative to the cost of living. Yet, tip jars in ice cream parlors, the local deli, and carry out diners have become almost ubiquitous. A local Subway store recently removed its tip jar. The cashier indicated that the franchise owner considered it "unprofessional."

$ $ $

Denise has worked for the last eight months at a Starbucks in Oakland, California. Here is what she had to say about the tip jar in her own words.

    I like this job. You meet a lot of people. I like being busy, and we are constantly moving. There is no waiting around.

    I earn $10 an hour. About half of the customers will leave change. Thirty-five percent will leave nothing at all, and the remainder (15%) will put in a buck or more. We are across from a federal center and have a lot of regular customers. Some of them will give us $5 or $10 once a week. They just drop it in the tip jar.

Men tip the most when there is a girl at the register. Women tip the least when there is a woman at the register.

On Mondays, we divide up the tips for the week. This is based upon the hours worked. It comes out to $1.75 to $2.50 an hour. I average $60–$70 a week in tips and work a 35 hour week.

On Christmas and Thanksgiving, people are very thankful we are open, and we average $3 an hour in tips. The tips are divided on those days and not by the week.

When I go to a restaurant, I tip 15–20%. When I go to the Starbuck's near my house, I usually leave my change.

We do all right with tips because we have a good location. It would not be that good if we were across from a college.

$ $ $

Daniel is a musician who also works at a Starbuck's in Cincinnati, Ohio when he is not touring. This is what Daniel had to say about the tip jar.

I love working at Starbuck's. It is very busy. People want their coffee immediately. I like the people who work there. A lot of them are musicians. I am paid $8 an hour.

People put their tips in the square Plexiglas container. About 80% will leave a tip. About half of them will simply put in their loose change—leave 20 cents for a $1.80 coffee. The other half will leave a dollar bill.

At the end of each shift, we do tip-drops. We put the tips in the safe. At the end of the week, one person will take the change to a bank and use a coin counter, as well as count up the bills that were left as tips. The tips are pro-rated according to the number of hours that are worked. I get $60–$70 in tips in a typical week in which I work 37–40 hours. We get our tip share weekly in cash. The biggest tips are given during the holidays. On Christmas Eve, I got $2.50 in tips for every hour that I worked. People were happy that we were open on the holiday.

The regulars almost always tip, and they tip the most. People with nice cars also tip the most on the drive-through. People who pay with credit cards or Starbuck's cards don't tip as often. About 20–30% of those with cards will leave a tip. They can't leave the tip on the card so they have to go into their pocket to get tip money.

When I am on tour and go to a coffee shop, I leave my change. I have to watch my budget. When I am at home, I will definitely leave a dollar.

We appreciate tips a lot. When we are swamped and really working hard, it's nice to know that people recognize it.

[We re-interviewed Daniel when the recession began.] I used to make 7–10% of my income from tips. I get $25 less a week than I did a year ago.

$ $ $

Bernice works at a Dunkin Donuts in Hartford, Connecticut. This is her story.

I've been there about six months. It's just a job. It helps pay the bills.

I get $8 an hour. I usually go in around 2 pm and leave at 8 pm. Yesterday, I made $5 on tips. It depends upon the day. On the weekend, I usually make $10 on tips while on a weekday $5 is the average. We split the tips at the end of each shift, and we share the tips equally.

Seventy-five percent of the customers will leave a tip. The average is probably 17 cents. They leave change. About 10% will put a bill in. My biggest tip was $10 from a regular customer. Regulars tip the most. They tip a lot around Christmas. On Christmas Eve, I made $50 in tips. I wish everyday was Christmas.

We have a drive-through. They don't tip much. We are next to a post office. The postal workers tip more. People who are in-and-out quickly don't tip well. Only about 25% of those who just get coffee will leave a tip. If people get food, they tip.

$ $ $

Janice also used to work for a catering company as a server. Now she works at an ice cream store. This is what Janice had to say about the tip jar.

I've been working at an ice cream store in Easton, Pennsylvania for the last two years. I get paid $6 an hour. I like the job even though it has long hours and not great pay. I have a lot of authority. I sometimes open up the store, and I like the people I work with.

We have a tip jar which we split according to hours worked. Less than half—maybe 40%—of the customers will leave a tip. The average tip is a dollar or two. Of the 40%, 25% will put in a bill, and 10% will just leave their loose change. I know that does not add up to 40%.

In a six–seven hour shift, I get $15–$25 in tips. On a really slow day, I get $8 in tips. On really good days, I might get $35.

Large families with dads tip the most. The regulars also tip well. Teenagers and kids don't tip well.

I always tip at least a dollar. If I am with a big group, I will leave two dollars. If the other people in my group don't tip enough, I will make up the difference.

Tipping is not done enough. A lot of people neglect tips because they don't realize that people depend on it.

$ $ $

Daniel worked at a deli in Northfield, Minnesota. He had this to say about the tip jar.

I worked at the deli for six–eight months. I made sandwiches. We had ice cream and beer on tap. I made $6.50 an hour. With tips, it made it $8 an hour. On the very first hot day in Minnesota, you could sell a lot of ice cream and do very well.

No one liked the job because the owner was a jerk. However, I liked the other workers.

We had a big sign on the tip jar about Minnesotans being great tippers. Older couples tipped the best. College kids were bad tippers which surprised me at first. I was raised to be a good tipper because my mom was a server in a restaurant.

About 25% of the customers left a tip. The average was their change. Maybe 10% would put in a bill. In a typical five hour shift, I would get $3–$4. The manager did not take part in the split.

We split up the tips whenever anyone clocked out.

$ $ $

Paul worked for seven months at a Chipotle in Chicago. This is his story in his words.

I loved working at Chipotle. The food was awesome. I am trying to find one down here where I can work. I was paid $7 an hour. About 80% of the customers put something in the tip jar. This was usually their change. About 40% put a bill in. Ten percent of those who paid by credit card put something in the jar.

We split the proceeds at the end of each shift. On a good day, I got $5.50, and on a bad day, I would get $2. There were six of us who shared the tip jar. Everyone got a share except the manager or shift supervisor. The manager would split up the tips and give us cash out of the drawer.

We had a lot of business people for lunch. They tipped the most. Teenagers tipped the least.

TIP JARS

Occasionally, we would get no tip because the manager would use the tip fund to replenish the emergency fund where about $200 was kept. I was very confused about this.

$ $ $

Carla worked at a restaurant attached to a miniature golf course in Bethlehem, Pennsylvania. This is her story.

I did this for a summer. It was a family affair. My brother, mother, and mother's boyfriend also worked there. We had more than the usual food at such restaurants. We had burgers, pirogues, club sandwiches, chicken fingers, fries, and ice cream. The golf course was owned by a cousin, and we rented the restaurant. It changed ownership at the end of the summer and that was very stressful at the end. However, I liked working with my family, and the customers were friendly.

I was paid $8 an hour. Ninety-five percent of the customers would leave some type of tip. Most would leave a dollar or two. Some would just put in their change. The average was $1. The biggest tip I received was $10 on a $5 meal.

I worked a seven hour shift, and when I got the tips, I would get $30–$40 per day in tips. The splitting up was a little different. If I was working only with family members, I would keep all the tips. If my brother was working alone, he would keep all the tips. There was one other person who worked with us who was not family. If he was working with us, he would keep all the tips. It was my mom's rules. It did not always make a lot of sense. My brother did not like the fact that I kept all the tips when I worked with him. However, when he was alone he kept all the tips. Because I worked there the most, maybe it evened out in the end.

We had two prominent tip jars. Most tipping occurred when people picked up their food at the counter or when they had finished eating.

Families with young kids tipped the most. Teenagers tipped the least.

When I go to a place with a tip jar, I tip more than I used to. If I am with other people, I try to talk them into tipping more as well.

Tipping is important. It was not as important for me because I got $8 an hour. Nevertheless, it was still important. People should keep it in mind.

$ $ $

Julia worked in Wilmington, Delaware at a deli counter for a gourmet catering service over the summer. She is discussed elsewhere as a babysitter. This is what Julia had to say about her experience with the tip jar.

The store was actually a deli. The deli had tables and chairs. People ordered their food at the counter, waited for it, and then took it home or to their tables. I was paid $6.50 an hour. I liked the job because it was laid back. I liked the five girls who worked there and the manager. The food was good, and we got free lunch. We knew a lot of the people who came in.

There was a tip jar, and people would put their change in or occasionally a dollar. About 25% gave us a tip. It made no difference if we brought the food to the table or not. People did not leave tips on the tables. We divided the money in the tip jar among ourselves throughout the day. We averaged $20 per day split among four of us. On my biggest day, I got $7 in tips.

Men tipped more than women. We were young and cute girls. When we had a guy working at the counter, we used to joke that our tips would go down. I'm not sure if that was true or not. We were also more likely to get tips from people we knew.

$ $ $

The narratives of those who rely on money from the tip jar are telling. Although many of them make at least minimum wage (unlike many other food service employees), the tip jar is both a means for them to supplement their low wages and a method by which employers are able to diffuse more costs to the consumers. It should be pointed out though that in the tip jar setting, management seems to engage in behaviors that attempt to retain control over wages. In most cases, management determines how the tips are divided. This is true with tip jars, but in settings with tip jars, managers exercise a greater degree of control over tip distributions, including changing the policy regarding the tip jar altogether. The most poignant example is Paul's experience with the manager at Chipotle who treated the tips as corporate property distributed or withheld at the manager's discretion. It is also interesting that a number of the respondents note the peak in generosity during the holiday seasons, and they state similar reasons. Customers apparently express an appreciation for the fact that they are working when most people are with their families.

Part 2

SERVICES

More than 90% of Americans say that they tip restaurant workers, but the tipping system in the service industry is much less consistent. Some people make a habit of giving cash to anyone who helps them out in any way. It's a strange curiosity that people tend to tip for those services that are not directly related to our well-being rather than tipping people who provide services directly related to survival. Patients almost never give tips and rarely give gifts to medical professionals; although other medical professionals may exchange gifts, particularly during the holidays. For example, pharmaceutical sales reps regularly bring lunch to medical offices on sales calls. In fact, most medical professionals have come to expect this, and many consider this an acceptable business practice. Yet, others express concern about the extent of what they consider inducements in the relationship between health professionals and the pharmaceutical industry.

Alternatively, it is fairly common for customers to tip for furniture delivery or even the painter and plumber. Perhaps the most interesting oddity is the professional practice of providing gifts to customers. For example, no one tips the dentist, but customers often get toothbrushes, floss, toothpaste, and sometimes even sugar-free gum in U.S. dental offices.

The vast extent of tipping practices related to the provision of services is inconsistent. If cash is given to a homeless person who washes car windows at a stoplight without solicitation, is that payment, a tip, charity, or extortion? If a tip is left for a housecleaner (a tip that is often provided before the quality of the job is even known), what is the purpose of the tip? What are tippers trying to accomplish? More importantly, what do people who receive tips for the services that they provide say about the effect of tips on the quality of service?

The disarticulated and decentralized nature of the current extent of the private contracting of government services in the United States has resulted in some interesting changes in the tipping protocol for some services that were once exclusively public services. Many jurisdictions have historically restricted tips for government employees. Such regulations may prohibit workers from soliciting or accepting money or gifts for doing their salaried jobs. Standards of professionalism in government established during the progressive movement attempted to limit the disparate influence of money in the provisions of services in a democratic society. Consequently, it was uncommon for people to tip postal workers, city sanitation workers, and so forth. Although, some homeowners have been known to put cash or gifts out for sanitation workers during the holidays where sanitation workers have also been known to honk their horns in expectation of such tips. These practices have become increasingly common as cities and counties contract services to private firms. However, there are generally firm prohibitions against tipping private ambulance drivers.[1]

A number of etiquette guides advise tipping service gratuities that are based on the tipper's "station in life," the building's pedigree, the guilt and anxiety quotient of the tipper, the income and budget of the tipper, and the number and type of requests made of service professionals. Etiquette is of course a mechanism by which the social status quo is maintained, so it should come as no surprise the etiquette guides address quite directly the extent to which tipping promotes and reflects social status. Most of the etiquette advice is related to the tipper and not the service worker or the quality of service. Notably, etiquette guides have very little advice on the protocol for accepting tips and have almost nothing at all to say about the experiences of those who receive tips.

Rational models have even less to say about tips for services. Tipping rituals do not follow from strict models of rational economic behavior. The rituals seem to perform regulatory and redistributive functions in society. Do voluntary regulation and the "emotional" enforcement of redistributive efforts leave those who receive tips more vulnerable in their experience?

NOTE

1. The "wallet autopsy" is not a tip and is also a clear violation of policy.

9

Household Services

In this chapter, household services are divided into services provided in high rise settings such as apartments, hotels, and office buildings and those services that might be utilized by people living in single family homes. Although people living in apartments may use some of the same services as those who own a single-family home, it is less likely and is not reflected in this sample. For example, the use of cleaning services is becoming increasingly common in larger cities, but is most often used by those who own their home or condo and less often by people renting apartments. In addition, the distinction between household services in high rises versus single family homes reflects different organizational dynamics. For example, janitors clean office buildings at the behest of the building management and not at the request of any given tenant.

The U.S. Census estimates that there are approximately 993,990 janitors and building cleaners, making an average of $25,000 annually. Furthermore, there are an estimated 437,190 maids and housekeeping staff, making an average of $18,000 annually. However, there is no reliable way to distinguish between those who work in homes and those who work for hotels. There are 29,990 baggage porters, bellhops, and concierges, making an average of $26,000 annually, and approximately 12,740 ushers, lobby attendants, and ticket takers who make $28,000 on average annually. These categories are represented in the data collected regarding tips for services provided in high rises. The narratives included in this study flesh out how tipping norms are perceived in the two distinct contexts of high rises and homes.

There are also about 108,720 personal and home care aides with average annual earnings of $20,000. Personal and home care aides lump together in-home childcare workers and home health aides for the ill and/or elderly. It is likely that the Census category for personal and home care aides significantly underestimate this market because babysitters who are often young people within the broader community network regularly receive cash and are not tracked in this category. Each of these categories is represented in the narratives included under the single family home subheading in this chapter.

Hollywood has socialized Americans to understand that bellhops and lobby attendants customarily receive tips. There is tremendous folklore about how much lobby attendants in apartment and condominium buildings make around the holidays. In *New York Magazine*, Brian Farnham (2000) tells the story of a doorman who was given a Nissan 300ZX. Farnham goes on to say that in high rise buildings, superintendents in New York City receive between $100 and $300 per tenant around the holidays, and this can total over $10,000. However, $30 to $50 is commonly considered the appropriate tip for a doorman, but the protocols for tipping household service workers are quite variable. There is a lot of confusion about tipping people who help around the house.[1] In the Washington Post, Annie Groer (2006) reports "the 'rules' for tipping for household services appear totally arbitrary."

HOUSEHOLD SERVICES IN HIGH RISES

Rod has been a lobby attendant at a high rise with 450 units in Yonkers, New York for the past 17 years. This is his story in his own words.

The job is OK.[2] The morning hour shift is hard, and I just got to change to the night shift which is better. My job is to open the door for people, get packages, help outside with groceries, and a little security. In general, I like the job. I get $17 an hour.

Tips during the week are not that great. I get tips for helping people load groceries into the shopping carts, getting packages to them, and watching cars in the driveway. Most of these tips are $2 or $3 and only amount to $10–$15 a week. I get tips maybe 30% of the time when I help someone with a grocery cart.

Today, I got my first tip of $5 for delivering a package. Most people don't tip for packages. If I know they usually tip, I am more likely to call them.

I occasionally will help someone bring something down during my dinner hour. I might get a couple bucks for this.

I get better tips from whites. Some blacks are OK. Hispanics (I'm Hispanic) don't tip very well.

During Christmas, the tenants (there are 450 apartments) are supposed to give $75 each to a common fund which is then distributed. I got about $2,000 from this in two different checks before Christmas. I also got about $1,000 in envelopes from individual tenants. These were mostly from people that I helped over the year. I got maybe 200 envelopes from about half the tenants. Most of these were $5s, $10s, and $20s. Two people gave me $50. The more you know someone the more you are likely to get tipped.

$ $ $

Reed has been a lobby attendant near the University of Chicago for 30 years. The following narrative details his responses regarding receiving tips for his services.

I also teach sociology. The management of the condo building where I work calls my job a "greeter" or "monitor." I work 32 hours a week. It is the simplest job in the world. I sit at a desk with six TV monitors and open either the front door or the rear door. I will help people put items on carts. I wear a white shirt and a tie. The building is mostly upper-middle class.

I take home $621 every two weeks. I usually refuse tips outside of the holiday season. I feel I live pretty frugally, and I have more money than many people in the building. Being an old socialist, I would feel uncomfortable taking their money.

At Christmas almost half of the residents give me a tip. The average is $20, and the range is from $5 to $100. I get a total of about $800. We don't share these tips. I also get a $200 check from management as a bonus.

Upper-middle class people give more. Whites give more than blacks. Those on the higher floors give more, and those who come from a family history of having more money are more familiar with tipping. Ninety percent of the tips are in cash, and most are put in an envelope with some type of card. I also get some presents ranging from cookies to umbrellas. I write people thank you notes.

$ $ $

Simon is a valet working at an upper-middle class high-rise condo in South Florida. The residents are generally older and tend to make more regular requests of the service staff. Simon had this to say about his experience.

I've been a valet for 11 years. I like it. The company helps me out a lot.

I get paid $7 an hour. I get tips from a lot of sources. My daily average in tips is $80. I park cars. About 80% will tip me. Almost everyone gives me a dollar. Only 2% or 3% will give me more than that.

I take groceries up to apartments. Everyone will give me something for that. The average is $3. My best tip for taking groceries up was $20.

I also fix things. People ask me to change light bulbs or to fix a closet door that is off its tracks. They don't want to wait for the building engineer. I don't charge them, but they will usually give me $5 or $10. Every bit helps.

People who are on vacation or traveling for work sometimes ask me to watch their apartment. I might water some plants or bring in their mail. I usually am given $20 a month for this. They will often give me $100 when they get back.

I get two types of holiday tips. About 70% of people give me an envelope. The average in the envelopes is $20. The biggest was $200. I also get a holiday bonus from the building. Newer employees get a minimum of $200 from the building, and more senior employees get $500–$600. The envelopes that I get are all for me. In general, we don't share our tips at all. Only a couple of residents say to share the tips.

The best tippers are the tourists. The people who live at the building full-time always give the same amount. It makes no difference if the quality of the service is good or bad.

$ $ $

Fred is a concierge in an office building and shared the following story.

I've been a concierge for eight years. I like it. It is good to be paid to be nice to people I would be nice to anyway. The salary range for people in my position is $25,000–$35,000.

I am a dorm mother, Santa Claus, and a bartender. I am there to let someone know that I can help them and to show that I care. I arrange for flowers, gift baskets, etc. People ask me where to find things, such as a good restaurant. I get left packages and let people into offices. It is a lot of little-little things. I have a huge collection of catalogs, and I give one person a car magazine and another person a clothing magazine, etc. We do security in some buildings. I always found that irritating. It is important to have the gift of gab. You can't be shy and must have been raised in a caring and loving home. You also need to know how to problem solve. Some people cannot even run a screwdriver or fix a light bulb.

We are not allowed to take tips except around the holidays. Our company advertises that. I only take tips in very unusual situations, for example, if I drive someone somewhere. I also occasionally take coffee or lunches when they are offered.

I just started working at this building, so I did not receive tips for the holidays. My last building had 1,200 tenants in 35 offices. I received a total of three tips which totaled up to $150 for the holidays. I had only been there for two years.

Prior to working at the last building, I worked at another building for six years. There were ten offices, and they all gave something for Christmas. The average was $50, and my total was $500–$600.

There is no great pattern in who gives the most. However, the smaller offices seem to give more. It is proportional to how much interaction you have with those in the office.

$ $ $

Carla cleans the common areas (stairs, elevators, lobbies, and so forth) of several office buildings in Northern Virginia. She is from Honduras, speaks little English, and has two jobs to support her three kids. Her previous experience as a babysitter is included in the narratives categorized under the household services in single family homes. She also currently works a second job as a busser in a restaurant, and that narrative is included in the restaurant section of this book. Her husband left her a year ago, leaving her legal status in this country tenuous. A translator was utilized in conducting this interview to minimize interpretation errors because she does not have a conversational knowledge of English. The following narrative reflects the responses provided by Carla regarding her experiences receiving tips for providing janitorial services in office buildings.

I've been cleaning buildings for the last 14 months. The job is OK. I have to work. There are a lot of important people in this building, and some are very nice to me. I earn $716 every two weeks.

The cleaning company I work for has me working at several buildings. I never receive a tip outside of Christmas. For Christmas, four of the offices at one of the government buildings pooled together and gave me $500. There are 200 people in that building, and there are 42 offices in another building. My employer gave me a $50 gift certificate to Giant. I received no other presents besides the general tip from the pooled government office.

$ $ $

Abasi has been a concierge for four years at a large hotel in downtown Washington, D.C. He is originally from West Africa and shared the following story.

The job is OK. I am able to make a living while I go to school. I am studying to get a degree in information technology. As a concierge, I get information for people at the hotel. I make reservations, book trips, find out what is open and closed, give directions, and try to make our guests happy. We are a convention hotel, and I help between 100 and 150 people per day. I get paid between $13 and $14 per hour.

About 2% of the people I help will give me a tip. I probably average between $5 and $8 per day in tips. There are days when I get no tips.

Doctors and attorneys don't tip. I get most of my tips from regular people—not upper class people.

My biggest tip was $100. I got that two years ago when the person needed a late reservation at a good restaurant, and I was able to get it for him. And, I also arranged for transportation. I never got a tip like that again.

$ $ $

Quincy has been a lobby attendant for five years at an exclusive resort hotel on the Delmarva Peninsula (the peninsula shared by Delaware, Maryland, and Virginia). The following narrative details his responses regarding tipping norms.

I love it. The owner is good to us. We get treated like human beings, and I make good tips. I get paid $6.15 an hour. On an average day, I bring bags up for six guests. The average tip is $6–$7. It really depends. Ten percent don't tip at all. I especially don't get tips from people who come on package deals, and they think that all tips are included.

I also get tips when I fix someone's air conditioning, unclog a toilet, bring up an extra chair, and so on. Eighty percent will tip me for one of these services, and the average tip is $2.

I average $80–$90 a day in tips. My biggest tip was $180 from a gentleman who asked me to park his car, take up his bags, unpack them, and bring him some ice.

Younger people definitely tip the best. The older generation holds onto their money more.

I don't share my tips.

I am always talking to the guests. Schmoozing helps. I like people.

I very seldom get a tip for just opening the door.

$ $ $

Kenneth is a bell captain at a swanky hotel in South Miami Beach. This is his story.

I've been at this hotel for three years and was recently promoted to bell captain. I maintain the front area. My main job is to provide service to the hotel

HOUSEHOLD SERVICES 95

guests. It is a good job. I meet a lot of people. People are here to have a good time (which is good for me), and I make a good living.

Most bell boys make $6–$7 an hour; while bell captains make $350 a week in salary. We also get a lot of tips.

There are a variety of ways we get tips. I take people up to their rooms. I bring up the bags, show them the services that are available, and provide basic information. Ninety percent of people will give me a tip. Most will give $5–$10. The average is $6.

When people check-out, I help load the cars. I get more at check-out than check-in. People have gotten to know me as I provide them information on restaurants and other services throughout their stay. I get a lot of $20s at check-out and the average is probably $20.

I usually get a couple of bucks for calling a cab (50–60% will tip for this). I might get a couple of bucks if I give someone an umbrella when it is raining. Although we have building engineers, I might get a couple of bucks when I help someone do a quick repair.

We have a lot of production groups that stay at the hotel. They often come with 20 or so boxes. We have a standard rate of $10 per box. We split this up among the bell staff.

Unless someone is assisting me with a specific chore, there is no pooling. People who are more outgoing tip the most. They come down and talk to you. Some celebrities are good tippers, and some are pretty bad. People on vacation are here to have a good time, and they tip well.

Sunday is our best day for tipping as people are checking out. I average $125–$150 on Sundays. On other days, the average is $60.

$ $ $

Doris worked at a Holiday Inn in Colorado for a year and a half as a housekeeper. This is her story in her own words.

I worked my way up to head housekeeper. I did not like cleaning rooms, but it was not bad being the head housekeeper. The Holiday Inn had both a lot of tourists and business people.

I worked an eight hour day and cleaned 10–15 rooms. About 20% of the guests would leave a tip. The average of those who left a tip was $2–$3. It really varied though. Occasionally, I got $10 or $20. If people stayed longer they were more likely to leave a tip. However, sometimes someone would stay a long time and not leave a tip. On an average day, I would not get over $10 in tips.

I rarely saw the people. If they came and asked for something like an extra towel, they were more likely to leave a tip. People who left a tip usually did it on their last day.

There was no sharing of tips unless we cleaned the room together.

Whoever cleaned the room got the tip. If someone cleaned the room for several days and the guests left while the cleaning person was on vacation, it was still the person who cleaned the room that day who got the tip.

When I now stay at a hotel, I leave at least $5 a day.

$ $ $

Doris has been a part of the housekeeping staff at a nice hotel on the Delmarva Peninsula for 17 years. She had this to say about tipping norms.

I also help supervise, so now I am on salary. I like what I do. I like my co-workers. We all get along and work together as a team. Most of the people on the staff make $7.75 an hour. Many are young and are foreign students.

About half the hotel guests leave a tip. The average is $5 for their entire stay. The biggest I ever got was $50 from a person who stayed an entire week.

Older people tip the best. Those with kids are less likely to tip. I guess they can't afford to tip. Those who make the biggest mess (have kids) leave the smaller tips. Those who stay longer leave a bit more in tips, but not that much more.

On an average day we get $10 a day in tips. On check-out day, we average $120 for an entire floor split among three staff members. You have to be working that day to get a share of the tips. We share the tips, and everyone here is honest.

We are satisfied if people leave $5. At least they are thinking of us.

$ $ $

Olivia has worked for over 20 years as a chambermaid at a resort hotel in the Deep Creek Lake area of Maryland. The area has a ski slope where families from around the region often go for weekend getaways. During the interview, Olivia invited three other chambermaids from the hotel to demonstrate the common experience shared by chambermaids in this particular hotel. The following narrative attempts to capture the interview as it unfolded.

We almost never get tips. Maybe one out of 100 guests leaves a tip. For those who leave a tip, the average is a dollar or two. Sometimes we clean an entire floor, and no one leaves a tip. Someone once left $20 for two rooms.

[Over the course of the interview, three other chambermaids walked by as it was the end of their shift. Olivia called them over.]

Violet—how often do we receive tips? Sometimes an entire week goes by without a tip. I've been working here 30 years.

[All four chambermaids agreed that only 1 or 2% of the guests leave a tip.]

Occasionally, someone might give me a few bucks if we help them with their bags. We once had a convention here and we had to make up 15 rooms extra nice. We set flowers and put in fruit. You know, we didn't get a single tip!

The few times we get a tip it seems the poor people tip the most.

[One of the women who said she was the manager added the following brief story.]

Once we had a chambermaid who put out envelopes. We had to fire her because she seemed to only work for tips. If people did not leave tips, she wouldn't clean their place. People should work because that is their job and not because of tips.

$ $ $

Millie is originally from Jamaica and is a chambermaid at a casino-resort hotel in South Florida. This is her story.

I've been there for a year, and I like it because I love housekeeping.

I clean around 12 rooms a day, and I get paid $8.50 an hour. Some days there are no tips at all. I might get a tip in perhaps 10% of the rooms. The most I've ever gotten is $20. The average is around $4 or $5. Some people leave a note with the tip thanking us for our hard work.

I average at most $20 a week in tips. Some weeks I get no tips. If I work with someone else, we share the tips. Otherwise, there is no sharing.

People are more likely to leave tips if they are here on conventions or seminars. The typical tourist does not leave a tip.

$ $ $

Todd was a houseboy in a guest house, a bed and breakfast. He has also worked in restaurants and on a schooner. His experiences in those jobs are discussed elsewhere in this book. The following narrative reflects Todd's responses regarding his experiences receiving tips as a houseboy.

I lived for free at the bed-and-breakfast and had to work 15 hours a week in return. For any amount over 15 hours, I got $10 an hour. I averaged ten extra hours per week ($100).

I was a chambermaid. People thought $5 a night was the standard tip. Sometimes they also left a thank you note. My biggest tip was $80 for four nights.

We left an envelope that said we appreciated gratuities. We got stiffed about 30% of the time. Some would act as if they never received the envelope. They threw it away. Others would put the "do not disturb" sign up the entire time and feel they did not need to tip. Some were what we called, "big verbal tippers." They would say how appreciative they were but not leave a tip.

There were three other maids, and we shared our tips. They were all retired, and they may have mistrusted me. So, I made a big show of always showing them the tips. The tips were given to the owner who recorded them in a "master sheet." He split up the tips weekly on a pro-rated basis determined by hours. The money was kept in a silverware drawer.

In May, I averaged $50 a week in tips. This went up to $100 at the height of the season in July and August.

The demographics were the same as with the restaurant. Lesbians tipped the least, and gay men tipped the most.

$ $ $

HOUSEHOLD SERVICES IN SINGLE FAMILY HOMES
Bianca is from Bolivia and has been cleaning houses for 15 years. She has also been a nanny. This is her story in her own words.

When I started, I cleaned 15 houses a week. I recently had another baby, so I am only cleaning a couple of houses now. Just before the baby, I was cleaning five houses a week.

I charge $80–$130 per cleaning. It depends upon how big the house is and how much work needs to be done. About two times per week, I get more than what I charged. When I get paid extra, it is usually an extra $10 or $20. I get tips because I do something unexpected such as clean a closet I don't normally clean, or I work really hard that day. A woman gave me $20 because she had a cat that was shedding a lot of fur, and I was sneezing a lot.

Everyone gives a Christmas bonus. Last year three gave me an extra week's pay, and two said there was no need to work during that week but they would pay me anyway. Over the many years I've done cleaning, I've gotten extra pay outside of Christmas about 30% of the time. Usually, the extra pay is $10 or $15. The Christmas bonus is almost always an extra week's pay.

I've also been a nanny. During my time as a nanny, I also got an extra week's pay for Christmas.

$ $ $

Jonathan, whose experiences as a server is explored elsewhere in this book, ran a housekeeping business in Washington, D.C. for seven years. The following narrative details Jonathan's perspective on tipping norms in household services.

I worked alone and had 20–25 clients. I was very high-end. I used to interview the clients before I started. I asked what kind of vacuum cleaner they had, what were their pet peeves, etc. I was very intimate with people. I spoke English, and I showed up on time.

My clients were very powerful people: a member of the House of Representatives, several vice presidents of large corporations, and so on. I charged $75 a week on average. Almost always they gave me $90–$100. I was really good at what I did and was usually tipped at 20%. Around the holidays, I probably got $500–$600 total. One couple gave me a month's salary.

I had a housekeeper of my own during this time period. She charged me $60, and I use to give her $80.

$ $ $

Rosa is a housekeeper for five separate families in Chico, California. She is Hispanic and speaks perfect English. This is Rosa's story.

I've been cleaning houses for five years, and I like it. Everyone is very nice, and they allow me very flexible hours. I charge $15 an hour. Outside of Christmas, I am almost never given more than my $15 an hour. Sometimes, I might get $5 for gas if I am running errands.

For Christmas, all five clients gave me a bonus. This ranged from $20 to $300. The family that I work for all day gave me the largest bonus—$300. I charge $115 for working for them all day. I also got two gift certificates. One was for my children, and one was for a food store. They were both for $100. The average bonus was $50–$60.

$ $ $

Barbara does childcare for three different families in New Jersey. She had this to say about her experiences receiving tips as a childcare worker.

I've been doing childcare for five years. I love it. I get to work with wonderful little people and help parents guide them. I go to people's homes. I make $10–$15 per hour, and I get paid every week.

Between the three families, I get about $600 a week. I don't often get extra money during the regular year. Sometimes I get an occasional $10 or $25.

During Christmas, I get the equivalent of one week's salary from each of the families. I get a bit more from the people who appreciate me the most. I have good relations with the parents and the kids.

$ $ $

Julia was interviewed about her work at a deli in Delaware. That narrative is included in the restaurant section of this book. She also had several jobs as a babysitter, and her responses during the interview about her work in childcare are included in the following narrative.

I started babysitting when I was 14. I really like babysitting because I really like babies. I babysat for two sets of families in high school. They both had twins. One set of twins was three years old, and the other was ten years old. I charged both of them $10 an hour. The first family never asked what I charged. They just assumed I charged $10 per hour. They both always gave me the exact amount. The second family often gave pizza to me and the kids.

I babysat occasionally for other families. One gave me $10 an hour—also exact. One other mom never asked what I charged and simply gave me $9 an hour. I never went back to the second family because she never asked me what I charged.

In college, I babysat over a summer for two boys, ages 10 and 13. I picked them up at camp and took them places. I charged $12 an hour ($2 was for gas). They also gave me the exact amount.

I also babysat for another family during the fall. They had a three and four year old that I picked up from pre-school. Sometimes there was another girl. The parents occasionally rounded up when paying me. If I worked 2.5 hours, they would pay me for three hours. I got $14 an hour from this family.

$ $ $

May has worked with children since she was 15. She lives in Winston-Salem, North Carolina and shared the following story about tipping norms.

I did tutoring at a private school. Most of the kids were in kindergarten or first grade. I was paid $8 an hour. Over the year, I tutored about 15–20 kids. About half of the families gave me tips over the course of the year (non-holidays). The total over the year was $250–$300. Most of the tips were in the $20 range. For example, one kid did poorly on a test. I tutored him, and he got an A. I was given an extra $20.

Over Christmas, very few gave me cash. I got a lot of gift certificates. Most of the certificates were for $30–$50. Seventy-five percent of the parents gave me either cash or a gift certificate.

The next year I was 16, and I started working at the same school in their after-school program. I was paid $9 an hour. I got very few tips during the regular year. However, I got the same gifts for the holidays as in the previous year (mostly gift certificates).

Over the summer, I was a camp counselor at this school with many of the same kids. I was also paid $9 an hour. I received no tips during the summer. However, at the end of the summer I got the same type of gifts as I did at Christmas.

For my sophomore and junior year, I did a lot of babysitting. I babysat maybe three times a month. I charged $7 an hour for one child and another $2 an hour for each additional child. I was almost always paid in cash, and the families usually rounded up. Therefore, if they owed me $17, they gave me $20.

When I was in college, I did childcare for a family of four in North Carolina. They paid me $12 an hour and gave me extra money for gas. I got $100 for my birthday and $100 for Christmas as well as a personal gift. We were very close.

After I moved to D.C., I worked for a law firm but realized I liked kids more. I've been working for a family for the last ten months. I charge $12 an hour. I got $50 for my birthday, $75 for Christmas, and a $50 gift certificate. They always round up. If they owe me $513 they will give me a check for $520.

There are only a few patterns in the tipping. Parents of girls tipped a bit more at the school. This was because the girls looked up to me. I bonded well with the girls. The boys were more likely to get into trouble.

I did not expect any form of tip when I was at the school. They knew I was paid. Some acted as if they were doing me a favor—especially when they paid me after their kid passed. Some parents were very condescending, and it was awkward.

$ $ $

Carla babysat for two families for three years in Northern Virginia. She speaks very little English. Her experiences as an office cleaner and as a busser in a restaurant are included in other portions of this book. Carla's experiences receiving tips for her work as a babysitter are detailed below.

The families brought the kids to my home. I got $140 a week from one family and $130 from the other. They never gave me more than the required amount.

For Christmas, they gave some gifts for my kids. They were pretty poor themselves.

I liked babysitting, but it was not enough money.

$ $ $

Linda has had several home care jobs in Western Colorado. She also received tips for her work cleaning resort condos (essay not included). The following narrative details her responses during the interview about tipping norms in home care.

I work for about a dozen senior citizens as a home health-care provider. I clean up their homes, run errands, give sponge baths, and so on. I like the health care part but do not like being a maid. I like the people, and I like working with senior citizens.

I am hired by an agency that pays me $7.15 an hour. I don't know how much the agency gets paid. In a typical week, I might work for seven–ten people. I have never received a tip or gift during the week or around the holidays.

I also work as a respite care provider to parents with special needs children. When the parents need to get away, I come and help. I like this work because it is one-on-one, and I can really connect with the kids and see their progress. I am now working with three families.

I get paid $10 an hour. On average, I spend two hours with the kids per visit. The parents pay me directly, and they get reimbursed in some way by a community agency. I don't know the details. I get something extra every time I work with these families. In an average week, I am given $20–$30 extra. Around the holidays, I got a total of around $100 from the three families.

$ $ $

The stories shared by those who provide household services reveal some common themes. There are also some similarities and differences between the high rise and home settings. In all forms of household services reflected in this study, tips are more often than not fairly small, and conformity to tipping norms appears to be less consistent than in the restaurant industry. There also seems to be a relationship between the ability or willingness of the customer to perform the task themselves and the likelihood of tipping for services, particularly when it comes to tasks performed by building employees. When it comes to cleaning services, the people who provide those services note that the likelihood of getting a more sizable tip seems to be associated with the work effort. Employees cleaning both high rises and houses state in various ways how they are more likely to get a tip or a bigger tip when they work extra hard or do something special. On the other hand, Doris reports that those who have kids and make the biggest messes leave the smallest tips. Some of the narratives also indicate that increased interactions with staff may correspond with increased tips; while those who speak very little English and have little interaction with the people in the building (like Rosa) tend to receive few tips.

The contextual differences indicate that tipping norms are related to the prestige of the work environment and the social status of the job. For example, nannies appear to be more likely to receive tips than babysitters, and lobby attendants seem to expect a correlation between the social status of those who reside in the high rises (a proxy for the prestige of the building and a reflection of the customer's ability to pay) and tips. Moreover, the tips for jobs that involve a higher degree of interaction tend to be understood in relation to the quality of the service; whereas tips for domestic services with little interaction between the worker and customer are not as likely to be accounted for in the evaluation of the quality of the work provided. This finding is also consistent with the literature on how workers manage the emotional value of labor. Domestics tend to evaluate themselves by criteria other than that of society or even their employer (Macdonald and Sirianni 1996). There is no evidence that domestics consider themselves inferior because of the work that they do despite the common tone set by employers that tends to reinforce the inequality of the relationship. Domestics focus on a job well-done; rather than praise from employers or customers.

NOTES

1. For a wonderful book on what it is like to be a housekeeper, see Ehrenreich (2002).
2. Bearman (2005) has written an excellent book describing what it is like to be a doorman. He says the Christmas bonus is a thank your for the previous year of work and a sign of expected attention for the next year. It is both past and future. It is a summary tip. He notes that some buildings pool tips, which raises the floor. But, some doormen do not like this because the tipping becomes taxable.

10

Deliveries

The Census Bureau reports the number of people employed in the following relevant occupations and their respective annual earnings: 103,970 couriers and messengers ($31,000), 282,690 postal service mail carriers ($39,000), 2,130,980 driver/sales workers and truck drivers ($36,000), and 50,870 non-restaurant food servers, ($21,000). The non-restaurant food service category is a catch-all classification that includes pizza delivery drivers among others. Newspaper delivery people are also subsumed under the door-to-door sales workers, news and street vendors, and related workers (56,450, $31,000) classification.

Tipping for delivery services is one of the more confusing and variable practices. Some stores have explicit policies that are often clearly posted so that customers are also informed of the standards and expectations. For example, Safeway has a firm policy that strictly prohibits accepting tips. If a customer insists, the employee is required to inform them that the tip will go to the charity that the store is currently supporting. The punishment for failing to follow the policy is up to and including termination. Such rules in retail used to be common practice. However, many of these policies are changing as well. Giant Food stores used to have signs reading "No Tipping," and many Whole Foods stores posted "Please No Tipping" admonitions. Yet recently these policies have been revoked, and the signs removed by stores of both chains.

There are also numerous gray areas. For example, UPS "frowns on" the practice of tipping delivery drivers but finds the practice of offering gifts perfectly acceptable. Etiquette advisors contend that consumers should consider the volume of the delivery, the degree of difficulty of the delivery, and the policies of the firm among the personal factors associated with the tipper when calculating the tips for delivery services. People may even ask the service provider or their employer directly about the customary tipping standards in the profession and policies of the agency. People are generally honest, even modest in their responses to such questions. However, this may pose a problem for those who prefer that the tipping system reduce uncertainty.

$ $ $

Lance delivers pizza for a Domino's pizzeria that is located outside of St. Louis. He has been doing it for three years and had this to say about his experience with tips from pizza delivery.

It is a fun job. I get paid OK, and I listen to music. I get paid $5.15 an hour and something for mileage. There are two shifts. Rush shift is from 5 pm to 8 pm, and I average ten deliveries in that time. The average tip is $3. Ninety-five percent will give me a tip. I get $30 in tips during that shift. The day shift is from 11 am to 6 pm, and I get $60–$100 in tips.

Working people tip the most. You go to a rich person's house and expect a big tip. But, you don't get it.

We don't share our tips. All the drivers get along. We are not competitive. We cooperate.

$ $ $

Larry delivered pizza in St. Louis for a year. This is his story.

It was a local pizza place. The job wasn't bad. I did not have to work very hard. During lunch time, I was paid $5 an hour. For the evening shift, I was not paid by the hour but was instead paid $2 per delivery.

Everyone tipped something. The tips were $1 or $2 and up to $10. During the lunch shift, the average tip was $2 and maybe $2 or $3 for the evening shift. I would do about 10 deliveries during the lunch shift and 12–20 for a weekend night shift. We were very happy if we got the $2 delivery fee and a $3 tip. Then we made $5.

I delivered in a nice part of St. Louis. People tipped more in the apartment complexes. I guess they are used to working for tips. Some ridiculously rich people only gave me a dollar.

My biggest tip was from a drug dealer. His bill was $23, and he gave me $50 and said, "Keep the change." I guess he had good business that day.

When I order pizza myself, I always give a minimum of a $5 tip to the driver. I will give a $5 tip for an $8 burger at a restaurant.

$ $ $

Carter delivers pizza for a Domino's pizzeria in Washington, D.C. He is from East Africa and has been in this country for five or six years. This is what Carter had to say about his experience with tips for deliveries.

I do not like my job. I don't make enough money. I am paid $4 an hour. Domino's does not help with gas. The average tip is $2. For a $20 pizza, most people will leave $2–$3. During a typical night, three or four people will give me no tip at all. Some people will occasionally give a $5 tip. For a really big order like a birthday, I might get $5 or $10. I work a four hour shift at night and averages $20 per night in tips. I work 40–45 hours a week for Domino's.

Companies and organizations pay the most. A school once gave me $40 when I delivered a whole lot of pizzas. About once a month, I deliver 20 or so pizzas to schools, and they usually give me $25.

Most people are nice. There is less tipping with cash and more tipping if they are paying with credit cards. The wealthy tip more. People who work with the public also tip well. Babysitters and kids don't tip very well.

Sometimes I am lucky. I get more than I expected.

[He refused to take the $10 for the interview.]

$ $ $

Joseph delivers furniture for a mom and pop store in Brooklyn. His experience selling furniture is discussed elsewhere as is his experience as a preparer in a hookah lounge. This is Joseph's perspective on tips for deliveries in his own words.

I get tips 70–80% of the time I make a furniture delivery as long as it was NOT my order. I almost never get tips when it was my commission. I also get tips 95% of the time when I assemble an item. If we are bringing up a sofa we are usually given $40–$50 to split. One guy gave us $200 to split because he said he was very meticulous and did not want anything scratched.

If I assemble a bedroom, we are usually given $30 to split. If I assemble after the store is closed, the owner lets me keep the assembly fee. If I assemble something during store hours, I give the assembly fee to the store. A quick assembly might take 20 minutes, and you can get $10–$20.

Hispanics tip the most. Whites rarely tip. Once I did a three-story walkup with some huge sofas and got a $1 tip. I was so mad because the owner had given free delivery.

The main delivery guy has a truck and will sometimes just give us a base pay of $20 a delivery as long as he can keep the tip. He might even just ask someone on the street to help him for $5 and save giving us anything. Everyone has to hustle.

It can get a little complicated on big deliveries over two days. Once, the guy who worked the first day did not get a tip since the tip was handed out on the second day. He complained. The owner gave him $20 out of his own pocket.

$ $ $

Bob worked for two years delivering furniture in Oakland, California. This is his story.

It was a good job. I kept in shape, and it was rewarding to give people their furniture.

I was paid $14 an hour. About 25–30% of the time, we got a tip. The average tip was $5. Our biggest tip was $20 a piece. There was one other guy I worked with. We shared the tips equally. About half the time, they gave the tip to one of us and said to split it. The other half of the time we were given the tips directly.

We made five deliveries a day on average. I probably averaged $10 a day in tips. You could not rely on tips for a living.

People who were most likely to tip were those who bought the least and had more modest houses. Once we rolled up to a big house we knew we were not likely to get a big tip. Sometimes a person getting two chairs would tip $20 and the person with two truckloads of furniture would not tip. Those with more modest houses had more compassion for working people. The richer people did not connect to us. We were not seen as equals. The quicker we left the better.

Some rich people would give us a couple bucks and say go get a few beers. They knew we had to work for another ten hours. How absurd.

$ $ $

Daniel has had several jobs delivering appliances in New Jersey. His job pumping gas is discussed elsewhere. This is what Daniel had to say about his experience receiving tips for delivering appliances.

I now deliver appliances for my brother. I deliver and hook-up refrigerators, ranges, washers, dryers, and dishwashers. I also delivered appliances for another company that paid me $800 a week. My brother pays me depending upon how hard the day is. There is no set amount. The job is for the birds. It is a bad job.

The problem is that the salespeople lie to the customers about what is included. They say everything is included, and in fact, a lot of the items needed to hook-up the appliance are not included. People need to buy water lines, shut-off valves, and other parts. The customers take it out on us. We are constantly ragged on. The salespeople really screw things up.

We get tips about 20% of the time. The average tip for a fridge is $20 and $5 for a stove. We get more for the fridge because it requires more work. The stoves are lighter. We get more tips if more work is required. There are two of us in the truck. The helper keeps the tips, and the driver keeps the proceeds from selling the extra parts. The same people tip the most and least that I described pumping gas. Wealthy people don't tip. I used to deliver pizzas. Wealthy people didn't tip much for that job either.

$ $ $

Abdul is a driver for a moving company. He also does estimates. His experience providing estimates is covered elsewhere. Abdul had this to say about receiving tips for delivering items for a moving company.

When I am driving long distance, I make $22 an hour. We get tips on 40–50% of the moving jobs. The typical tip is $20–$50 per person. This depends upon the size of the job. We don't get a lot of tips for apartments. About 75% of the time, the person gives the tips to each one of the movers. The other 30% of the time the customer gives the tips to the crew chief [We realize this does not add up to 100%]. Sometimes they put the tip on the credit card. When the crew chief gets the tip, he divides it up in proportion to the amount of time worked. This can get complicated as sometimes there are packers who work before the day of the move.

A few times we got $100 per person.

People from higher income brackets tip the most, but it varies. Sometimes you are not expecting a big tip, and you get one.

Corporate moves are usually by invoice. The estimator sometimes will give a hint that they need to take care of the movers. It often depends upon the cash policy of the company. Do they allow the office manager to disburse cash? It ends up that about half of the corporate moves will give tips. They also tip in the $20–$50 range per person.

On most large jobs, the customer will offer to get pizzas or sandwiches. On small jobs that are three–five hours, we are rarely offered food, but we might get sodas and water.

$ $ $

AJ has been delivering groceries for Peapod/Giant in Washington, D.C. for the past six years. This is his story in his own words.

I like the job because I get to meet a lot of people. I don't have someone on my back all the time, and I get to help the elderly and disabled. I don't like the hours. I have to get up at 2:30 in the morning, and I don't get off till 5:00 pm. I have no social life. Some customers are also pains as they complain about everything.

I get paid $16.20 an hour. About a third of the people will tip me. The tips range from $5 to $20. Today, I will make 17 deliveries and will get $20–$30 in cash tips and $30–$40 in tips added on to credit cards or checks. Only about 20% of deliveries to offices will result in a tip.

If someone is helping me on the truck, I will split the tips with him. I mostly work by myself unless I am training someone.

The average order is $150 and the size of the order does not seem to affect the tips.

Poorer people tip more. I get more tips from the smaller houses. People in businesses and mansions don't tip as well. I see about half of my customers. Those in the mansions will leave the tip with their nanny or maid when they tip.

I have about 200 regular customers. I did not get as much in tips on the holidays this year as compared to last year. I only got $300–$400 extra.

It amazes me that so many people don't realize that they can tip you. There is a space on the credit card and other paperwork to leave a tip.

$ $ $

Anonymous makes deliveries for Staples in Washington, D.C. He walked into an office, vented for a minute, and left before a full interview could be conducted.

I make 50 plus deliveries a day. I never get a tip. Well actually, I got one tip from a lady when I helped her set something up. We set things up and drag heavy boxes of Xerox paper up five flights of stairs. And we don't get shit. They say it is part of our salary. I got to run.

$ $ $

Charles has been doing deliveries for a florist shop in Washington, D.C. for 30 years. The following is what Charles had to say about making tips for flower deliveries.

It is an OK job. It pays the bills. I get paid $12 an hour. The summer is slow. I make 6–7 deliveries per day. On Valentine's Day, I make 25–30 deliveries.

I get a tip once a month. When I get a tip, it is for $2 or $5. I get no more than $10 a month in tips. Last month, I did not get a single tip.

Most of the time when I deliver flowers, the person is at home or at an office. In the suburbs, people are not often at home during the week, and they are at home about half the time during the weekend.

Regular customers tip the most.

I take a lot of flowers to weddings. I've gotten two tips in 30 years at weddings.

You don't get a lot of tips delivering flowers.

$ $ $

Thomas has worked for a pharmacy in Maryland for the past two years. He had this to say about tips for deliveries.

I work as a cashier and do inventory. I also make deliveries. I get paid $11 an hour. The pharmacy is in a poor suburb of Washington, D.C.

I make about 40 deliveries a month. About ten or less of those people will give me a tip. The average tip is $3 to $5. People who are most likely to tip are older and black. Whites don't tip [Thomas is black].

$ $ $

Abigail had a paper route for the Philadelphia Inquirer for 2½ years while she attended graduate school. Here is her story in her own words.

The job was something that I had to do. I could not work full-time while going to school. I was paid 15 cents a day for each daily paper and 40 cents for each paper delivered on Sunday. I had about 250 customers. I did not collect the money. There was a person who "owned" the route. People sent him the money, and he paid me. He was OK. I needed flexibility because I sometimes had to go out of town because of my schooling. He would find someone to fill in for me.

It took about two hours to deliver the papers, and I made $1,300 per month. The customers all lived in various apartment buildings.

Outside of the holidays, I rarely got a tip. One customer gave me about a dollar a week.

During the holidays, I got gratuities from 80% of the people on my route. The average amount was $10. Some mailed me the tip. Some left it at the door, and others sent it via the person who owned the route. I got between $1,000 and $1,500 in holiday tips. The amount I received in holiday tips increased each year.

Most of the people who lived in the apartments were wealthy and retired. There was little to distinguish those who gave a lot from those who gave a little. I expected to get more from those who got daily delivery. However, this was not the case.

[She refused the $10 payment for her participation.]

$ $ $

John sells the Washington Post on a busy one-way street in a rapidly gentrifying neighborhood in Washington, D.C. This is his experience.

I have been selling papers at this location for over 15 years. I was living at a shelter, and a man said he was looking for people to sell the "Washington Times." I've been homeless for most of these years. I switched to selling the "Washington Post" because I found I could make more money.

I like what I do. I get a little change in my pocket, but it is mostly about the people. I meet a lot of very nice people, and I like talking to them. Some have been buying from me for 15 years. This starts my day. I work from 6:00 am to 8:30 am selling papers, and after that I sometimes do odd jobs such as cutting grass or pulling weeds.

I usually get a packet of 25–35 papers. It has been a little slow this month because of the road construction. I pay the distributor $10 for the packets on Sundays. The papers sell for 35 cents, and I keep all proceeds and tips.

About half of my customers give me more than the 35 cents. Most of those who tip give me 50 cents, and a lot of my regulars give me a dollar. I even have a few people who pay me by the month. Look, [he pulls money out of his pocket] the four dollar bills are from people who said to keep the change, and the coins [about $4 in coins] are from other people.

Around Christmas, a lot of my regulars give me cash as well as presents. Some of the presents consist of food and clothes. One guy gives me $40–$60, and a lot of others give me $5 or $10. This helps me give presents to my family and friends.

My regulars are the most generous. They are middle-aged.

Half of the people who buy from me are drive-bys. The other half walk by me on the way to the Metro.

I also cut grass and pull weeds for people who live in the neighborhood. Depending upon the size of the job, I charge between $10 and $25. Very rarely will they give more than what I charge. Last month, I worked all day pulling weeds for $85. The guy gave me $100 and a pair of hedge clippers.

$ $ $

Tammy has worked for the U.S. Postal Service delivering mail in a suburb of Cleveland for the past 13 years. This is her story.

I like the job because it is outdoors. I dislike it because of dogs—and birds that attack you after their babies have hatched. All-in-all it is not a bad job.

I get paid $15 an hour, maybe more. I deliver mail to 210 households. I get very few tips during the regular year, maybe one or two a month. I might get $5 or $10 for someone whose mail is being held while they are on vacation. Other than Christmas, tips are fairly rare.

Of the 210 households I deliver mail for, 75% will give me a tip for the holidays. If you are a new mail person, the tips are not as common. Last year they changed the routes and that reduced the tips for some carriers. The average tip is $20. My biggest tip was $100. I got a total of $1,500 in tips. We are not supposed to take tips, but most of us do.

The best tippers are Jewish people. Jewish people know how to tip. You are not going to use my name—right? Black people don't tip [the respondent is black].

We don't share out tips.

Most of the tips come in a Christmas card. We get presents as well—mostly candy. I sometimes get a more personal present, such as something from Bed Bath & Beyond from people that I know more.

We go the extra mile for people who tip. We put their papers closer to the door in bad weather, so they don't get wet and so on. We treat everyone right, but we help them a bit more.

$ $ $

Scott has delivered mail in New Jersey for 27 years. He had this to say about his experience receiving tips for delivering mail.

I am a third generation postman. I don't like working there now. They have rules and regulations going back to Benjamin Franklin when it was vital for our country to have the mail delivered. But, do you need to put your life on the line in order to make a timely delivery of TV Guides or a bill from Macys? We drive trucks without collapsible steering wheels, have homeowners who don't tend their dogs or get rid of the ice in the winter, and as you can see with the Anthrax issue, they had employees working a week after it hit.

I get paid $48,000 a year, but I get paid by the hour. Other than Christmas, I get tipped two or three times a year. Maybe if I hold someone's mail, they will give me $10.

I have 260 mail stops. About a quarter will give me a tip during the holidays. The average tip is $10. Some give $2, and some give $20. I get about $500 during the holidays.

Several years ago Avon had cologne that was in a toy Post Office jeep. I got a lot of cologne that year. Fortunately, that is no longer being made.

Some guys get $2,000 in tips. They really work at it. They bring in the garbage cans and the newspapers. I am in the middle of the road. I have a heavy volume route and don't have time to play.

The working class tips the most. Doctors and lawyers are more extravagant. Teachers are the worst. They are very demanding and degrading, and they expect perfection. The highest percentage comes from the working class, but the rich tip most when they do tip.

Apartment buildings are OK. People want more favors. They want you to ring their doorbell if they have an express delivery instead of making them go to the post office. Recently, the post office has been putting in curb boxes. People don't like it because they have to go out to the street, so they tip less.

It is dangerous being a mailman. You must have rapport with the people you are serving. Some mailmen get close to extortion. If the tip is not right, they will lose the social security check.

[Scott would not take the $10 for his participation, stating that he was thankful for the opportunity to vent.]

$ $ $

Carolyn has been a mail carrier in Kansas for 20 years. She lives outside of Kansas City and had this to say about her experience.

The bad side of being a mail carrier is dealing with the government mentality which causes a lot of inefficiency. On the other hand, I really like what I do. I like my customers a lot.

I only get tips around the holidays. I have 475 deliveries. Some are in apartments and others are with banks of mailboxes on the road. About 10% of customers will give me a tip around the holidays. The amount of cash ranges from

$5 to $20. Most give around $20, and the total that I take in is around $150. We are not supposed to take gifts worth more than $20, but nobody pays much attention to this. I know that some mail carriers in really affluent areas will get $1,000 around the holidays. We often compare with other mail carriers what happens with holiday tips.

Older people are more generous. They give either cookies or candy or money. I get a lot of home-baked goods. Because I am so busy delivering mail, I don't have time to bake, so this is really very helpful and thoughtful. For those who give cash, they will usually place it in an envelope with a nice note and a Christmas card.

It is really amazing that people give. They don't have to. I look out for the older people on my route. Sometimes it seems that those who have the least give the most. I get a lot from single moms and retired people. Maybe I get a lot because they are at home, and I see them a lot. I know them personally. I don't often see the people who work.

$ $ $

David has recently retired from working for UPS in South Carolina. This is his story.

I worked for UPS for 11 years. I enjoyed working for them. I interacted with a lot of people. I received good wages, and I was able to give quality service. I was getting $22 an hour when I retired.

Other than holidays, I only got occasional tips. On a typical non-holiday week, I might get $40–$50 in tips. These all came from snowbirds from the North who came to Myrtle Beach to retire or to vacation. I almost never got tips during the week from Southerners.

I had about 100 regular customers. Seventy-five percent of these gave me a present for the holiday. I got money, gift certificates, wine, handicrafts, and food. Forty percent of those who gave me a gift gave me money or a gift certificate. The average was $50. In a good year, I got $600 in cash and gift certificates for the holidays. Some years I received only $300 or so. If I had a new route, I got less in holiday tips. I always got more from regular customers.

I also got more gifts from business owners who had a lot of deliveries. Basically, I did really well with regulars.

$ $ $

Dale is a bike courier in Philadelphia. The following narrative details his experience with tips for deliveries.

I've been doing this for 2½ years. It's a pretty decent job. It is easy. I have a lot of flexibility, and I am self-employed. I generally work 9 am to 5 pm, but I can take a week off whenever I want. Of course, I am not paid when I take a week off.

I am an independent contractor who is really on commission. I get 50–60% of what the client is charged. The larger the job the higher my percentage. Most of my jobs are within zone 1, the central business district of Philadelphia. Clients get charged $5.50. Two-thirds of my deliveries are for this fee. The other third range from $5.50 to $15. I do 2–35 deliveries a day.

I get few tips. Most people pay on accounts. We have a lot of big law firms. Usually, there is no money that is handled, and I get paid a check every two weeks. About twice a week, I get a tip. Smaller businesses or people who are paying with cash will more often tip. If they pay with cash, I actually expect a tip. About half of the cash jobs will give a tip, and the average tip is a dollar or two. However, I have received $5 tips on a $5.50 delivery. Sometimes, I will be given a tip for a rush job—when someone really needs it fast.

$ $ $

These narratives reveal a few common themes. Tips for delivery services are more common where a relationship between the server and client is well-established. The stories told by the respondents indicate that people that they have repeated and regular interaction with tend to tip more. Additionally, tipping appears to be more common during the holidays for some type of delivery jobs (postal delivery). The holidays are a time when people tend to spread money around, and tipping is a form of gift exchange.

There are a number of differences between the tipping norms in restaurants and tipping norms in the delivery services. Perhaps the most evident difference is in the consistency or common knowledge of the norms of tipping. In restaurants, the structural and social norms are fairly clear. The structural norms defined by the restaurant are clear matters of policy that employees typically follow. The structural norms defined by several of the organizations responsible for making deliveries are often clear matters of policy that the narratives indicate employees consider guidelines or even ignore altogether. In fact, some employees making postal deliveries are described as actually violating policy by "extorting" the public through practices like withholding mail or providing poor service when tips are not received for services that the policy clearly prohibits mail carriers from accepting.

The social norms in the delivery business are significantly less clear and consistent. However, the structural norms appear to be as clear as they are in the restaurant business; although the structural norms in the service industry seem to be more likely to be ignored. Why might restaurant workers be more likely to follow the agency policies that establish the tipping system? Perhaps it is a matter of monitoring and enforcement. Delivery personnel operate under relatively independent conditions when performing their jobs; while restaurant personnel are directly and consistently monitored by management, customers, and other employees in a context in which the hierarchy is clear and known to all participants. It appears that the social transmission and enforcement of norms is associated with a greater degree of variability. The institutionalization of tipping systems is likely most firmly established in a hierarchical context in which structural norms are socially reinforced. Future research may examine the relationship between social and structural norms in the establishment and maintenance of the tipping system.

11

Loading and Carting

The Census Bureau does not have obvious codes for workers who help load cars. A grocery store courtesy clerk is classified under packers and packagers (177,890, $22,000). Employees who help load items into cars at grocery stores, liquor stores, department stores, and electronics stores are not generally included in estimates of the economic value of the tipping industry. Moreover, the loading and carting practices vary as much as the tipping policies and practices.

Some economists compare tips with handshakes and similar societal customs that keep things running smoothly and civilly (see Ben-Ner and Putterman 1998). It is also important to note that emotional labor and its management reveal a great deal about how fragile civility can be (Hochchild 1983). Given the theoretical role that tipping rituals and emotion management play in civil society, the unique set of behavioral expectations that have developed deserve further exploration. Whether or not people who help load items are tipped and the amount of the tip is fairly uncertain. There are expectations that customers have an awareness of and conform to the social norms of a tipping system that is not well-established. In addition, there are protocols that those who might receive tips for loading and carting such as care for the customer's property, modesty, and posturing in a manner that implies that tips are not in fact expected (when most often they are expected). The fascinating aspect of these interactions is that the tipping system persists in the absence of clearly defined structural norms and weak social enforcement. If tipping does in fact contribute to or facilitate civil relations, to what extent must the practice be present to "keep things running smoothly"? How does society interpret and understand smooth relations in a context in which direct communication on the issue is inhibited? To what extent are those who receive tips subjects of the system, and to what extent are they able to define the boundaries of the relationship? How do people in the loading and carting services perceive their experiences as the possible recipients of tips?

$ $ $

Malcolm has been working part-time at a Giant Grocery store in Maryland for 12 years. He does not do deliveries. Malcolm's job is to help customers load groceries into their cars and keep the parking lots clear. In some cases, he may even be required to collect carts that have been removed from the store property. This is his story.

I also have a full-time job working for the local school system keeping HVAC systems working. I put groceries into cars and return carts to the store. I am part of the old contract. I get $16 an hour. The union just negotiated a new contract where people who would have my job get $6 an hour. This is the same for Safeway and other stores.

I used to get a lot of tips. The cars used to line up for me and six other workers to put groceries into the cars. I would load a couple hundred cars per day and would earn $100 to $200 a day in tips. Ninety percent of the people would tip me. For Christmas, I would get over $1,000 in tips. A lot of people would give me envelopes.

Now, they put these cart corrals in, and most people bring their own groceries to the cars. I still load a hundred cars per day, but only 15 or so of those people will give me a tip. I get only about $20 per day. Some will give me a dollar, and some will give a quarter or just say have a nice day! This is really hard for new people who get few tips and only get paid $6 an hour. These cart corrals are hard. We work hard bringing carts in from all over. We get a call that there are 50 of them at a local university. We have to go pick them up.

Working people tip more. Rich people don't tip unless they have known you for a long time. I put these bags in Hummers, BMWs, and Jags and get no tips. We get nothing.

We don't share out tips. I learned the first day that we keep all the tips for ourselves. That was the system.

$ $ $

Kwame is a redcap at Reagan National Airport in Washington, D.C. This is what he had to say about tips for loading and carting bags.

I am from Ghana and have been working at this job for four months. I get baggage when the flights land but not at check-in.

I like my job. I am able to pay my bills and take care of my family. I earn $2.13 an hour. I depend on tips. I help about 40 people a day. I don't charge them for the bags. The tips are voluntary. They must tip from their heart.

Four to five people a day will give me nothing. The average tip is $3. I get $65–$70 a day in tips. In the summer, I can get a bit more; perhaps $80–$100 a day if I am lucky.

The biggest tips come from those from Orlando or W. Palm Beach. People from La Guardia or Boston don't tip very well. They come in all the time. The number of bags does not make a difference. Yesterday, I got $5 for ten bags from one person and $10 from another person for one bag.

I get bigger tips when I bring bags to the curb or taxi stand and wait. If they just ask for the bags to be dropped at the curb, I get just a few bucks.

My biggest tip was two days ago when a woman gave me $30 and said it was for my Easter.

$ $ $

Akbar has been a skycap for United Airlines at Dulles Airport for 20 years. He is originally from South Asia. This is Akbar's story in his own words.

I like what I do. I see different people everyday. People come from different states and countries.

In a typical day, I help 50–100 people check in their bags. About 70% will give me a tip. The tipping process changed a lot in the last few years. Before 2005, United did not charge people for using curbside check-in. Now, United charges $2 a bag. I used to make $100 a day. Now, I average $80 a day. People don't want to pay above-and-beyond the $2 a bag.

The average tip is $2 per bag. Eighty percent of customers have only one bag, but the tip does not vary much according to the number of bags. A big family with six bags will often give me $15 total, and I get $3 of that for the tip [$2 a bag x 6 = $12 for the United Airlines fee for checked baggage].

I used to get an hourly wage of $2.15 an hour. When they went to the new system, they increased my hourly wage to $6.25.

Every once in a while an international passenger will give me $35 or $40 and say, "Take care of my bags." That helps a lot.

You never know who will tip. Sometimes a person that looks really nice will give you nothing, and others who look like they are poor will give you a good tip. If it is really freezing outside or raining, I will sometimes get a bigger tip as well as a thank you.

$ $ $

Olivia worked in the Atlanta Airport moving people in wheel chairs. This is her story.

I picked up people who could not walk and brought them to connecting flights or to meet people who were picking them up. I had this job for one summer, and I hated it. It was hard physical labor. I was pushing heavy people and also trying to deal with their bags. I worked an eight hour shift at $5.25 an hour.

In a typical day, I would help 15–20 people. Seventy-five percent gave me a tip. The average tip was $3. Every once in a while I would get $20. On an average day, I made $60 in tips. On my best day, I made $85. One of my coworkers once got a $100 tip. I could have made more if I hustled. I did not want to work too hard.

Older people tipped the most. Sometimes a family member would give the tip when we got down to baggage claim. I got less in tips for taking people to connecting flights because people were usually in a hurry.

There was a lot of competition. For example, the airline [Delta] would announce that they needed five wheelchairs for a flight. We would all try to get there because we survived on tips. People who really needed the jobs got very competitive. Sometimes, someone would curse someone else out. I never asked for tips. Other people would let the client know that we lived for tips.

People who did not tip probably thought our compensation was built into the cost of the flight ticket.

$ $ $

Fred is a retired police officer who works as a bagger at a specialty grocery store in Massachusetts. He had this to say about tips for his work loading and carting.

It is a good place for a retired worker. We have our own deli and catering. I bag groceries and take stuff to cars. Once a week, I make deliveries. I get paid $9.50 an hour.

I take stuff to cars about 25–30 times a day. Fifty to seventy percent of the customers will tip me. The average tip is $2. One lady always gives the bagger $20 or $30. She gets $300–$400 every week. On an average day, I make $40 in tips. Around Thanksgiving and Christmas, I will get $50–$70 a day and on some days close to $100.

Once a week I do deliveries. Seventy-five percent will tip me. The average tip is $2–$5. I will get on average $45–$50 in tips on delivery day. I like doing deliveries. I work at my own pace, and nobody is there telling me what to do.

The average person tips the most—those with families. There are some with a lot of money who drive BMWs and Jags, and they don't tip at all. Younger people tip more than older people.

We don't share our tips.

$ $ $

Kwame has been a clerk at a liquor store in Washington, D.C. for the past three years. He is from Ghana and told the following story about his experience.

The job is OK. It pays the bills. I get paid between $9 and $10 an hour. I stock the shelves, help put liquor into bags and boxes, and help people take their purchases to the car. I help 25–30 people a day. They don't have to tip me, but about half will give me a tip. I also get occasional tips from people in the store when I give them advice. The tips range from $2 to $10. On an average day, I make $30–$40 a day in tips.

The people who tip the most are the quiet people. I am much less likely to get tips from people who start conversations.

We don't share our tips.

People are not obligated to tip me, but I appreciate it.

$ $ $

Samir works as a stocker at Best Buy in Pennsylvania. He has worked there for the last six months and had this to say about loading and carting electronics.

I like working at Best Buy. There are some good people, and I like the environment. I make $8 an hour.

I help people take items to their car. Three out of five people will give me a tip. It depends on how big the item is. The average tip is $3. My biggest tip was $10. The guy didn't really need any help. He just wanted to give a big tip. I was very surprised.

In a typical day, I make $10–$15 in tips.

Men in their late 40s and early 50s tip the most. Older women in their 60s and 70s tip the least. They think they have a right to get help.

There is some competition among the stockers for tips. Sometimes they will jump on customers. I'll do it!! I'll do it!! The competition is friendly. We see who made the most money at the end of the day.

If I went to a Best Buy type store, I would tip if I got a large TV. I know what the stockers go through.

$ $ $

Paul worked at Wal-Mart for a year collecting grocery carts and now works at Home Depot. His work at Chipotle and at a Mexican restaurant is discussed in the restaurant section of this book. This is what Paul had to say about loading and carting.

I worked at Wal-Mart in Tennessee for almost a year. I did not like it because of management issues and scheduling conflicts. I was going to school at the time, and they were not very flexible on my hours. I collected carts and helped load items. They had a huge parking lot, and I was expected to clean too many carts in too short a time. I started at $7 an hour and eventually got up to $7.40.

In a typical six–seven hour shift, I loaded 20–30 cars with items. About 20% gave a tip. The average was $1–$2. In a typical day, I would get $5–$8 in tips. Older women tipped the most. In fact, the only tips I ever got were from little old ladies. My biggest tip was $10, and we did not share our tips.

I've been working at Home Depot for the past 3½ months. I work in the garden department, and I love it. I learn about plants, landscaping, how to build ponds, and I get to help people. I get to interact with people; which I rarely did at Wal-Mart.

Lately, I've been loading a lot of mulch and grills. I get $8 an hour and will soon get a raise to $8.50. In an average weekday, I load 40–50 cars, and on the weekend, I load 150–200 cars. Twenty percent of people give a tip, and the average tip is $3–$4. On weekdays, I average $20 in tips, and on weekends, I get around $40.

People with big loads tip the most. If they come back later in the day for another load, they are also more likely to tip.

We don't share tips. However, if I had a good day or a big tip I will buy Coke and Powerade for those in my department.

$ $ $

Toni worked for one year at Johnson's nursery in Washington, D.C. This is Toni's story.

I worked there during vacations and summers when I was in high school. It was very long hours. I earned $7.25 per hour. I was a cashier, and I wrapped flowers, made bouquets, and brought mulch and plants out to cars of the customers and sometimes to their houses.

LOADING AND CARTING

I NEVER received a tip, and my brother who also worked there for two years never received a tip. We talked about it and did not understand why we never received tips.

$ $ $

Hani was born in Manhattan and went to college in Northern New York State. His regular job is working with a general contractor as a project engineer. He is selling Christmas trees because he is trying to make extra money to pay for his wedding. This is what Hani had to say about loading Christmas trees.

I work at two Christmas tree places owned by the same company. The first is in Bethesda where I am paid $6 an hour. The average person tips $5. About 10% will stiff me and give me no tip. Sometimes I get a $10 tip and every once in a while $20. Last weekend I made $100 in tips on an 11 hour shift. On a weeknight, I will make about $30 for a four hour shift.

I will share my tips with the other guy who works at the lot when he helps me load a tree onto a car. I also give a few bucks to the cashier because she rarely gets any tips. I just suggested to her to put out a tip jar, and now she gets a few tips from that. I sometimes give her $5.

I work well with the other people on the lot. You have to work well with people you see 11 hours a day. There is no fighting over customers. We usually rotate customers. If I get a really big tip, I will let the next customer go to the other guy on the lot. Sometimes there are college kids working on the lot. They don't work as hard. They are more interested in conversing.

I also work at a Christmas tree lot on a military base. I get paid $7.50 an hour instead of $6. This is because they tip less. I only get tips from about 25% of the people who buy trees from this lot. The military base made us take down our sign that tips are encouraged. The military does not allow tipping on the base at other stores. I make much less from tips when I work at the military base. I make much more money working in Bethesda.

$ $ $

These narratives reveal a few features worth consideration. One of the themes evident in the loading and carting services is the extent to which firms can make changes that significantly affect tipping practices without the necessity of a policy regarding tipping. For example, the standardization of cart corals creates a situation in which self-service becomes common practice. Today, customers usually load their own purchases, but the employees are still responsible for wrangling carts. This reduced interaction between the employee and customer decreases the likelihood of tipping. There are a few related implications. First, the more people tip the less they have to spend on consumer goods. Second, if tipping is a way of diffusing the cost of keeping employees happy (so that presumably they are less likely to steal and more likely to stay in their job), one might wonder if the enhanced monitoring mechanisms available to employers results in a reduced motivation for employers to concern themselves with the "happiness" of their employees, at least relative to the benefit to the firm of increased consumer spending. In other words, do the managers of tipped employees spend less time or provide fewer noneconomic benefits that might affect the happiness of employees when compared to managers of employees who do not receive tips?

It is also worth noting that the trends in tipping for loading and carting services follow relatively closely the broad etiquette guidelines. Customers are understood as having based their tipping decisions at least in part on the difficulty of the job and the level of service provided. Additionally, the perception of tipping practices by those who work in the loading and carting services generally attribute the instances in which people do not tip to system failures. In other words, their belief seems to be that people who don't tip are most likely unaware of the customary standards.

12

Cars

The Census Bureau reports the number of employed people and their average earnings for the following relevant occupations: 144,590 cleaners of vehicles and equipment ($24,000), 22,540 parking lot attendants ($23,000), and 112,180 taxi drivers and chauffeurs ($28,000). Most people know that the people who park our cars, wash our cars, and drive us in cabs and limos are "supposed" to be tipped. However, tipping is not universal, not all car services are equal, and the amount of the tip varies quite a bit.

Most etiquette guidelines contend that car service drivers that serve businesses charge rates that already include a service charge, and car services for individuals have also already included a tip in the form of a service charge if the fare is higher than what would be charged by a taxi for the same route. Limousine services usually include a 20% service fee, and etiquette guidelines usually advise an additional tip of $10, $20, or $30 if the driver provides some special service, depending on the service and the total bill. However, there are also those who contend that it is customary to tip at least 10–20% for these car services because they are luxuries. In addition, there are corporate car services that do not include gratuities, and the rider is rarely aware of the contract. It is also the case that customers who are unhappy with the service and complain to the agency may have the service charge reimbursed. It is not clear whether this cost is absorbed by the driver or the firm.

Although this is not the norm, parking attendants, car washers, and even some garage mechanics have been known to attempt to compel tipping by negatively affecting the quality of service for those customers who did not tip or did not tip adequately. For example, some garages post "gift-giving" charts that list the name and contribution of each customer on the wall of the garage. In addition, those who refused to "contribute" the recommended sum might find that the attendants have trouble retrieving the car and returning it to the customer in a timely manner. Many customers presume that an adequate tip might ensure that the employee will take special care of their vehicle. Do these employees feel entitled to a tip? If employees do indeed feel a sense of entitlement to the extent that they might provide poor quality service to coerce compliance with tipping norms, can this tipping system truly be considered voluntary, and how is quality control actually managed?

$ $ $

Teclu is from Eritrea and has been parking cars at the same garage in Washington, D.C. for the past eight years where the clientele is fairly well off. This is Teclu's story.

The job is survival for me. That is how I make my bread. I started out at $7.15 an hour and now make $8.75.

About two-thirds of the customers will tip me. The average tip is a dollar. Out of 30 people, two or so might give me $2 or more. There are four–five attendants, and we park 60–80 cars. My share of that would be $15–$20. We do not share our tips. Those who work the morning shift get very few tips; maybe one out of ten will give a tip.

Around Christmas, some of the regular customers will give me $5 or $10. This totals to maybe $100 or $150.

Average people tip better. Some people who are very wealthy don't tip. They often give nothing.

$ $ $

Pablo is originally from Guatemala and has been parking cars in Washington, D.C. for 23 years. He speaks perfect English and tells the following story about his experience receiving tips for parking cars.

I get paid $8 an hour. Seventy-five percent of the customers tip, and the average tip is $1. Everyone once in a while I get a $5 tip. I average $60 a day in tips. I know this is higher than at other garages, but I give really good service. I also get $1,500 in bonus tips at the end of the year for the holidays.

I keep all my tips and do not share them with the other attendants or the cashier.

$ $ $

Eric has been a car valet in Washington, D.C. for the last six months. This is his story in his own words.

I enjoy the job. It is convenient for college students (I am studying engineering). I work when I am available and get paid every week. I have money in my pocket. I get paid $7 an hour. We mostly do events such as parties, museum openings, and fund raisers. Tonight, I worked at a fund raiser at the Library of Congress.

In a typical night, I park 10–15 cars. The average tip is $2. My biggest tip was $20. About 30% will not tip at all. The biggest tips seem to come from those with fancier cars—I often get $5. The smaller tips come from those who are driving by themselves.

In a typical night, I get $15–$20 in tips. We pool all our tips. There were four of us tonight. I don't trust everyone. I know for a fact that some people have put tips into their pockets rather than the pool. I have not seen fights or confrontations about this.

We are supposed to give the tip directly to the supervisor who then puts the tips into the tip bag. We are never supposed to put our cash tips into our pocket. If someone gives us coins, we can keep the coins.

Some people will give us $20 and ask for change. When we say we don't have change, they will look around for loose coins in their car.

$ $ $

Cory has been a free-lance valet car parker in St. Louis for the last year and a half. He told this story about his experience about tips for parking cars.

By free-lance, I mean that I work on an ad hoc basis—as needed. I work for restaurants, hotels, office parties, and charity functions. The job is OK, but it gets chilly during the winter.

I get paid $6 an hour. Eighty to ninety percent of the people will tip me. The average tip is $2 or $3. I get good tips because I rush. The tips almost always come when we get the car and not when it is dropped off.

In a typical shift, I work six hours and get about $40 in tips. My biggest tip was $100 from a man who owns a tire and auto store. I was shocked.

The bigger tips come from those who are upper-middle class. The rich don't tip well and neither do those who are poorer. We get bigger tips at charity functions when alcohol is served. I don't do as well at restaurants.

We pool all our tips. They are put in a pot and divided at the end of the night. I trust the other people. We all know each other.

$ $ $

Larry parks cars at a ski resort in the Maryland/West Virginia area. This is his story in his own words.

I've been doing it for two years. I like it. People are nice, and it is a nice place to work. Unfortunately, it is seasonal. We only offer valet parking on holidays or weekends. We charge $10 a car for non-members, and club members park for free. About 75% of our customers are non-members.

I get paid $8 an hour. Fifteen percent of people will not tip at all. The average tip is $3–$4. People pay on the way in. Less than 20% will tip on the way in. The average tip upfront is about $5. It is possible that people who tip on the way in don't tip on the way out.

On President's Day, we had 72 cars. We usually have 30 cars on a Saturday and 20 on a Sunday. Over the entire weekend, we got $170 in tips. We have one or two runners and one money man. We split the tips equally. When we get a tip, we give it to the moneyman. We trust each other. The moneyman is my father.

Regulars tip the most. Orientals don't tip very well. You are lucky to get a dollar. It is really hit-or-miss. You don't know how much a person will tip by looking at them. If I have time, I try to help people put their skis on the car and help with the kids. This usually happens after they tipped. This is probably why regulars tip better. They know we are trying to help.

We offer a cheap service. People don't think they are overpaying. They really appreciate the service. Late in the morning it is really hard to get a parking spot.

Last year was sluggish. Our business is up 50% over last year. People are more likely to know that we are here. Weather does not affect the number of customers or the amount of the tip. I thought people would tip more in bad weather, but is has no effect.

I also do security for the resort. The resort contracts us to do both security and parking.

$ $ $

Jack's story as an ice delivery driver and locksmith are presented in this book and in a subsequent volume on commissions. This is what Jack had to say about receiving tips for his work as a hotel valet.

I've been a parking valet at a Hilton hotel in Ohio. I like it. I am very self-motivated. The harder I work the better my reward. I make much more than I would with an hourly job.

I get paid $6 per hour. Eighty percent of people leave tips when they pick up their cars. You can tell who will tip by whether they make eye contact with you and their manner. We help load up their luggage, give directions, and help on restaurant choices. We take the bags to the lobby. We never go to the rooms.

The average tip is $3. My biggest tip was $20. During my shift, I expect to get a minimum of $50 to $60 in tips and up to $100. On my biggest day, I made almost $200.

We don't share tips. Whoever drives the car gets all the tips.

There are three shifts. The first shift has businessmen coming and going. They tip the most consistently. When they drop off a car, about 50% will leave a tip. It is not unusual for a guy with bags to give us $10. Businessmen always give $2 or more. They usually will give $5.

We get much smaller tips from those who come for conventions. They are not familiar with high-class hotels and don't know how to tip. They think because they are charged $18 a day to park that the attendants are doing well. At a recent horseshoe convention and another motorcycle convention maybe 2% tipped. With businessmen, 90% tip. Businessmen are used to eating at three and four star restaurants and not McDonalds.

Tipping is a cultural thing. I am twenty-one, and I think a lot of people my age don't realize the common courtesy of tipping. Older people always have the tip ready and plan for it. When older people go out, they think ahead of spending $10 for the server's tip, $3 for the bellhop, and $5 for the parking valet. Younger people are not as money conscious. They want more instant gratification.

$ $ $

John drove a charter bus for six months in Colorado. This is his story.

I did not like this job. It was a lot of work. The weather could be bad, and people did not have much patience. Their only concern was getting to the destination. I mostly drove from Denver to the ski resorts or to the casinos. All destinations were in Colorado.

I was paid by the mile, and I was paid a pre-negotiated sum. The typical charge was $50–$150. The gratuity was up to the group leader. There was no set amount. It usually depended upon how satisfied they were. The typical tip was 20%. Sometimes they would pass the hat, and other times, the group leader would have it built into the basic charge and then give me an envelope. Two-thirds of the time I got a gratuity.

Skiers gave more than gamblers. The gamblers were usually coming back broke.

$ $ $

Pierre is a courtesy driver for a car dealer in the Washington, D.C. area. The following reflects his experience as a tipped employee.

I've had this job for two years. I drive people back and forth to their homes and the Metro. The job is good in that it is peaceful and low stress. No one gives me a hard time. The problem is that the pay is low. I get $8.50 an hour. I'm from Gabon, and I am also going to school.

I make about 30 trips a day. About one-third of the people will give me a tip. The average tip is $2 or $3, and I average about $20 a day in tips. My biggest tip was $20. I was surprised. He was simply a nice guy.

Women tip more than men, but older men tip the most. Young people tip the least.

$ $ $

Nathan worked as a car valet at a dealership in the Washington, D.C. area. He also had experiences receiving tips as a summer camp counselor, pizza delivery driver, deli employee, and as a server (essays not included). Nathan had this to say about receiving tips for his work as a valet for a car dealership.

Being a car valet was a good summer job. I washed cars and brought the cars to where the customer came to pick them up after a service call. I got $5.50 an hour. About 25% of the customers would tip me. The average tip was $2. I would bring down about 30 cars a day and on average made $15–$20 a day in tips.

The middle class tipped the best. Those with fancy cars tipped the least.

$ $ $

Anton is from Senegal and works at the same car dealership as Nathan, whose story is presented in the previous narrative. Both Anton and Nathan perform the same job at the car dealership but make somewhat different estimations of their experiences.

He brings cars to people whose service work is complete. The difference in their base pay is a function of their seniority. Anton's report indicates that he receives significantly fewer tips compared to Nathan. Something that might be explained by the fact that Anton is an African who speaks English with a heavy accent, while Nathan is the "all-American" white kid going to college. This is Anton's story.

I work a nine hour shift and get paid $8 an hour. I receive very few tips. On some days, I receive none, but on other days, I get as much as $7. I get my biggest tips when I drop someone off at the Metro or their house after they drop their car off. I once got a $5 tip.

On a typical day, I get $2–$3 in tips. About 10% of people tip. Today, I delivered 15 cars, and you are the first to tip me.

$ $ $

Jean-Pierre is a cab driver originally from Haiti. He drives a cab in the Ft. Lauderdale area of Florida. This is his story.

I have been driving for two years. I also have a part-time job fixing computers. It is a living, and I have flexibility. I do not like driving a cab. It is not a job for life. It is sometimes dangerous and scary.

The average tip is 10%. If you treat people well, you can sometimes get more. The rich tip well. Minorities don't tip well because they are not educated correctly. They are not taught how to appreciate.[1]

Ninety percent of people give me a tip. I work mostly out of the airport and get 10–12 fares a day. I work for eight hours. I pay $75 a day to rent the cab, and I buy gas. On a good day, I will make $120–$150 in profit. I get about $30–$50 a day in tips.

The dispatcher at the airport looks out for me. I give him $5 several times a day. I don't give the dispatcher at Yellow Cab any of my tips.

Tips come from my attitude. If I'm on the phone, I don't deserve a tip. I need to make the customer comfortable. They understand what I do. I work hard.

My biggest tip was on a three and a half hour cab ride. The meter said $550. I said he did not owe me for the return trip. He gave me a huge tip because I was so honest.

Men tip the most. If a guy is going to South Beach, he will give me $100 for a $65 fare.

We are not treated right by the company. The owner of this cab is charged for a lot of extra things. In addition, if you buy a car they will put an advertisement for another company up top, and you get none of that revenue.

I pay $75 a day to the owner. He pays $550 to Yellow Cab every week. The only way he can make it is to have the car out most of the day. I drive it, and he drives it. The cab is almost always on the road. We are all Haitian and work together. If you go back to Haiti, someone will help you and drive your cab.

$ $ $

Majd has been driving a cab for two years in Washington, D.C. and had this to say.

I am also a full-time electrician. I like it because I am my own boss, and I own my cab. D.C. is making it more difficult because they are requiring that you live in D.C. to own a cab. They want everyone to rent from the big companies.

About 20% will not tip me at all. Latins tip the most (even if they are 15 or 16), and blacks tip the least. Black women are the most likely to jump out of the cab and not pay at all. They say they forgot their money. Not getting a tip is OK because our fares are OK. If a poor black person does not tip, that is OK with me. This morning a black lady gave me a $5 tip for an $18 fare while a rich white lady gave me $10 total for a $9.80 fare. She didn't get rich by giving it away!

I work for Yellow Cab. They are a good company, and their owner is a black man from Haiti. He will send cabs into the poor parts of Southeast where the other cab companies won't go.

I pay $97 a week for dispatching services, the license, and insurance. I work ten hours a day on the weekend and when my carpal tunnel syndrome won't allow me to work as an electrician.

I pray twice a day. I am an African-American Muslim.

I get $50 a day in tips. My average fare is $14. Most people tip me a dollar or two.

$ $ $

Tesfaye has been a car driver in Washington, D.C. off and on for ten years. He is originally from East Africa and shared the following experience.

I do not like being a cab driver. Some people rob you, and others won't pay.

I rent my cab for $185 every week. I pay for gas and car washes. The cab is old, and there is no dispatcher. Sometimes I work two hours, sometimes four, and sometimes eight or ten. I also have another job.

If I worked eight hours, I would usually have 15–20 customers—about two or three per hour. We charge by zone. Zone 1 is $6.40 and zone 2 is $8.80. [Note: The zone system in D.C. has changed since this interview.] My average is between $7 and $8. In an entire day, I get $10–$12 in tips. About half the people give me no tip. The average tip is a dollar. I pick up at lot of people near the Ft. Totten Metro. The people who live near there are poor, and they don't tip well. Sometimes I get ten cents, sometimes a quarter.

From downtown hotels, I get tips that are a little better—a dollar or two for a $6.50 fare. Even there sometimes I get very little. The doorman at the hotel will often ask me for money. I say no.

Whites tip the most. Poor people and Hispanics don't tip very well.

There is a lot of competition among cab drivers. I have not seen any fist fights. Other drivers will steal a fare from me. I will let it go.

I am not allowed to pick up at the airports. My cab is too old, and I don't have the proper airport license.

[He would not take the $10 payment for his participation.]

$ $ $

Alem is from Ethiopia and has been driving a taxicab for a year. This is his story.

I have been in the United States for seven years, and I am an American citizen. I drive only from the BWI airport. The typical ride is $50, and I average 15% on the tips. Occasionally, I get no tips. My biggest tip was $20.

To drive from BWI, you need a permit. The owner of the permit pays BWI $162 a week, and I pay BWI $262 a week. It is not fair. He lets me use his permit in case he ever wants to go back to driving. He does not charge me for the use of his permit. I pay for gas and insurance, and I own this van. We are required to own a Windstar or a Saturn.

I work ten hour shifts, seven days a week. I have not taken a vacation in a year. I average four–five rides per shift and make on average $150–$200 per day. Sometimes I make less than $150.

All white people tip. A lot of black people don't tip. I sometimes ask them why. Then, I might get $1 or $2. They say they don't have much money.

Sometimes, I have to wait two–three hours at the airport. Sometimes, I wait 15 minutes. There is a taxi stand, and they call us up by radio one line at a time. There are seven or eight cabs in a line. Sometimes there are 300 cars waiting.

Ninety percent of the time I go back to the airport empty. We are not allowed to pick up passengers for rides to the airport except by appointment. I could lose my license.

I tip the dispatcher. That is the person who puts you in the cab. He also tries to help with bags so he might get $1 or $2 from the customer. I give $2 to $5 to the dispatcher. He knows what is going on—who is going a long distance, who looks like they might tip, and so on. There is no obligation for me to tip the dispatcher, and he is the only person I tip.

I like the idea of tips. It is very encouraging and helps a lot.

$ $ $

Omar has been a limousine driver for a year and a half. He is about 25 years old. His family is from Pakistan, and he speaks perfect English. This is his story in his own words.

Tips are supposed to be 18%. In fact, the owner says we should tell customers that they should tip 18%. We charge $85 to go from D.C. to Baltimore Washington Airport. Sometimes I get a $5 tip. The average is $13. My biggest tip was $150 when I was driving someone for the presidential inauguration. Sometimes someone will pay extra if I have to wait for a while.

I pay the owners half of everything, including half the tips. I also have to pay for gas, tolls, parking, and the mandatory car wash. It is not fair that the owner takes half my tips. The driver should get the tips. I have to write the tip amount on my sheet and they give me a paycheck every two weeks.

I make $300 a month in tips, and it would really help if I could keep my tips. Please tell your readers that we should keep all our tips.

My average shift is 12 hours. The most I ever made was $450 in 18 hours. Once, I was stuck in traffic for six hours on a trip to Richmond and two hours back. She gave me $108 total. I had to pay $35 for gas.

Most people (80%) are nice. Others try to order you around.

$ $ $

Margaret has been a limousine driver for the past two years in the Washington, D.C. area. She told the following story about her experience as a tipped employee.

I like my job very much. I meet a lot of nice people, and it is not very stressful. I like to travel, and the pay is good. I work for a company, but I am trying to open my own limousine service. I do a lot of long trips—Atlantic City, New York, Charlestown races, Philadelphia, and so on.

I get paid a gratuity that is a percentage of the bill. I get at least 20%. If I meet all my requirements, I get 30% of the bill. These requirements include being 15 minutes early, filing all the proper paper work, and so on. I almost always get the 30%. I get no other compensation. If we charge $160 per hour for eight hours I get 30% of $1,280 or $384. The price charged the customer is affected by the day of the week, time of day, and type of limo. It usually comes out to $20 an hour. I get more if they rent a Hummer limo.

The company pays for all expenses including gas, insurance, and so on.

The amount of cash tips that I get are determined by the type of event. With proms, I get cash tips 10% of the time ($20 average when given). Anniversaries, weddings, and girls-nights-out tip about half the time ($40 average), and with out-of-town trips, I almost always get a tip. The average is $50. I do really well with out-of-town trips if I don't get lost. My GPS comes in handy. With funerals, I average $10.

Being a female driver, I get somewhat better tips from men. I get better tips from those who have more money. I must be honest with you. I am African-American, and whites tip the most.

If there is more than one driver, we usually split the tips. This occurs for weddings when there are several limos.

$ $ $

Janina was a taxi dispatcher at JFK airport in New York City for 16 months, working for the Port Authority. The following narrative details her story.

I'm a college student, and it was a great way to make a lot of money. But, I did not like being looked down upon by the customers.

I spent 25% of my time in a booth working the radio. I might call 20 cabs to Terminal 3 or a wheelchair cab to another terminal. I was paid $11.00 an hour when I started, and I was getting $11.45 when I stopped.

We also got bonuses. If Port Authority did not spend its full budget, the remainder would get distributed in proportion to hours worked. I got $600 in bonuses over my 16 months and another $600 when I quit.

We were not supposed to take money from the drivers or the passengers. However, some dispatchers would take $100–$500 a week from a driver in order to "get taken care of." The driver would be allowed to go to the front of the line or not write them up for infractions. If a driver took a passenger to Manhattan, the driver was guaranteed a minimum of $45. However, if the passenger was only going to Queens or Brooklyn, the driver might only get $10 or so in fare. Therefore, if a driver was taking someone to Queens or Brooklyn, they were given a ticket to allow them to go to the front of the line. These tickets were often sold to other drivers. About a quarter of the dispatchers participated in these scams. Arrests were made in some cases. When I worked the line, I put over 60 parties an hour into cabs. Ten percent of the customers would offer me something. Half the time I would take the tip that was offered. I was more likely to take the tip if I felt I really deserved it, if I was pissed off for some reason, or I needed money in my pocket. The average tip was $2, and I would typically get $5–$6 a day in tips.

Wealthy people tipped the most. Europeans also tipped. They thought tipping was standard. The locals knew better.

Twenty percent of the dispatchers were in college. Sometimes we did not get along with those who were "lifers." They worked to support their family and needed the money to survive. I knew that this was not my lifetime job. I could not do it. That is why I am in college.

$ $ $

David is a shuttle bus driver for an airport hotel in Colorado. He takes people back and forth from the airport. David shared the following information about his experience receiving tips for driving a hotel shuttle bus.

I've been at this hotel for seven months and was a shuttle bus driver at another hotel before. I truly enjoy what I do. I am a people person, and I enjoy going out of my way to help people. I used to work for the federal government, and now I don't have to deal with a bureaucracy. I help people directly and have instant accountability.

I get $11 an hour, which is really good. Most shuttle bus drivers get $7.50–$8.00 an hour. I don't know why my wage is so high. You are not using my name—right?

I do a run every 45 minutes. In a typical day, I do ten runs and will give rides to 45–55 people. I have put every day in an Excel spreadsheet. Ninety-three percent give me a tip. The average tip is $1.50 per person. Today, I got $53 in tips while my average is usually $60. Five to ten people per day will give me more than a dollar. This has been down in recent months because of the economy. Today, three people gave me five-dollar bills. However, one family of four gave me no tip at all. I feel hurt when I don't get a tip that I deserved.

Usually, families and businessmen tip the best. Asians and Europeans until recently were bad tippers. Lately, their tipping has been much better. People from New York are the best tippers.

I connect with people. I engage them in conversation and try to establish a bond. I go out of my way. I bring a cooler with ice onto the bus and offer people free water. I give them a lot of tourist advice and so on. I never, never put a tip jar in my shuttle. You are not supposed to solicit for tips. People know when they should tip.

My biggest tip was $30. The number of bags makes a difference. At the hotel, I offer to help them with their bags. If they say no, you know the tip will be lower, or I will not get a tip at all.

I personally don't tip people who are not giving me a service. I don't tip hot-dog vendors.

$ $ $

Karl is a pedicab driver in Washington, D.C. Although he pedals a bike instead of driving a car, it makes sense to present his story with the cab and limo drivers because the service provided is most similar. This is Karl's experience in his own words.

The company just started about three weeks ago, and it is a great job. It is different. I am out and about. I meet a lot of interesting people. It is good exercise, and I make good money.

The drivers are independent contractors. We are given general guidelines, but we are not instructed how to charge. We are told that the going rate is $4.50 per person per ten minute ride. I will sometimes charge more depending on the distance, the time of day, and whether I will have to ride uphill. There are almost always two passengers in the cab. The average fare is $10, and 75–80% will tip. The average tip is a couple of bucks. It comes out to between 10 and 20%.

In a six–eight hour shift, I get around $150 in fares and tips. There is no sharing of this except what we give the owner.

We pay the owner 25% of our total fare (including tips). This is on the honor system. However, the owner has told us that since he is also a driver he knows what to expect in fares.

Yuppies are our most common type of rider and are the most generous. We have two foci. During the day, we work the mall where there are tourists. At night, we do the bar scene.

A lot of the tip depends upon how good of an experience the person has. You need to make it fun, be courteous, and be efficient. If the customer is drinking, that helps.

[Karl refused the $10 payment for his participation.]

$ $ $

Josh has been working at a car wash in St. Louis for the past two years. This is his story.

I like working at the car wash, and I like working with cars. I've been fixing cars since I was six. I started out at $7.00 an hour, and now I get $8.50 since I also have a minor supervisory role.

We have a tip box, and we encourage customers to use the tip box since it is unfair to tip only those at the ending station. Those at the other stations would rarely get a tip.

We charge $8 for an outside wash and up to $15 for outside and inside. We also do detail cleaning for up to $120.

It is hard to know how many tip since many customers use the tip box, and we don't see who puts money into it. I guess 85%–90% tip. I've gotten a $25 tip on a $35 wash. The average is $2–$4 for a $15 wash. Sixty percent put the tip into the tip box. The other customers give the tip to the people wiping down the cars. Some customers will give a tip into the tip box and give directly to a person. Middle class people tip the most. Upper class people don't tip. They don't care. They made their money by stiffing other people.

The average tip is $1 a car. On a typical day we wash 200 cars, and we get an extra $2 an hour in tips. This is for each crew member as well as the booth person. On a really busy day like after a snow melt, we average $4 an hour in tips. For a slow day, the average is $1.50 an hour in tips. We get the tips with our paychecks since they must be taxed.

Our policy is that if you are given a direct tip it must be put into the tip box. We tell all employees the first day that if they don't put the money in the tip box they will be fired. Even if it is only fifty cents that they take, they will be fired. Last year, we fired someone who didn't put a $50 tip in the box. This guy had detailing done and gave a $50 tip. When he asked if we got it, we realized that it was never put in the box. This is not a common occurrence, but it does happen.

$ $ $

Juan is the assistant manager of a car wash in an affluent area near Washington, D.C. He was working at the time and had to rush through the interview as quickly as possible. Juan told the following story about his experience with tips at a car wash in an affluent neighborhood.

We charge $15 for a regular car wash. Most of the employees are Hispanic and are paid the minimum wage of $7 or $8 an hour.[2] They usually don't stay very long. Tips are dependent upon how busy we are. Business is dependent upon the weather. Today is a very slow day, and we will only wash about 100 cars. The tips are divided up at the end of the week according to the number of hours worked.

We get a lot less in tips than you would expect. In a typical week, a worker will get $20 from tips. On some weeks, we have only $200 in the tip box.

We don't take individual tips. There is a very prominent tip box. About 30% of the customers won't even put a tip in the tip box. You would be surprised about who is more likely to give us tips. Regular people are more likely to tip. People who drive the fancy cars are less likely to tip.

$ $ $

Daniel pumps gas at a BP service station in New Jersey. His job delivering appliances is discussed in another chapter. New Jersey is one of the two states (the other is Oregon) where people are not legally allowed to pump their own gas. Daniel's responses are presented in the following narrative.

My aunt owns the filling station, and I've worked here all my life. I dropped out of high school and have had many jobs since then. The job is all right. It is not what I want to do. I want to race motorcycles. I don't have a wage. My aunt helps me out and supports my motorcycle racing.

Less than 5% of the customers tip me. I average $6–$7 a day in tips. I get almost no tips from people who live in New York or New Jersey. I get most of my tips from out-of-staters and from cab drivers. Jewish people don't tip. I hope you are not Jewish. Wealthy people almost never tip. Italians tip the most. I often give my tips to the other guys who work at the station. They need the money more than I do.

It makes no difference whether you help someone check their tires or oil. They don't tip any more than other people.

There is no need to send me the $10. Please don't send it.

$ $ $

Edward drove a courtesy cart for two summers for the San Diego Fair. His work experience running games at Sea World is discussed in another chapter. This is what Edward had to say about tips for his work driving a courtesy car.

I drove elderly people from the parking lot to the front gate in a golf cart. If they walked, it would take them 15 minutes. I earned $7.35 an hour.

People would ask how much the ride was. They were happy when I told them it was free. Three quarters of the people would give me a tip. The average tip was $5. In an eight hour shift, I would give rides to 40 people and make $50–$60 in tips.

Older black men tipped the most. They would talk about the problems of gang violence and how happy they were that I was well-groomed [respondent is black]. They would say they were happy to help me out. My biggest tip was $20.

$ $ $

These responses reveal a few common themes. There seems to be a pattern in which people rely heavily on one's appearance (i.e., style of dress, type of car) to assess the wealth of potential tippers. Several of the respondents conclude from their assessments of economic status that wealthy people do not tip as much as some employees determined that they should or could tip. Alternatively, the perception of the relationship between race/ethnicity and tipping are largely inconsistent. In some cases, minorities are perceived as better tippers and perceived as poor tippers in other cases. Interestingly, the respondents regularly conclude that wealthy people are miserly or shrewd and that minorities[3] are unfamiliar or uneducated. Such judgments of the character of customers are based on assumptions about class and the notion that tips somehow reflect a concern for the well-being of others. And, in the one case when, for example, minorities were asked why they did not tip, the responses indicate that they may in fact have fewer resources to tip. In addition, recent research reveals that minorities are also less likely to be tipped (see, e.g.; Ayres, Vars, and Zakariya Forthcoming). One conclusion that may be drawn from this is that people do not seem to theorize from the perspective of the other very readily.

NOTES

1. Ian Aryes and his colleagues recorded tips from over 1,000 cab rides in New Haven. In the study, they find that black riders tip less than white riders, and black cab drivers are less likely to be tipped than white cab drivers (see Ayres, Ian, Vars, Fredrick E. and Zakariya, Nasser, "To Insure Prejudice: Racial Disparities in Taxicab Tipping." Yale Law School, Public Law Working Paper No. 50).

2. The minimum wage in Washington, D.C. for most employees is $7.63 per hour and $6.15 in Maryland. The minimum wage for federal employees in the District is $5.15 per hour.

3. It is unclear from the respondents' descriptions the extent to which these categories are perceived as mutually exclusive.

13

Animals

The Bureau of the Census reported that there were 22,620 animal trainers and 50,410 nonfarm animal caretakers earning an average salary of $23,000 and $29,000, respectively. Generally, these pet service workers are not well paid. There is also no established protocol for tipping people who provide this service; although it does appear to be common for people who use these services regularly to give a gift or cash during the holidays. Some even give regular cash payments that correspond with the service fee. It is often described as a bonus for taking good care of a beloved animal. It remains a curiosity that such bonuses are common for dog walkers and pet groomers but not very commonly offered to someone like a home health nurse taking care of one's aging parent for example. It is likely positive in an ethical sense that tipping is uncommon in health care settings. Imagine if tips were expected in the nursing profession. Would people who tip get better health care, or would their tip simply reflect an appreciation of the quality of care? Regardless of the implications of the tipping norm, the fact that the norms exist in some settings and not others remains an oddity.

Dog trainers are more likely to receive tips in an individual setting but not in a group setting, which seems to indicate that tipping for these kinds of services is not intended as a display of wealth or to show off. It is often described in the context of a relationship in which concern over the economic well-being of someone who has helped an individual achieve a goal.

As a general rule, etiquette dictates that tips for these services are regularly given during the holidays. However, this is largely at the discretion of the customer. It is also interesting that dog walkers and pet groomers are more likely to receive tips than veterinarians (who are, after all, doctors). Do those who receive tips for the services that they provide for animals perceive the tipping practice as an issue of economic well-being or class?

$ $ $

Eileen grooms horses at a stable in Maryland. This is her story.

I've been doing this for two years, and I love it. It is a job you cannot do if you don't love horses. The hours are long, and the work is hard. It is very rewarding getting a horse ready to show. I went to college so that I could do this.

I get a salary from my boss. I work six days a week. Most days I earn $70. On days that we show horses, I earn $75. My employer pays my hotel bill, and I receive $100 per week for gas. On average, I show horses 18 days a month. In the winter, we show horses in Florida. During the rest of the year, we show in Maryland, Kentucky, and Virginia.

At a typical horse show, I take care of four–six horses. Sixty percent of my riders will give me a tip. The average tip is $10 per day, but a few will give me $20. I generally get $20–$60 per person for two–three days of showing (from those who tip).

At a horse show, I do all the care. I clean the stalls, feed the horses, ride them an hour per day, run a line for 30 minutes, bathe them, meticulously clean them, and warm them up before the show.

During the week, I ride the horses, take care of them, and train. I almost never get tips during the regular week.

On holidays, I get gifts but prefer cash. I got a total of $400–$500 from six people over the last holiday season. I work closely with ten people.

Parents of junior riders tip the best as well as adult riders. Teenagers are very bad tippers.

The grooms help each other out. You cannot get two horses ready for a show at the same time. It is a team operation.

$ $ $

Paula is a dog walker in a New Jersey suburb outside of New York City. The following details her responses during the interview.

I've been walking dogs for nine years. I love it. Most everyone is terrific with a few exceptions. You have to trust animals. Some people were not honest about their dogs before I started working for them.

I charge $15 for a half-hour walk. I have six full-time people that I work for, and 15–20 people who I occasionally walk for. They almost always give me the exact amount. Very, very rarely will someone give me extra.

During holidays, I get a lot of very nice presents such as china bowls and candle sticks. Ninety percent of my full-time customers give me cash. The average tip is a week's wage. I got a total of $300–$400 during the holidays.

Who tips the most—it really varies. One person started in December and gave me a full week's salary two weeks later for the holidays. Some people will pay you when they tell you not to come such as when their dog is being groomed. Most do not. If they cancel at the last minute, most will pay me. If they go on vacation with their dog, they usually don't pay me.

It is not a big tipping business.

$ $ $

Sandy is a dog and cat groomer in New Jersey. This is what she had to say about her experience receiving tips for her grooming services.

I've been grooming dogs for 14 years. I like working with animals. It is very satisfying. The work is not that hard. Another woman owns the business. We charge between $20 and $80 for a grooming. A Jack Russell might go for $20, and a Standard Poodle for $80. It depends upon the amount of work. We groom between 12 and 20 dogs a day. I get paid $15 an hour.

About 10% of the people will give me a tip. The average tip is $5. During the holidays, about half my regular customers will give me a present or a gift for my daughter. The average is around $20 but some give $50 or $100. I probably got $400–$500 in tips last holiday season.

Men tip more than women. I guess men are more generous, and women have more things to spend their money on [laughing]. Most of those who tip are regulars. If they know you, they tip you. Cat people also tip more. With cats you are somewhat more likely to get scratched. Those with big dogs like Labradors or Goldens tip more. These are more likely owned by men.

The tips don't affect how hard I work. Wait a minute. I guess I work faster when someone tips me.

I know the owner sometimes steals my tips. I can't catch her, but I know it has occurred. But, I'm still with her after 14 years.

$ $ $

Mari has been a dog groomer in South Florida for 33 years and had the following to say about tipping from her perspective.

I've worked for the same salon for 18 years. The job is very rewarding for the money. You must be able to get along with dogs and understand them.

The average grooming charge is $50–$55. This covers cut, nails, conditioner, and bath. I get 50% of the amount that is charged. It is very much like a hair salon.

About half my customers tip me. The average tip is $7. My biggest tip was $20. I have about 100 regular customers. Ninety-nine percent gave me something for Christmas. The average amount of cash was $100. I got WELL OVER $1,000. You are not from the IRS, Right?

People are more likely to tip if they are very fussy, and I do exactly what they tell me to do.

There is no competition among the groomers. There is more than enough work to go around.

We don't generally share our tips. I will occasionally give something extra to the bather or the fluffer (dryer) if they do an exceptionally good job. There is a tip jar in the front which is for them.

$ $ $

Steve is a dog trainer in South Florida. This is his story in his own words.

I've been training dogs for 16 years, and I love it. I love dogs, and this is all I ever wanted to do. I started when I was 12 years old when I did competitions.

There are several ways that I train dogs. I have individual lessons in which I charge around $120 a session for normal training. Most people get four–six sessions. I will charge $150 for aggression issues, and I can go up to $200 for some other issues. I get less tips now that I am self-employed. I used to work for another company and was paid by the hour. I got tips from 10–15% of the people. Now that I am self-employed, I get tips 5% of the time. The average tip is 15–20% of the cost of the session. About 15-20% will tip me over the holidays. Fifty dollars is the customary tip, and I total about $500–$600 over the holidays.

People who are more affluent give more. I get more from those who understand the industry. I am not an auto mechanic. We are a service industry, and we are trying to teach people how to get control over their dog. Those who understand this tip more. One thing that is odd is that I've had situations when I used to turn down tips and that always ruined the relationship. I would say, "You don't have to tip me." They would almost never call back.

I have group lessons where I charge $150 for six weeks. I have never been tipped in a group setting. It is a different environment. It is more of a teacher-student relation. For someone to tip they have to step out of formation, and people don't like to stand out. I also do boarding training. I charge $2,500 for three–four weeks, and I get tips from around 10% of my clients. The average tip is $200–$300. I also have some dogs that I keep overnight by invitation. I will charge $200–$300, and maybe 10% will tip me.

I occasionally share tips when the person asks me to. Last week someone gave me a tip and asked me to share it with my office manager.

It is a very difficult industry. You become very intimate with the family. You teach the entire family. They have to be comfortable with you. It is a very relationship based industry.

[Steve would not take the $10 payment for his participation.]

$ $ $

These stories present a somewhat different perspective. Several of the narratives indicate that the tips are experienced by those receiving them for animal caretaking services as a part of a relationship. Tips are described more as a function of the difficulty of the work and how well the animal is cared for, an experience that seems to be perceived through the lens of a relationship between the caretaker, client, and animal. Tips are often understood by the caretakers to reflect an appreciation of that relationship. It is unclear if the hierarchical ambiguity expressed in these essays is a cause or effect of the nature of the work. It does appear however that the hierarchical ambiguity does mask issues of class evident in the difference between who receives tips for their work with animals and who does not, at least from the perspective of those receiving tips.

14

Cosmetology

Cosmetology is the study and application of beauty treatments, including but not limited to hairstyling, skin care, cosmetics, manicures, pedicures, hair removal, and massages. There are 48,680 barbers in the United States whose average earnings are $25,000. The Census Bureau also reports that there are 305,440 hairdressers, hair stylists, and cosmetics professionals, whose average annual earnings are $23,000, and 100,140 massage therapists with average annual earnings of $24,000.

Tips for beauty services can be as numerous and extravagant as the services themselves. A full spa treatment is expensive in itself, but the price quickly escalates when the full range of employees that may require tips is considered. Ten to twenty-five percent of the cost of each service to the stylist, colorist, shampoo person, maestro's assistant, manicurist/pedicurist, nail technician, wax professional, esthetician, and masseuse is common in urban areas. There are also numerous gray areas in salon tipping. For example, many people tip even when they are unhappy with their haircut, including when they do not intend to continue to be a client. Many people do not know whether there is a tip out system or if they should provide tips to each individual. In addition, there is a range of behavior related to the act of tipping itself. Some contend that discretion is the most sophisticated method for disbursing tips; while others prefer pretension.

The tipping system for beauty services operates in a unique context. Generally, beauty services are luxuries and are highly gendered both experientially and economically. Usually, salon owners do not have strict policies regarding tipping, but encourage the practice as a means by which customers may express satisfaction with the service. While the structural norms are relatively weak, the social enforcement can be quite coercive in a circumstance in which a number of employees expect tips from individual customers. Another noteworthy point about the context of beauty services is the extent to which the work is perceived (at least by some of the providers) as an artistic skill and a profession centered on human relationships. Consequently, service providers might feel a sense of vulnerability in the subjectivity of customers' judgments; which logically leads one to wonder what the tip represents to the service provider.

$ $ $

Mary Ann has been doing hair for 40 years. She is now in South Florida and shared the following story about her experience receiving tips.

I like my job very much. I love to create and make someone look nice. It is great to work with people.

I only work with women. I charge $47 for a haircut and a blow. Some stylists are cheaper than me. I'm on commission. I keep 55% of what I make, and the salon keeps the rest. The average tip for a $47 cut and blow is $5. Some of the customers are cheap and feel that $5 is enough. A lot of my customers come in every week. Most of my customers are over the age of 60.

Young people go less often but have bigger jobs (more work done on their hair). The old people tip more. They understand what working is about.

On a busy day (Friday and Saturday), I do 20–22 jobs. On Thursdays, I do less jobs, but the jobs are bigger. I would rather do the big jobs. Someone gets a color, a haircut, and blow for double the bill, but the time is very similar. They spend a lot of time in the chair waiting, but we charge more. And, I get a bigger tip. I can charge $167 for a color, cut, and blow.

On a Saturday, I usually make $100 in tips and $300 in commissions. I make half of that during the week.

I do not share my tips. The shampoo girl gets a dollar or two from the customers. I never give them anything extra. Some of the other girls will give the shampoo girl extra. I don't do it. That is their job.

The tip is very important. Some girls really work for the tip. I like my job, and I will look in my drawer at the end of the day to see the tips. The tips make you feel appreciated. You talk to these women every week and hear their problems. Sometimes it is too much.

Around Christmas, all of my 60–70 regulars will give me something. I get $10, $25, $50, and a few will give $100. Most give $25. A few will give you chocolates or a gift certificate. I do favors for them all year long. I get about $1,500 in tips for Christmas.

We all have money in our pocket, but we never have big money.

$ $ $

Ruth works at an upscale hair salon in Washington, D.C. The following details her perspective on tipping in cosmetology.

All the senior stylists are on commission. A man's haircut is $40, and a woman might spend $200 for a color. I get 60%, and the salon gets 40%. Most of the other stylists get 45–50%, but I am more senior. I receive no salary.

Some of the stylists are on salary. They get $250–$700 per week. The people in the back (those who sweep the floors and give shampoos) are paid by the hour. My average tip is about 20%. I usually give 10–15% of my tip to the service staff (people who wash the hair, sweep the floors, etc.). I give a little more if the client does not tip the service person themselves. Sometimes instead of giving the service staff money, I take them out to lunch. Usually, I give money to the service staff, and the money is given after each client.

[When asked how she knows how much to tip the service staff she said, "I just know."]

If they do a bad job in the back, I will let them know. However, I will usually still tip. There is a lot of teaching that is going on. Most of the senior hair stylists tip in the same manner.

I will also give 20%—sometimes more—to the receptionist for a referral. The system is fair and most people are happy with it.

At the end of the year, the owner gives out bonuses. I give out gifts or bonuses for Christmas.

I have about 300 regular customers, and they all tip me for the holidays. The holidays begin before Thanksgiving. The men give around $50, and the women between $25 and $50. Yes, the men tip more. My total over the holidays is between $2,000 and $4,000. I share 20% of what comes in with the assistants (the shampoo person and the person at the front desk). I also get presents such as candy, candles, clothes, and jewelry. I am very good to my clients. I treat them like royalty.

$ $ $

Marissa has been cutting hair for 12 years and lives in South Florida. She is originally from Colombia. Marissa's responses during the interview are presented in the following narrative.

There are five cutters at the shop where I work. There is one assistant for shampoos and sweeping the floor.

I am paid straight commission. I get 45%, and the salon gets 55%. If I make more than a $1,000 per week, I get 65% of the amount over $1,000. I also get 10% on selling of products. I get paid each week.

The average tip is 15–20%. Sometimes I even get 30%. I have never gotten completely shafted. A typical haircut for a male is $35, and they tip $5–$10. Women's haircuts can range from $55 to above $100.

The salon takes $10 a day from me for the assistant, and I also pay $5 for each color. I also tip out. I give the assistant $20–$30 a week depending upon the week. She also receives an hourly wage. Only two of the five of us cutters tip out the assistant. The other three are cheap bastards. They say she makes enough money. Of course, I get better service when I tip out. I usually tip out at the end of each week; although sometimes I do tip out daily. It depends on how I feel.

I make sure that the customers give her a tip. I hint by asking, "Did you take care of the assistant?" Most of the time, they get the hint. Otherwise, I pay her myself. Some blacks and Hispanics either under-tip or over-tip. They don't know what is the appropriate amount. Some Jewish ladies try to get breaks on the price. I never told anyone that they tip too little. However, once I got a $2 tip for six hours worth of work that I charged $200. I said, honey, give it to the assistant.

I do real well for Christmas. Almost all my regular clients tip me. I start getting the tips a couple months in advance since I see some of them only once every two or three months. They essentially double their regular tips. I am off the norm, and I get $8,000–$10,000 extra in tips during the two–three months before Christmas. On some days, I walk out with $400 in tips in my pocket.

If I cut at someone's house, there is no split with the salon, so I tell them there is no need to tip. Ten percent will still tip. I won't lower my price for a home visit. Some cutters will lower their prices for cuts out of the salon.

$ $ $

Betty has been working as a hair dresser at a mall salon in suburban Maryland for five months. This is her story.

I like my job a lot. Most of the customers are women, but there are also some men. The cost for a haircut for both the men and the women is $40. Most customers tip $5 or $10 for this. If they get a hair color, the total cost is between $50 and $90, and the tips are usually around $20. Tips make a big difference to me. I live off my tips, and then when I get my biweekly check, I almost forget it was coming. Tips are money in the pocket.

Females that get their hair colored tip the most. These are mostly women who do not work. Men are great. They are easy to please. They tip well, and they get in and out quickly.

There is only one client who does not tip. She only gets blow dries.

I split 50–50 with the shop and keep all my tips. The shop also charges me $3 per customer for water and products.

Although I don't have to, I always give the shampoo assistant $3 for anything she does. We really overwhelm her. Most of us give her this amount.

The shifts are six–eight hours, and I take home half of $300 ($150) plus tips of $40–$60.

$ $ $

Roxanne has been a hair stylist in Berkeley, California for 29 years. She also owns the salon. This is what Roxanne had to say about her experience.

I like my job. I help people create a good image of themselves. I make them feel good. I like making beauty.

The salon is unisex. We charge $16 for a man's haircut and $20 for a woman's. Men always tip me even though I am the owner. About 60% of the women tip me. The average tip for men is $2 for a $16 haircut, and most women get a full do which costs $45. The full do includes a shampoo and a curl. The average tip is $3–$5 for a full do.

I have an assistant on Saturdays who helps with shampoos and other related services. Some don't tip her very well. I always tip the assistant about $1 a person just to show her I appreciate her work. I pay her $7 for her work on the full do plus the $1 tip.

About 80% give me something for the holidays. Often it is a gift or a Christmas favor. I got maybe an extra $50 in cash for the holidays.

$ $ $

Wilma has been working as a stylist in a hair salon in West Philadelphia for the last three years. This is her story.

I do not like my job. It is physically tiring. I don't know what else I would like to do.

A women's haircut goes for $12. I keep $8, and $4 goes to the salon. A color goes for between $14 and $50. The salon keeps 35%.

For a $12 haircut, the tip is between $2 and $10. The average is $5. With a $50 color, the average is still $5. People are cheap. A lot don't have the money. Our clientele is mostly middle class. Only about 5% do not tip at all. My biggest tip was $50 for very little work that I did. She just liked how her hair worked; although I didn't do anything.

In an eight hour day, I get about $150 from working on hair and $25 in tips.

I do not share tips. The person who sweeps the floor gets her own wage, and we do our own shampooing. I do not give tips to the person at the front desk who makes the appointments.

Those who are better dressed tip the most. Teens don't tip.

$ $ $

Alvin has been going to barber school in St. Louis for about a year. The training takes at least one year but no more than two years to learn a trade that specializes in cutting male and female hair. Typically, schools of barbering are different than cosmetology schools because schools of cosmetology train people as colorists, manicurists, and in hair removal in addition to hairstyling. Alvin had this to say about receiving tips for his services as a student in a school for barbering in the Midwest.

The school charges $5 for a man's haircut and $5–$7 for a woman's haircut. We do both kids and adults. The school keeps all the money from the haircuts.

Ninety percent of the customers will tip us. The average tip is $2. On a slow day, I might only have five customers and get zero in tips. On really busy days like Saturday, I will see 15 people and make $25–$35 in tips. My biggest tip was $15.

Grown people (over the age of 18) tip the most. Some regulars don't tip at all. We try to avoid them. They pay $5 for a haircut and can't leave a dollar or two!! I pay $3,000 to the school to learn how to be a barber. The program lasts for 14 months.

$ $ $

Peter is a student at Howard University. The following narrative details his responses during the interview.

I've been cutting hair since I was 16. I used to go to the barbershop in Jamaica Queens, New York every day after school and just watch the barber. Eventually, I got to cut hair. I worked there for two years until I went away to school, and I still cut hair there when I go home for vacation. Most of the customers were African-American, and there were a few who were Spanish. The customers were all male.

It was hard to begin because I looked so young. However, the quality of my cuts was good.

We charged $12 for a faded haircut; $12 for a shave; $10 for all around even; and $5 for shaping a line. Fifty percent of this went to the shop, and the rest went to me. Thirty percent of the customers left no tip. Of those who did tip, I got $2 on average. My biggest tip ever was $10. I kept all my tips.

Kids tipped the least. When they came in without their parents, I got tips from less than 50%.

In a typical week, I earned a total of $100 for 35 hours of work.

Since I got to Howard University, I've been cutting hair in the dorm. I charge the same price, but I don't split it with the shop. I keep 100% of it. I get tips from about 20% of the customers. That doesn't matter. My tip is for them to keep coming back. I average $125 a week for 18 hours of work. There is no sitting around. People come to my room. I love it. I have flexible hours, and it's my own time.

$ $ $

Daniel has worked as a barber in Washington, D.C. for 14 years. This is his story.

I love it. I like to make people look good. It's an art thing. It is a challenge cutting hair for different cultures, but it is great to satisfy others.

A man's haircut costs $25 and with a shampoo and style will cost $25–$35. A woman's haircut depends on the length of the hair. An African-American woman with short hair will take six–seven minutes, and I charge $12. For longer hair, I will charge up to $35. I don't do coloring.

I keep all the money. I pay a booth rent of $150 to $200 per week. My average tip is $5 to $10 on a $25 haircut. In a week, I make $400–$800 for the cost of cutting the hair and $300–$600 in tips.

The amount of tips and business depends upon the clientele and how good you are. Location is important. I worked at another shop at a not-so-good location and got $100–$200 in tips a week or a total of $400–$600.

Older people tip the most. Females tip more than males because they come in less frequently. The youngest tip the least. Seven and eight year olds sent by their parents don't tip. Ten to thirteen year olds rarely tip. Kids are not responsible enough. They will save the money and spend it on themselves.

I don't share my tips with anyone. I pay someone $20 a week to take my towels to the laundromat. I also have a kid who comes in on weekends. I want to keep him out of trouble. I don't pay him anything, but he sweeps the floor and brushes hair off of people. He gets 50 cents or a dollar from the customer. By the end of the day he gets $40 to $80.

Tipping comes automatically. If people are satisfied they tip. A few people won't tip because they are not satisfied. Others will say they don't have the money and say they will make it up the next time. They usually do make it up.

$ $ $

Carissa has been a manicurist for 25 years in a salon in Berkeley, California. She had the following to say about receiving tips for her services as a manicurist.

I like my job. I have a great feeling for what I do.

I charge $15 for a manicure and $25 for a pedicure. I don't split my fees with the salon. I rent my booth for $90 a week. Ninety percent of my customers will tip me. The most popular procedure is a pedicure. I charge $25, and the average tip is $5. In a typical day, I get about $150 from what I charge and $20–$30 in tips. I don't share these tips with anyone.

Eighty percent of the customers gave me something for the holidays. The average was $25. I took in $300–$350 for the holidays.

The average person tips more than the professional. They know about the service field. A lot depends upon how personable you are. If you are likeable all round, you get a better tip. Likeable all round means you do good service, and you are nice to people. You need to be personable.

$ $ $

Lannie has been a hair assistant for a salon in Oakland, California. Hair assistants can have a variety of responsibilities in a salon and are usually working their way up to stylist. This is Lannie's story.

I drape clients and give them shampoos, color, and relaxers. I've been working there for a year and I love it. I meet a lot of people and I like the lady for whom I work. The stylist pays me directly. Each shampoo is $8, color $5, relaxer $10. I do 15 hairs a day. Everyone gets a shampoo. Half get a color, and half get a relaxer.

About half the clients tip me. The average tip is about $10. Today a lady gave me $20, and another one gave me $2. The better a job I do the better my tip. I talk with them and laugh with them. It is all about selling yourself.

You would think that the regulars or those with more money would tip the most, but that is not the way it works. There is no way to predict who will tip well.

A little less than half of my customers gave me something for the holidays. Three gave me $20. I also got food and champagne. My total extra for the holidays was $130. I work mostly for the owner of the salon. There are two other stylists. I sometimes work with them as well. The owner always gives me a little something extra. I'm a good worker. She pays me weekly; although I could take my payment daily if I wanted. Last week she gave me $400 of which $20 was extra.

$ $ $

Long has been doing nails and skin care for one year at an upscale hair salon in Washington, D.C. She is Vietnamese, and her English can be somewhat difficult to follow at times. But, this is her story in her own words.

I like my job. People are very nice. The owner takes good care of me, and she really cares about what we do.

I do manicures for $18, and people tip between $3 and $5. If I do full nail sculptures, I charge $70 and the tips are usually $10. Sometime the tips are zero. People think the cost is too high, or they give it to the front desk; and the tip gets lost. The tips really range and are affected by how happy the customer is with the work that is done. I keep 50% of what the customer is charged for work on their nails.

I also do skin care. This might be defoliations, waxing, cleaning, and putting on masks. The typical skin care charge is $75. A typical tip is $20, but it really depends upon the quality of the service. Again, sometimes I get zero. I get to keep 60% of the amount charged for skin care.

Wealthy people tip the most. I really can't say who tips the least as it depends so much on whether or not they feel comfortable.

In a typical day, I take home $160 from the commissions and $30 in tips. However, it really depends. Last Saturday, I had two customers and made $50 plus $2 in tips. Everyday is different.

The hair stylists do not give me extra tips. Sometimes if work is slow, I will work on them, and they might give me some money. We all get along very well, and there is no competition with the other nail technicians.

Most of my regular clients give me something for the holidays. The average is $5, and last year I got about $200 in holiday tips.

$ $ $

Irene is a licensed esthetician in Western Colorado. Her job as a musician is discussed elsewhere. Irene had this to say about receiving tips for her skin care services.

I work with skin: acne, dry skin, beautifying treatments, light acid peels, and so on. I've been doing it for 15 years, and I like it. I am a people person. This work is one-on-one, and it also satisfies my scientific bent.

I charge between $45 and $100 depending upon the treatment. If I worked for a salon, the salon would get 50%. I own the building where the salon is located.

For a $45 treatment, I get between $5 and $10 for a tip. If the client gets the $100 treatment, I get $10 or so.

It is not always those with the most money who tip the most. Sometimes I get a great tip from the college kid on a budget. It depends if they are trained to tip and if they appreciate my work. I get better tips from those who have been around. They are more savvy and know that my prices are low. If people are getting treated because of a medical condition they don't tip. If they see the treatment as beauty, then they tip.

In a full day of work, I get $250–$500 from direct billing and $25–$40 in tips.

I do not share my tips with anyone.

$ $ $

Mercedes is a manicurist from Brazil who lives in South Florida. This is her story.

I love being a manicurist. I see different people every day. I have had clients for 15 years, and we have become friends.

I go to people's homes to do manicures. I charge $15 for a manicure, $25 for a pedicure, and $100 for a full waxing. I usually go every week to a person's home. Each week they get a manicure, and every two weeks they get a pedicure.

Ninety percent of clients give me more than the list price. Most will give me $18 or $20 for the manicure. For a $40 manicure and pedicure, most will give me $45. Often, when they give the tip they say, "This is for you." A few people don't tip. They say I work for myself, and I don't have to tip you. I get tips from most people because I know them. We are friends. I've seen their babies, and I've seen their kids who are now 15. I get good tips because I have a relationship with them.

My biggest tip was $40. It was a new client who had no time and had to get the work done the next day.

I have 60 clients. Almost everyone gives me something for the holidays. Half give me a gift for the holidays, and half give me money. I get more money from those who don't tip much during the year. The average holiday tip is $25. Some will give $40, and some will give a $100. I get an extra $800 during the holidays.

The people who tip the most are the people who work the hardest. People with a lot of money tip less.

$ $ $

Barbara is a massage therapist in Washington, D.C. This is what she had to say about her experience receiving tips.

I worked as a therapist for eight years in Indiana and now on Sundays in D.C. I also work full-time for a hospital doing other work.

It is a very physical job. There is a financial cap on what you can make because the work is so hard.

In Indiana, I charged $55 an hour and worked for a spa. I got 65% of that total. About 40% of my clients would tip me, and $5 was the average tip. I had about 50 regulars. Seventy-five percent gave me something for Christmas. I got a couple of hundred in cash and gift certificates. I got another couple of hundred in gifts such as from Bath Body & Beyond. People were more likely to be generous if they saw the massage as a luxury. Those who came for medical reasons were less likely to tip. People in Indiana were more likely to give gifts over money.

In D.C., I also work out of a spa and charge $85 an hour. I keep 45% of the $85, and the spa gets 55%. Ninety-five percent of my clients give me a tip. The average tip is $15. It was very nice to move to D.C. In D.C., more people come to reduce stress and to treat themselves. There is no profile of who tips the most.

Cash tips are always better because you don't have to declare them.

$ $ $

Toni has been doing massages for 12 years in Nevada. This is Toni's story.

I love it. It helps me stay connected with God. My massages are spiritually based. My main purpose is to be of service to others.

I work for myself. I used to be an independent contractor renting space at a spa. They charged me $600 a month. Four years before that it was $350. People now come to my house. I charge $90 for a 90 minute session. I do two–three sessions per day. I've had to cut back because of injuries not related to work.

Seventy-five percent pay more than the $90. The tip range is $5 to $35, and the average is $10–$20. People who look at massage as a medical treatment very rarely tip. Those who see it as a personal service are very likely to tip. If someone comes in with a doctor's referral, I do not expect a tip. They see it as a medical charge.

Around the holidays, 75% of my regulars will give me something. Twenty to thirty percent of these gifts are gift cards or cash. The total in gift cards and cash is $100–$150. I also get body lotions, scarves, jams, teas, etc.

The best tippers are those who earn tips. They understand the importance of tips. People who receive tips count on them. I put mine aside and use it for weekend getaways and services for myself.

Tip jars annoy me. I worked 20 years in bars and restaurants. I am happy to tip for service but not for Starbuck's. It makes people less generous to restaurant people.

$ $ $

Mani is from Brazil and has been shining shoes in New York City for the past 12 years. The following narrative details Mani's experience receiving tips.

I work inside at four different banks. Of course I like my job. I feed my family. It is good. I have no complaints.

I charge $5 to shine shoes. It takes about ten minutes to shine a pair of shoes. I do 30–40 pairs of shoes per day. Everyone gives me a tip. The average is $1 or $2. My biggest tip is $5. By the end of the day, I probably get $50 in tips.

I have a lot of regular customers, and around Christmas I get a lot of $20, $50, and even $100 tips. I probably get $2,000 total from around 100–200 people.

I also fix shoes. I will take them home and put a pair of heels on them for $10 or $50 for a full sole. Very few people will tip me for this.

The middle class people are most likely to be generous.

$ $ $

These narratives illustrate vast gender differences in beauty treatments. It is a firmly established finding that women not only pay more than men for the same beauty services; women also pay for more services overall. On top of all that, this research reveals that some beauty professionals perceive women to be worse tippers than men without accounting for the tax on gender reflected in the differences in price and overall costs. In addition, few of the respondents recognize the complexities of class or interaction of class, gender, and sometimes ethnicity. People who receive tips tend to make judgments about the character of the customer more than they evaluate the quality of the service. Often, these judgments are lumped into stereotypical categories. For example, the participants in this study seem to collect data on the class, gender, and ethnicity of clients and describe tipping norms in ways that reinforce pre-existing stereotypes; like when Marissa says, "Some Jewish ladies try to get breaks on the price."

The difference in how male and female beauty service providers describe their work is also interesting. Women tend to express satisfaction with "helping people look their best." Men tend to describe the value of their work in terms of the freedom and sense of independence the work provides them.

Many of the respondents in cosmetology also say that they love their jobs and note the artistic elements of the job more than the economic value. A number of them describe himself or herself as a "people person." There is also a good deal of variation in terms of the tipping norms within the work context. Some of the respondents tip those who assist them and some do not. In some cases, there are organizational rules that determine how workers in the organizational setting are tipped out, and in other cases, there are only informal customs. Some of the narratives reveal the logic that determines when, who, how much, and why those who assist a cosmetologist might be tipped. That logic appears to be dictated by the formal organizational rules, the informal organizational norms, the wage structure, perceptions of the quality of the work, and personal relationships.

It is an interesting, yet somewhat consistent finding across sectors, that tipped employees seem to conclude that some people do not know how to tip or are unaware of the standards; rather than drawing any correlations between the tip and the quality of the service. Several of the narratives indicate that some people are perceived as being better socialized or "trained" to tip. In general, most of the tipped employees tell stories that describe their work as consistently of high quality and presumably deserving of the full tip amount at all times (something that is highly unlikely). Another interesting finding has to do with the fact that people do not tip if the work is seen as a medical service; a finding that supports the notion that tips are inversely associated with a more complex interplay of professionalization and socio-economic status.

15

Teachers

The Census Bureau reports that there are 224,730 pre-school and kindergarten teachers whose average salary is $21,000. The Census also registers 2,143,750 elementary and middle school teachers whose average salary is $38,000. Teaching is not thought of as an occupation where receiving tips is standard procedure. However, tips for teachers are becoming increasingly more common as educational opportunities have become more competitive. There are also a few trends in education broadly that may contribute to the increasing occurrence of tipping in educational contexts. First, the increasing privatization of educational institutions might result in a higher likelihood of tipping. Second, there is a general perception that educators are underpaid relative to the value of their work. Tipping teachers is more common in private schools and schools in which parents tend to be wealthier. It is not likely that this reflects a difference in the value parents place on education; rather a difference in the parents' ability to pay. Third, the higher rates of dual income households also correspond with higher rates of tipping teachers. Today, the vast majority of parents participate in market labor, and there is a significantly smaller pool of available volunteers, who used to provide a considerable amount of assistance to educators. Financial contributions may serve as a sort of replacement for the voluntarism that previously supported educational institutions.

It has always been fairly common for teachers, especially in lower grades, to receive gifts during the holidays; although cash and even gift cards that were once quite rare have become increasingly more common. It is also true that parents and teachers have had to bear more of the economic burden of teaching supplies and supplementing the needs of students who are less well-off. Holiday gifts may be an attempt to redistribute the costs related to these changes as well.

Parents may get together and collectively purchase gifts for teachers, or they may give individual gifts. Gifts may be given to all the educators involved in a student's education or only to reward specific educators. However, there is not much known about the extent to which teachers expect tips. There is also little known about what teachers think or how they feel about receiving tips. In fact, a considerable degree of debate went into the evaluation of the narratives in this chapter because it was extremely difficult to distinguish between gifts and tips. More importantly, understanding the difference between gifts and tips may reveal a great deal about the relationship between tips and professionalization and clarify class issues related to tipping. The narratives presented here explore those unknowns regarding the experiences teachers have with tips.

$ $ $

Karen is a pre-school teacher at a private school in Washington, D.C. This is her story.

I've been a pre-school teacher for 30 years. The kids are between 2½ and 5 years old. I like what I do because I can see the results of my work. It is different everyday. I like helping people.

My base salary is $35,000. We get gifts and presents three times a year: the winter holidays, Valentine's Day, and the end of the year. I have 12 children in my class, and there is one other teacher. The parents for the entire school team up, and parents voluntarily donate to a fund which is split equally among the teachers. I got $1,500 this year for the holidays. This was incredibly generous. I also got presents from four to six of the children. These presents consisted of chocolates, gift cards, and candles.

For Valentine's Day I got chocolate and candy—nothing substantial.

At the end of the year the parents again voluntarily donated money into a pool, and I was given a gift certificate for $1,050 to Amazon.com. One teacher got a gift certificate for the same amount to Home Depot, and another got several gift certificates to several restaurants. I also got flowers from some of the parents.

I don't like the system. I live a comfortable but not rich lifestyle. I would prefer that more was donated to the school. It is fun to get a couple of thousand dollars that you were not expecting, but the school also needs help. My colleagues who are living a little closer to the edge disagree with me. I feel some discomfort taking the money, and I appreciate other schools where the large gifts are discouraged.

The school is in a very wealthy neighborhood. I used to work for D.C. Public Schools in a low income area. I got a lot of little trinkets such as candles, picture frames, and other small things. It was very touching and meant a lot to me. It was as equally moving as a big gift and was a personal gesture of gratitude.

$ $ $

Martha has been teaching elementary school in the D.C. public school system for over 25 years. This is her story in her own words.

I like teaching. There is nothing like watching the light bulbs go off in the children's minds. It is instant gratification for me. The public elementary school where I teach is fairly affluent.

I get gifts three times a year.

For the holidays, I get gifts from about half of the parents in my class and perhaps 30% of the parents from the other classes in which I help team teach. I get mostly gift cards from Borders, Starbucks, and so on. The average amount is $25. I probably get a total of $200 worth of gift cards for the holidays.

I am most likely to get gifts from the room parents, parents whose kids I have helped with special needed attention over the year, and parents of girls.

For Valentine's Day I get a lot of candy.

At the end of the year, I get a group gift from all the parents of around $100 and perhaps 5% of the parents give something extra. In the past, 50% would give something extra. At the end of the year, I get more personal items such as candles, hand lotions, little cosmetic bags, and a few gift cards.

I suspect that fewer parents give something extra at the end of the year because more moms are working and have less time to volunteer. I suspect that the volunteer parents spend more time in the classroom and hence appreciate the work that I do.

I used to teach younger grades (first and second). I got more gifts then. I think parents of younger kids volunteered more. Older kids want more independence, and many don't want to see their parents in class. Or, the parents feel the kids should not be as coddled.

The gifts used to be more personal. However, since the advent of gift cards, they have become more the norm.

Please give the $10 to the first homeless woman that you see.

$ $ $

Doug was a teacher for eight years at an exclusive private (independent) school in Washington, D.C. and had this to say about his experience receiving tips as a teacher.

I liked coaching sports, and I really liked working with kids. It was just time to move on. I was paid $42,000 a year plus some stipends for coaching and other things.

Maybe 5% of the parents gave me something for the holidays. That was the only time I received something. I would get coffee mugs, books, and two or three gift cards that totaled $20. I got nothing for the end of the year. I was not surprised by this. There simply was not a culture of gift giving at this school. Once a year, there was teacher appreciation day, and we got food, massages, and other treats.

I mostly received gifts from parents of girls and mostly from those in middle school. I almost never received anything from parents of the high school kids.

$ $ $

Carol has been a special education teacher in Ohio for 22 years. This is her story.

I work in the public schools and make $70,000 per year. I used to teach grades one–three, but now I teach more pre-school. When I had my own classes, I got very few gifts. Most of my kids were from a lower socio-economic status.

Now, I travel around from school to school and help kids in the regular program. I see them once a week and I've worked with some for a couple of years. This spring I got two gift cards from Starbucks and Barnes and Noble. Each was for $10. I also got a purse and a flower pot. For Christmas, I got three gift cards for $5, $10, and $15. Over the year, 25% gave me something.

I am more likely to get gifts from those whose kids I worked with the longest, those who were the most trouble, and those for whom I spent the most time. I once got a very nice pair of earrings.

I enjoy my work more now that I am traveling around. I get to see progress with the kids. They are less handicapped than before. I do more problem solving and conflict resolution.

$ $ $

Patrick just retired after teaching high school math in Cincinnati, Ohio. The following narrative details his experience receiving tips during his tenure as a teacher.

I taught for 16 years. I made $65,000 a year. I liked it because kids were learning things, I had contact with young kids, and I liked the people with whom I worked. What got to me though was the amount of failure. With kids who did not learn, it was hard to feel successful. It was an inner city school.

I taught 30 kids a year. I got maybe one gift a year of something of value.

Before I taught in the high school, I taught at a Montessori public school that was more middle class. About one-third gave me something: a candle, a gift card, or a plant. The total value over the year was maybe $20. Parents of girls seemed to give more than parents of boys.

$ $ $

These stories reveal a few commonalities. First, teachers are much more likely to receive gifts or gift cards than money, and teachers are likely to receive gifts during the holidays and sometimes at the end of the year. It is also the case that there are a number of holidays when teachers might receive gifts, including Valentine's Day. Second, those teaching younger children are more likely to receive gifts than those teaching older children. Third, most teachers get a sense of satisfaction from student learning and not so much from tips. Although tips were described as a rewarding form of acknowledgment, teachers do not appear to expect them. Moreover, teachers often refrain from calling gifts and gift cards tips; although they are functionally the same thing. A teacher might likely perceive a tip as demeaning, a circumstance that supports the notion that tipping norms are conditioned upon a complex interplay between professionalization and socio-economic status. Some very intriguing questions about value (both social and economic) might be better understood by looking closely at the role that establishing and dismantling tipping standards has on the real value of wages in a profession.

The teachers interviewed in this study seemed to perceive wealthy people as tipping more. However, gifts from people who are less well-off are seen as a highly valued form of appreciation because people with limited budgets used some of their funds to express gratitude for the educators. Some teachers express a degree of apprehension about accepting tips that they believed they did not really need given their lifestyle compared to others and compared to the inequities in education. In general, parents may do more for teachers by partnering with teachers to facilitate student learning than may be accomplished with a tip.

These narratives, perhaps more than others, reveal a unique aspect of status reflected in tipping conventions. Teachers are more likely to receive cash in wealthier, private schools. If private school teachers might be more likely perceived by parents as serving them and their children, is the apprehension that some recipients of tips in the education system report a function of a sense that they are not in need as much as others or a feeling of discomfort about what this may reflect about the social status of teachers today?

16

Blue Collar Workers

Blue collar workers are members of the working class who are usually paid an hourly wage for manual labor. Blue collar workers are distinct from both service industry workers and white collar workers whose jobs are generally not considered manual labor. The total number of employed workers reflected in the Census in the blue collar occupations interviewed along with their corresponding average salary include: 533,790 electricians ($41,000), 185,460 radio equipment installers and repairers ($45,000), 232,880 heating, air conditioning, and refrigeration mechanics ($36,000), 21,830 locksmiths ($33,000), 50,590 refuse collectors ($30,000), 46,300 service station attendants ($22,000), and 144,590 industrial truck operators ($30,000). Often there is a distinction made between skilled and unskilled manual labor, which has less to do with the level of skill required for the job and more to do with the level of organization of the workers.

We had no idea that blue collar workers sometimes receive tips until a driver stated during an interview, "Hey, do you want to hear about the tips I received as a cement truck worker and as a school custodian?" Groer's (2006) interview of Angie Hicks who runs Angie's List (where consumers rate contractors and service companies) reports that it is more common to tip the painter than the electrician, but there is "no rhyme or reason for it." In this chapter, we scratch the surface of some blue collar workers who sometimes get tips.

$ $ $

David repairs appliances such as dishwashers, refrigerators, and washing machines. He shared the following story.

I've been at this job for 25 years, and it has its good moments and bad moments. Each customer is different. Some complain a lot and others are very nice. I enjoy the work.

I get tips from 2–3% of the customers. I probably get a tip two or three times a month. The average is between $10 and $20. People who are most likely to tip me are the middle class. I don't get many tips from poor people or those with huge houses. It seems that many of those with big houses are living beyond their means. I get tips from people who are nice.

I am paid by the hour, and I don't remember the amount. I also get commission. I get 2% of anything I sell and for services for which I charge. This comes out to $300–$400 a month. It is not a lot, so you are not selling just to make your commission.

When people tip it is very nice. It is funny. I seem to get tips when I really need them. My wallet is short, and I need gas. Or, I need to buy lunch.

[He would not take the $10 payment for his participation.]

$ $ $

Dan is an electrician. He has worked for a small electrical contracting company in the Washington, D.C. area for the past several years. He is from North Africa and had this to say about his experiences receiving tips.

I like my job a lot. I have a great boss.

I rarely get tips. I get a tip once every six months. The amount of the tip is usually $20. These tips usually come from middle-aged customers. I occasionally get a holiday tip when we are working a big job. The holiday tips range from $30 to $40.

$ $ $

Steve has been a plumber in the Los Angeles area for 18 years. This is his story in his own words.

I love being a plumber. It is something I always wanted to do. I love the challenge. I love working on a project and getting it right. I love fixing something that is broken, and I love helping people who have problems.

I work for a plumbing company and get paid a salary of $75,000 per year. I see about 15 clients a week. Two or three of these will give me a gratuity, and the average tip is $20–$30. It is enough to buy lunch. I don't expect a tip. I sometimes tell people I don't need or want a tip. Sometimes they have to force it on me.

Older people (over 40) are the most generous. I get tips from people who appreciate that I take the time to talk to them. I help them and find out their needs. The tip is a token of appreciation.

Please don't send the $10. I don't need the money.

$ $ $

Wayne has owned a small heating and air-conditioning company located in the Washington, D.C. area for the past six years. The following narrative details his responses to questions about tipping.

I've been doing installation and repair for 18 years. I like what I do. It is a challenge. Competent labor (or the lack thereof) is my biggest problem. It takes many years to properly train a technician. I pay them $12 an hour, and this has to be passed onto the customer. This can hurt when you are placing competitive bids. It can take several years to train someone, and it really hurts when they leave after they have been trained.

I see 25 customers a week. About 1 in 40 will give some type of tip. The average tip is $10 per worker. It pays for lunch. Since I am the owner, I don't take the tips, but I tell the customer to give the tip to the workers. There have been a few times when the tip has been as high as $50 per worker. This happens when they need a "rush" job. We are also more likely to get a tip for an emergency call. We are also given cookies, candy, and lunch. If it is real hot out people will give us drinks. Older people are more likely to give items, and younger people are more likely to give cash.

I refused to charge one older lady for a service call because her husband just died. She gave us cookies. Her daughter was so appreciative. She got us 20 new customers.

The middle class is more likely to tip. Rich people don't tip.

$ $ $

Davar was originally from Iran and does handyman work in the D.C. area. This is his story.

I've been doing this for two years, and I generally like it. I work with good people. In an average month, I have 10–15 jobs. They can range from a couple hundred dollars to $3,000 or more. I get paid either by the hour ($175–$200) or by the project. Three or four jobs per month will give me extra money. I get an extra $50 or $100. Once I got an extra $500. I get extra because I charge a fair price and do good work, and the people know it. I probably get $200–$400 a month in extra money.

Rich people are less likely to give extra than normal people. Rich people never give tips and always try to bring the price down.

I have workers who work for me. It is a problem when I get a tip. If I give them an extra $20 they then expect the extra every time. One time I got a $200 tip and gave an extra $60 to a worker. He spent his tip on liquor. He got drunk and threw up in the client's home. I never gave him part of another tip. He is not happy about that now, but I told him that is his fault.

I decide when to distribute the tips and how much. I sometimes give it to the workers, and sometimes I don't. It is not good to give tips to the workers because they then expect it all the time.

Please give the $10 to a children's charity.

$ $ $

John is a school custodian in Colorado. His job as a tour bus driver is discussed elsewhere. This is what John had to say about his experience receiving tips for his work as a custodian.

I work in a public school. I get gratuities above and beyond my usual work. This usually happens at graduation, extracurricular activities, or sporting events. I have to do a lot of setup and cleaning. About half the time the club leader or rep will slip me $10 or $20 under the table.

I get somewhat more from entertainment and sporting events. They take a lot of effort. Over the entire year, I probably got $100.

At Christmas, the school board gives us a bonus. I occasionally get a gift certificate from someone else.

$ $ $

John also used to drive a cement truck and had the following to say about tips for that work:

When I had to make a delivery on the weekend to a homeowner, I often got tips. This was about 25% of the time. Once I got to split $100 with another worker. The typical tip was $20. People knew that I did not want to work weekends.

$ $ $

José, has been a house painter in the Washington, D.C. area for over 20 years. He is originally from El Salvador and shared this story about receiving tips as a painter.

I paint 80–100 houses a year. I have a crew of six workers. I get tips from 10% of my clients. The average tip is $10–$20 per worker. They give me the money, and I distribute it to my workers. Only once did someone give it directly to the painters. Whites are more likely to give tips for my workers.

$ $ $

Dennis owns a small landscaping firm and only had a few minutes for a brief interview. This is what he had to say during the interview regarding receiving tips for his work as a landscaper.

We do landscaping and outdoor masonry. Most of my workers are Hispanic. We rarely get tipped. Out of a 100 jobs in a year, maybe three will tip the workers. The average tip is $10–$20 per worker.

I don't take tips for myself. When a tip is offered, I tell the client that I don't take tips and that they should give it to the workers. I won't even touch the tip. I say give it directly to the workers.

Tips are not offered very often because most people think we charge too much. Some really appreciate the workers and will comment on the good work that they did. Others don't even comment.

We get more tips from those who are in their 50s and 60s and have kids. They will sit and joke with you. The upper class does not tip. They will hardly talk to us. They get in their Jags and BMWs and drive off.

$ $ $

Rico washes windows at peoples' homes, and he is a carpenter. He is from Guatemala and has some difficulty understanding English. The following narrative details his responses to the questions about tipping with some minor edits for clarity.

I earn $12 an hour washing windows. About 20% of the customers will give us a tip. There are two of us who work together. The average tip is $20 a piece.

Americans are more likely to give the tips. Non-Americans, like Iranians, don't even offer us water.

$ $ $

Frank has been working for the sanitation department of Atlanta for the past 18 months. This is his story.

I pick up yard debris. It is a great job even though the pay is low. I like working outdoors. I earn $12.45 an hour. I can never save anything.

We are not allowed to accept gratuities. I service 3,500–4,000 houses. Around the holidays, I get something from members of seven or eight households. They usually give me candy or soda. Some will just say thank you. I've heard of others getting money, but I have never received any money.

$ $ $

Russell has pumped gas at a boat dock in Lake Ozarks, Missouri for the last four seasons. This is his story in his own words.

It is a very enjoyable job. I know the customers really well.

I get paid $9.25 an hour. About 75% of the customers will tip you when you put gas into their boat. The average tip is $5. My biggest tip was $50. It takes 25–30 minutes to fill up a boat. The average cost to fill up a boat is $250 to $300. Under state law gas locks are not allowed. Therefore, you have to keep your hand on the pump. I gas up four or five boats a day. I get $25–$30 a day in tips.

I also wash boats. I don't get tipped for that because people are charged a flat rate of $75 to $100, and I don't see them when I am washing the boat.

I also do occasional favors such as minor repairs, taking a boat out of the water, and helping someone guide their boat into the slip on a windy day. I'm occasionally slipped a few bucks for the latter.

Five or six people tip me $20–$30 at the beginning of the year and say, "Please take care of me."

I have friends who work at larger marinas, and they make $250–$300 a day in tips. There is much more volume. Ours only has about 100 boats.

I am the only gas jock, so there is no sharing of tips.

$ $ $

Jack is a locksmith. We also see his story as a server, ice truck driver, and valet in this book. The following narrative details Jacks experiences receiving tips as a locksmith.

I do emergency locksmithing. This is usually for cars or homes. I get there as quickly as I can. In a typical bill, I charge $45, and I split this evenly with the company. I also try to convince the customer to get other services. For example, if a woman had a fight with the boyfriend who locked her out, I suggest that she get the lock changed, or if a person lost their key, I suggest they get five additional keys made.

BLUE COLLAR WORKERS

About 30% of the people will tip me. If I charge $45, they will usually bump it up $5 to $50. They give an extra $5 or $10—almost never an extra dollar or two. I've also been offered dinner, wine, sex, and drugs.

I get more tips if it is cold and dark and depending upon how quick and courteous I am. A lot of times the cars break down in a bad area.

$ $ $

Edgar installs sound systems in cars at Best Buy. This is his story.

I've been doing this for two years, and I really like it. It is a quiet environment. I am my own manager, and I like the challenge of the work. Installing is fun.

I put in seven–ten systems per day. Most people give me a tip, and the average is $10–$20. I get $30–$50 per day in tips.

Whites are more likely to be generous [Edgar is African-American]. Females are also better tippers because they can't do a lot of the work themselves.

If the other installer helps me on a project, we split the tip, but we usually do not share our tips.

I get more tips than most installers because I am friendly and good at what I do.

If you are going to tip someone like myself, don't give me $2. I am not worth two bucks.

$ $ $

Adam has been a security guard and bodyguard for the past ten years. This is what he had to say about tipping conventions in the security industry.

I was a police office in the District of Columbia for over 30 years. I am also in charge of security at a hardware store.

As a bodyguard, I have two or three clients per month. I charge $40 to $50 per hour. Most of my clients are CEOs of large corporations, athletes, or entertainers. I love what I do. I meet a lot of people, and I get to talk to them. I find out how they got ahead.

We usually have a detail of two bodyguards per person. So, if a husband brings his wife, they would both get two bodyguards. While the husband is attending a meeting or something, we drive the wife to places to go shopping.

Ninety-five percent of my clients tip. The average tip is $100 for a day. CEOs are the most generous. Some of the athletes are pretty cheap. I picked up a CEO this week at Dulles in a limo and he gave a $500 tip. Sometimes we get tips from both the husband and the wife. It can be pretty funny when the wife says, "Don't tell my husband that I gave you a tip."

We split the tips evenly. If the husband gives a tip and the wife does not, the tip the husband gives would be split among the four guards. Most of the time, the tips are given in cash. We appreciate cash. I don't take any extra money for setting up the security. We have known each other for many years, and we are honest with each other. You never know when it will be your turn.

$$ $ $ $ $$

I jointly interviewed two hotdog vendors who were taking a break at the end of the day near a university. They both had been selling food for about 15 years. The ensuing transcript will make it appear as if I had interviewed one vendor. Hotdog vendors (and the subsequent interview with Irene who sells flowers on the street) are not formally classified as blue collar. Nevertheless, we placed them in this chapter as they are not the type of worker who we traditionally think of as tipped.

I like selling hotdogs, chips, candy, and soda because I work for myself. I get about 100–150 customers per day. About 10% will say keep the change and occasionally one or two will give me an extra dollar for my kids, etc. If I sell something for $1.75 they will give me $2 and say keep the change. In a typical day I get $10 extra.

The workers at the university are most likely to say keep the change.

It is getting more difficult to make a living selling hotdogs. I sell a soda, chips, and a hotdog for $2.50. My profit margin is 75 cents. On top of that I pay $100 a month to store my cart, $25 a day to have it transported, for license fees, ice, and so on. My stand cost $10,700 ten years ago. It would now sell for $25,000.

I buy a six pack of chips for $2.50 and sell them for 50 cents each. I make 50 cents total on the six pack. However, if one of the bags is ripped or someone drops it I make nothing. Just yesterday, the wholesaler said he was raising his price to $2.75. Customers won't allow 60 cents for the chips. It is a real challenge to stay in business.

I get extra change everyday but I also give people free food. They say they don't have money today and will pay me back. Some never pay me back.

$$ $ $ $ $$

Irene sells flowers at a stand in Washington, D.C. Her teenage son also participated in the interview.

I've been selling flowers for 19 years. I'm originally from El Salvador. I like selling flowers because I like flowers and I like talking to people.

On average, I sell flowers to 25 people a day. Half of my customers are men and half are women. I sell about $175 of flowers per day. The typical bunch of flowers sells for $5. I sell a lot of $10 mixes or six roses for $10.

People rarely pay more than what I charge. Maybe twice a week someone will give me an extra $5. This usually comes from regular customers. Over the holidays, I get presents from six–seven people. I usually get cards and chocolates. Very rarely will someone give me cash in the card. If they do, I get $5 or $10.

I go to the flower shop two–three times per week. Today I spent $300 at the flower shop. The $5 bunch costs me $3. But flower prices go up-and-down. If they go up, it is hard to pass the cost onto my customers. Sometimes I lose money. Look at this flower (she is pointing at what looks like a Flamingo Lilly). The cost of this just went up. But, my customers expect it in the mixed bunch. I will lose money on this bunch.

Sales are affected a lot by the weather. I don't sell much around Christmas because it is so cold. My biggest sales day is Valentine's Day. Mother's Day is the second biggest day. On Valentine's Day I will buy $5,000 worth of roses three weeks in advance. I have to prepare the bunches. Two years ago, it was cold and it rained and I lost a lot of money.

There is a lot of competition. There are three other flower vendors within two blocks of me. I don't know where they get their flowers. One is able to get his cheaper as I sell six flowers for $5 and he will give seven flowers. Although we compete, we don't fight.

It is a very difficult job. I leave the house at 5:30 am and return at 7:30 pm. My husband died three years ago. He used to help me. Now I drive the van myself in order to buy the flowers and to set up the stand. I have to sell or I lose money. On a typical day I earn between $40 and $50. The work is very dirty—look at my hands. I have to bring my children when they are not in school.

I am thinking of getting another job because I am not spending enough time with my children. But, it is hard to find a job.

$ $ $

The stories told by blue collar workers demonstrate that manual laborers seem to draw conclusions about the character of others based on their tipping behaviors. For example, David the repairman says, "I get tips from people who are nice." It also appears that blue collar workers who are salaried do not expect tips, but for those who like their jobs, a tip is generally perceived as a token of appreciation. They certainly do not appear to rely on tips as a source of income. Moreover, tips deemed too small are likely to be perceived as insulting. Many of the respondents indicate that simple forms of appreciation like small talk, jokes, and offering drinks go farther than a cash tip that appears to undervalue the skill of the laborer. The signals regarding the value of the labor and the laborer cannot be ignored. Offering male laborers "wine, sex, and drugs," liquor and beer, or a few dollars to "go get drunk" (as one customer had suggested in the middle of the work day to a delivery driver whose narrative was included in a previous chapter) exemplifies class-based stereotypes about manual labor. Offering wine, sex, and drugs to a laborer is at least potentially as offensive and oppressive a stereotype as cocktail servers might endure. Suggesting that a manual laborer might use tip money to get drunk in the middle of the work day likely reflects a degree of resentment or hostility. Unless the person giving the tip thinks everyone drinks in the middle of the day, the tip in such cases reflects a class-based stereotype and is an example of a tip used to establish status *over* another.

There is another interesting class-related pattern in the stories. A number of blue collar workers describe wealthy people as not normal, stingy, and imply that they might not tip because they are not nice or are living beyond their means. Curiously, some of those workers making these kinds of statements report annual salaries of around $75,000. What's rich? One of the most fascinating things about class-related issues is that many people seem concerned about the impact that perceptions of class have on their future economic prospects, and few people agree on the designations about class.

17
Officiants

According to the U.S. Census, there are 46,590 judges, magistrates, and other judicial workers with average earnings of $79,000. There are 285,580 clergy in the United States with average earnings of $34,000. Judges, ministers, and now officiants ordained online might be the recipients of tips. Ministers might receive tips for performing a wedding or funeral, but they might also receive tips from members of the congregation after a sermon. Judges are prohibited from accepting tips at any time, before or after performing services related to their justice system judgments. However, some judges are allowed to accept tips when they officiate a wedding. As more and more people are planning less traditional wedding ceremonies and more people are completing online ordination, friends and relatives are performing wedding ceremonies. Friends and relatives are less likely to be tipped for this service than judges and ministers are. They are much more likely to participate as means by which people personalize their ceremonies; although they may indeed be tipped. The norms for tipping officiants are tremendously inconsistent. There are generally no structural norms and very little, if any, social enforcement. Yet, the tipping convention persists.

$ $ $

Adam is a part-time judge in upstate New York. This is his story in his own words.

I've done about 100 weddings since I became a judge. People ask what I charge. I tell them I charge nothing to whatever. We are not supposed to take more than $75. Ninety-eight percent of people give me something. The average is $40–$50. They always offer me dinner. I only stay if I know the person. Then, I usually bring a present, so I break even.

People with more money give a larger gratuity. You know as you drive up to the swanker places that you will be given $75. If you go to a trailer or a small house or people come to my office—I might get $20 or nothing.

I don't look at the envelope till I am gone. A couple of times people gave me $100. I am never given presents. I sometimes get a nice card.

I don't love doing weddings. It blows out my Saturdays or Sundays. I have to put on a jacket and tie and meet the people somewhere.

I offer people a standard set of vows, or they can choose their own. I always tell them to keep their vows handy so they can read them when they get in a fight.

$ $ $

Terrence has been a judge at a state court for the past 13 years and had this to say about his experiences with tipping.

I like being a judge. It is challenging and exciting. I've married around 15 couples. I don't believe we are allowed to charge for weddings. About half of the weddings I've conducted are at the courthouse where there is a wedding room. I'm usually called on the spur of the moment to come up to the room. I don't charge for these.

The other half of the weddings are outside the courthouse. I also don't charge for these. I get a free lunch, and I suggest they give between $200 and $300 to a children's charity that I've named. One wealthy guy did not pay. He had the wedding in a swank hotel on a Saturday, but I had to hound him to pay up. It pissed me off. He had a lot of money, and he was trying to get out of giving a donation to a good charity.

I've heard that one judge takes money when he officiates at weddings. Most judges give donations they receive to an art fund for paintings that go into the jury rooms.

I like doing weddings. The couples are having a happy moment unlike most of the people who come through my courtroom. I've only had one divorce so far.

I can't take your $10.

$ $ $

Franklin has been a minister in the D.C. area for 17 years. The following narrative details his responses to the questions about tipping conventions.

My present congregation has about 60 members and is mostly black and poor. Previously, I had a more affluent white congregation which had 450 members. I like what I do because I have personal contact with people at significant places in their lives. I can be helpful. I enjoy teaching, preaching, and counseling.

For weddings, I never charge members, and I tell non-members that I have no expectation of receiving compensation. I only mention this in case they ask. If they ask what is appropriate, I tell them that my average is $100 to $200. One hundred percent give something, and the average is $150. I counsel the couple before the wedding, so they must feel that I am putting in substantial time that is beyond my normal pasturing duties on Sunday. The largest gratuity I ever received was $500.

I get more from those who have more affluent weddings. They are prepared and often give me the check the night before. They have more resources. I was initially surprised because I put in the same amount of time for affluent and less affluent weddings.

I never get compensated for Baptisms. These occur on Sundays during the worship service. Luckily, I have had few funerals. Of the five funerals that I did, two people gave me $50 each.

I do a lot of counseling. Members of the congregation don't compensate if they come to my office during the week. If there is a crisis and the counseling occurs at night, about half will give me something.

I receive less from the poorer congregation that I now serve. I am expected to be accessible, and I am more seen as a spiritual advisor. The wealthier congregation saw me more in professional terms, and I was hired to take care of tasks. Clearly race and class issues affect the process in some way [Franklin is black].

$ $ $

The narratives of officiants are told in a way that seems to convey a sense of humility. In these cases, tips are rarely perceived as a source of income. In some cases, the service is provided exclusively to promote and support charity work. Tips are not usually expected but are reported as being paid at very high rates. The most common theme from this perspective appears to be an orientation toward receiving tips that is consistent with their corresponding professional standards. At this point, the notion is that tip norms might evolve in these sorts of circumstances when no price is set, and/or the price is not perceived to reflect the full value of the service.

18
Medical Care

The U.S. Census reports 1,384,630 registered nurses in the United States with average earnings of $46,000. Office managers who supervise other people are considered "first line supervisors/managers of office and administrative support workers." There are 56,450 administrative support workers making approximately $31,000. Office managers with secretarial duties are classified as "secretaries and administrative assistants." There are about 2,409,830 secretaries and administrative assistants who make an average of $29,000 annually. In most cases, people do not tip for services that are perceived of as medical but will tip when the same service is considered a luxury. However, there are some instances when workers in the health care system receive tips, usually in the form of small gifts. Tipping in this capacity does not appear to be a convention. It remains relatively uncommon and is usually strongly discouraged in the profession altogether. The norm is actually reflected in professional standards that discourage tipping. Interestingly, tipping is so pervasive in American society that even when there are strong structural norms against tipping, the practice persists.

$ $ $

Margaret is a nurse. She has had two different jobs as a nurse and had the following to say about tipping in health services.

In graduate school, I was a registered nurse doing home health care. I worked for an agency, and I also did this for nine years after I graduated. I did skilled visits. Most of my patients were elderly who were housebound. Most were on Medicare. Some I saw daily if they required changes of dressing and so on. Others I saw weekly or monthly. I mostly worked weekends and was on call. I saw 20–30 patients per month. I was paid $50 per visit or $70 per visit if it was an assessment. I liked the job. It was OK.

I received a present twice in twelve years. I once got a bottle of perfume and a bottle of wine. This was for my birthday. I was not the regular nurse. I filled in on weekends, so perhaps the regular nurse did better.

I was also a nurse practitioner for nine years. I just changed jobs a few months ago. I worked for a medical practice of five or so doctors. I had a lot of flexibility. I wrote orders instead of following orders as an RN. I did both jobs concurrently to make money. I got paid $45,000 per year as a nurse practitioner. I loved my patients. I would see 15–20 per day and on a four-day week would see 70–80. I was never tipped per se. I got presents a few times a year—a purse, earrings, flowers—thoughtful presents. Around Christmas, I would get another ten presents of this type. When I left the practice, I got presents from maybe 25 people. I got two gift certificates for $50, jewelry, and flowers.

I never got a referral fee for referring patients to ENTs, cardiologists, GI specialists, dermatology, and psychiatric care. It would have been unacceptable and unethical to take referral fees. The drug companies were occasionally allowed to bring lunch in for the entire staff.[1]

Margaret would not accept the $10 payment for participation.

$ $ $

Nancy is a registered nurse who works at a "celebrity" asthma clinic in the Washington, D.C. area. This is her story.

We are a group practice and a lot of celebrities come here. I've been a nurse for 14 years. I am paid $18.50 an hour, and I'm underpaid. I don't complain because I am allowed to work part-time and go to school. I used to like the job, but it is very stressful. And, I am tired of it. That is why I am back in school. You bust your ass. If you are not white [the respondent is black] you have to work twice as hard. I prefer working for white doctors. Black doctors don't want to pay you.

I get presents around the holidays. These include cookies, pastries, and lunches. One patient gave us all $10 Starbuck gift cards. That was real nice.

I also get a bonus from the doctors. I have no idea how it is determined. Is it based on not having screw-ups, coming on time, or whatever? I have no idea. A lot of people don't pull their weight, and they got bigger bonuses. There are 15 of us in the office. The bonuses range from $100 to $2,000. I got $750. The year before I got $1,000, and the year before that I got $1,500. I don't know why my bonus went down. On the other hand, my bonus was more than that of my supervisor. That made no sense. There are a lot of unhappy people because of the bonuses. A lot of people who don't work as hard as me got a bigger bonus.

$ $ $

Jenny is the manager of a large doctor's office in Southern Florida and had this to say.

I've been managing this practice for ten years. I have ten people who work for me. I love working here. I lost both my parents at an early age, and most of our patients are elderly. I care for them and I like to help them out. The doctors are like family, and it is a great job. I get paid salary. There is no commission.

I get thank you tips. About twice a week someone will bring me candy or flowers. I'm also the surgical counselor. Yesterday, I squeezed someone in on an appointment, and she gave me a box of candy.

Around holiday time, I get about a dozen gifts. The cash total is about $100. I am uncomfortable taking the money. The patients are expecting free samples in return over the course of the year. Some of the prescriptions are expensive, and I am happy to give them out if we have any available. The doctors don't like that we take gifts, so we don't tell them.

$ $ $

The sample of medical professionals is very small because the number of individuals who accept tips for medical services is virtually nonexistent. In fact, these narratives make little mention of cash tips; although they may calculate the cash value of the gifts that they receive. One of the respondents speaks of her bonus as if it is a tip, but tips come from customers and not employers. Consequently, the conclusion that may be drawn from these narratives is that there is not a lot of tipping in the health profession. The tipping that does occur involves gifts that are generally unique circumstances and many times is a violation of the structural and social norm against tipping. It is also worthy of note that there is very little mention of the lunch, pens, notepads, cups, mugs, shirts, and other miscellaneous items that drug companies bring to medical offices and hospitals on a daily basis. These narratives make only passing mention of a practice that is a daily part the work life of medical professionals.

NOTE

1. See Stephanie Saul, "Drug Makers Pay for Lunch as They Pitch." *New York Times*. July 28, 2006.

19

Miscellaneous

There are a few interviews that do not fit nicely into any category. For example, this chapter includes party planners, which often involves the restaurant industry, includes a number of different kinds of services, and is also related to entertainment. Ultimately, we incorporate it into the miscellaneous category because of the unique nature of the work, which is primarily a service and not itself entertainment or a restaurant business. Party planners are considered "meeting and convention planners." The Census estimates 22,620 such planners with an average annual income of $42,000. We also include photographers within the miscellaneous services. There are 63,320 photographers in the United States with average earnings of $40,000. Although photographers are often hired for events that might be considered entertainment, it is a professional service. Many professions have norms that restrict or inhibit tipping, so the fact that this sample includes such a professional is additional evidence about the pervasiveness of tipping norms.

Some of the jobs included in this chapter are ones in which tipping obviously occurs, like coat check clerks. The Census defines coat check clerks as "miscellaneous entertainment attendants and related workers" and reports that there are approximately 30,900 earning an average of $25,000 annually. However, many of the jobs people receive tips for that are documented in this chapter might be unexpected. Several of the interviews resulted from statements made by respondents during an interview about their experiences in another job. Often, interviewees asked if we wanted to hear about tips that they received in a job that we might never have thought to ask about because we had no idea people received tips for that kind of work. A number of the narratives included in this chapter came about quite by accident. A lot can be learned that way.

$ $ $

Nick was a coat check clerk in a suburb of Philadelphia from the time he was 11 till he graduated high school. He also shared his experience as a raft guide and ski instructor. The following narrative details his experiences receiving tips for his work as a coat check clerk.

I received no salary. The restaurant was owned by my brother-in-law. It was a very fancy restaurant that had a harpist. I only worked Saturday nights.

I almost always got $1 per hanger. If a couple came in, I put both coats on the same hanger and got a $1. Every once in a while I would get a couple of bucks, and sometimes I would even get $5. I would average $50–$60 a night. On my best nights, I would get $120. I would get better tips from those who had been drinking and women who thought I was a cute kid.

There was no sharing of tips. I had to protect my tips from the busboys. I made more than they did. I had a basket and always kept $3 in the basket. I wanted to show the customers that tipping was encouraged, but I did not want them to see that I made a lot.

$ $ $

Paul worked at a Kinko's [now called FedEx Office] in Davis, California for five years. Tips for copy services are not standard. In fact, Paul mentions the fact that it is unusual to receive tips in this context. However, the following narrative does provide some evidence of the extent to which tipping is a strategy for exerting influence or attempting to affect the quality of service (in this case, in a market with limited competition).

I liked the job. It paid for my undergraduate education. I was paid $10 an hour when I left. Surprising to me, I got tips. People would want to do a promotion campaign, and I would help them design their flyers or posters. About a fourth of those asking for design help would give me a tip. The tips ranged from $5 to over $100. These were for the most part high income accounts. One person gave me a $150 tip for $10,000 worth of work.

A couple times a week someone having a problem with a copy machine would also give me a few bucks. In an average week, I made a couple hundred dollars in tips for working a 30 hour week. I shared my tips with the one other worker if he helped me with the project.

I know this tipping was not normal. We probably got tips because we were the only copy store in a small town. We were the only option.

$ $ $

Robin works at a clothing store in St. Louis. The following narrative reveals that retail employees do not only receive commissions in some cases, but they may receive tips. This is what Robin had to say about receiving tips for the services she performed in her interactions with customers in a clothing store.

We sell young adult and hip clothes. I've been working at this store since it opened six months ago. I like the people I work with a lot.

I am paid $9 an hour. I do not get commissions. However, I do get tips. We help people put together outfits, and we are a specialty store. About half of the customers will tip me. The average tip will be $5 or $10. I help about 20 people a day. During the week, I average $20–$30 in tips and on the weekend, $50–$60 a day.

I know it is unusual to get tips at a clothing store, but we are small and specialized. We put a lot of time into finding things for customers.

There are several of us who work at the store, and we pool our tips. They are placed in the safe by the manager and split at the end of the day. The manager also gets a share. The regulars tip the most. Some people come in three times a week.

Everyone is honest. If someone did pocket their tip, that would be OK because she earned it.

The company may not condone the tipping, so I would appreciate it if you did not use the name of the store or my name.

$ $ $

Ian works at an auction house. His experiences receiving tips for his work selling beer and food at sporting events is included elsewhere in this book. This is Ian's story in his own words.

I like working at the auction house. It's fun. I get a salary every two weeks of about $1,000 after taxes. I get tips from two different sources. I help load vehicles after an auction. I will be tipped from a couple bucks to as much as $50. Seventy-five percent of clients will tip me. The others just say thank you. Regulars tip more than new customers. On a typical sales day, I will make $150 in tips loading trucks. We have sales days once a week and auctions about once a month.

I also get tips by putting bids in for people who cannot attend the auction. If the bid goes through, almost everyone will leave a tip. The average tip is $5 to $20. I make a $100 on auction days by placing bids. It really varies on the type of merchandise on the floor. I will usually bid for two–three people and as many as ten.

$ $ $

Zachary works as a party planner at a private country club in Massachusetts. This is his story.

We have both private and public functions. People who are not members can use the country club for weddings, retirement parties, Bar Mitzvahs, and so on. I love working at the club and have been there for five years. It has a relaxed atmosphere. How bad can it be—planning people's parties?

My salary is based on a 50 hour work week. I get $39,000 per year. However, if I put in more than 50 hours a week, I get $25 an hour in overtime. I am usually really busy in the summer.

There are three of us who do the planning. We deal with the kitchen, the wait staff, and the vendors, such as bands and florists.

Tipping is not required beyond the 18% that is added to the bill for the servers. Most customers will round this 18% up to 20%.

We do 60 events a month, and the average event has between 30 and 300 people. About 30% will tip us. The typical tip is $300–$500. This is usually split up among the staff. For example, if the event has 200 people, we will split the amount among the 13 or so staff people who are there. There are also side tips. I get envelopes just for me, and the servers sometimes get envelopes just for them. Sometimes a customer will give an envelope for a particular person. We do what they want. It's their money.

The biggest envelope for me had $800 in it. It was a very complicated corporate Christmas party. In an average month, I personally make $600–$800 in tips. Men are most likely to tip for events, and those in their 30s and 40s are more generous. Weddings throw off the most tips. They are more complicated to set up.

A lot of our tips come around Christmas. Our own members give out individual tips throughout the club. We have a golf course and private dining. I get about $500 extra for Christmas bonuses. These are from people that I help throughout the year.

$ $ $

Griffin does photography at weddings, Bar Mitzvahs, and other special events. This is what he had to say about tipping norms.

I've been doing it for three years. It is a great job but a mediocre dream. I get to dance, eat, and booze on the job. The job is mediocre because I would like to shoot movies.

When I work for myself, I charge $1,200–$2,000 per event. I require $500 to hold the date and the remainder 14 days prior to the event. My costs are $300–$400 for photo shoots and $200–$300 for videos. I might also pay someone $200–$300 if I outsource it. My costs are albums and prints.

I sometimes get a job through another company. They charge $2,000, and I get $400. They pay for the costs.

I never get tipped directly from a client. About one in seven times I get a tip from what I call the drunken uncle. He will say you did a great job and slip me $30–$70. The average is $50. The tip is irregular. I don't expect it, and I am not upset if I don't get it. But, it's nice when it comes.

$ $ $

The miscellaneous narratives demonstrate the pervasiveness of tipping. In fact, the recipients are often surprised, do not expect, or acknowledge that it is unusual to receive tips in their line of work. These stories show that tips are a means for attempting to exert or demonstrate influence, and some of the responses indicate that tipping seems more likely in smaller settings where there is significant interaction between the customers and service workers.

It should also be noted that tipping norms are highly contextual. Paul, the copy attendant at Kinko's, points out that tipping may not be "normal" in the broader setting of copy services. However, there appears to be a strong tipping norm in that particular work environment. This example highlights the necessity of the methodological approach to understanding tipping norms undertaken in this study. Knowledge about the contextual norms obtained through structured interviews guides future exploration and facilitates a more accurate understanding of causal relationships.

Part 3

ENTERTAINMENT

The Bureau of the Census has the following categories relevant to this section with their corresponding number of workers and average annual earnings:

1. dancers and choreographers (5,960; $31,000),
2. entertainers and performers, sports and related workers, all other (11,490; $38,000),
3. musicians, singers, and related workers (50,450; $43,000),
4. recreation and fitness workers (106,550; $30,000),
5. tour and travel guides (9,900; $28,000),
6. athletes, coaches, umpires, and related workers (66,700; $45,000),
7. gaming and service workers (52,620; $30,000),
8. personal care and service workers (14,500; $27,000),
9. miscellaneous entertainment attendants and related workers (30,900; $28,000),
10. lifeguards and other protective service workers (12,710; $28,000),
11. ushers, lobby attendants, and ticket takers (12,740; $28,000), and
12. vendors at sporting events (classified as door-to-door sales workers), news and street vendors, and related occupations (56,450; $31,000).

There are a number of occupations that are not categorized in a straightforward manner. Consequently, the narratives of those occupations are organized as follows. Strippers are in category one. Clowns are in the second category. Camp counselors are in the third category. Cruise line greeters are in the fourth category. The narratives of casino dealers are in the fifth category. The narratives of prostitutes are included with the narratives defined in the sixth category, and beach attendants are among the narratives organized in the seventh.

Entertainers encompass a lot of different roles. In this section, a distinction is made between those who provide entertainment oriented toward children and families and those who provide adult entertainment. The largest category of entertainers sampled was musicians. Musicians who perform on the street, play at private parties and weddings, work in bars and restaurants, and those who provide music lessons are among those who might receive tips. We also separate sports entertainment and include another distinction for vendors and ushers, who usually do not work exclusively at sporting events.

The protocol for tipping people in these occupations is not particularly clear. When renting a chair and umbrella at the beach, the tip may be more obvious when compared to other forms of entertainment. Often there is a big sign saying, "tips are appreciated." Similarly, one may learn to tip at a casino when others are observed tipping, but tipping for many other forms of entertainment may be less obvious and more difficult to learn. For example, the interview of Shona in this section indicates that at least some people tip museum guides, and this tipping often occurs in streaks after observing someone else initiating a tip. A number of vagaries persist. Do people learn to "make it rain" by watching music videos? What relationship does this have on the quality of the entertainment? Why is it customary to tip dancers at a strip club but not dancers on Broadway?

The stories in this section reflect a variety of people whose job it is to ensure that people are entertained. Clowns, camp counselors, carnies, club promoters and party motivators, cruise ship greeters, parasail and schooner staff, museum guides, beach boys, casino dealers, strippers, cabaret performers, and prostitutes, among others were interviewed about their experiences receiving tips. These narratives provide a greater understanding of the tipping industry in a sector in which the entertainment is differentially utilized across society, tipping norms are more vague, and very little is known about the experience of most of those who are tipped for entertaining others.

20
Family Entertainment

Those who entertain children and families occupy numerous occupational categories and may or may not work in settings in which the structural norms allow them to receive tips. Structural norms that address tipping are most often described as being related to professionalism, but the social norms related to tipping in the entertainment industry are varied, not strongly adhered to, and are usually perceived to be mostly unrelated to the quality of the entertainment or entertainer (although tipping may be perceived as related to the quality of the overall experience).

    Family entertainment is a luxury for the most part. As such, some people can afford to be entertained and others cannot. However, this does not mean that those who are entertainers are not also consumers of family entertainment themselves in other instances. This is particularly true in the United States. It is a commonly held belief that Americans are the most entertained people in the world; although this is primarily based on the development and assessment of the entertainment industry. It may also be the case that comparable entertainment is quite common, even where there are not calculations of the industrial production of entertainment. In any case, family entertainment in the United States is exceedingly common. Consequently, tipping practices for family entertainment reveal a good deal about the custom.

    People who provide family entertainment work in an industry that is generally a luxury; albeit one that most Americans can access at least some of the time. Family entertainment requires workers to be patient, personable, responsive, and have the ability to make parents and children feel safe. These aspects of the entertainer in conjunction with the structural norms, the cost of the entertainment, the type and extent of direct contact with the entertainer, and the overall experience are among the factors that are likely to affect the tip. However, the social norms of tipping for various types of entertainment for children and families are irregular and inconsistent across the population.

$ $ $

Larry is a children's entertainer in Northern Virginia. The following narrative details his experiences in his own words.

I've been doing this since 1978. I like it. It's work, and I enjoy it. I am mostly a magician. Sometimes I am a clown, but that is also usually mixed with magic as well. I also do balloons. Ninety percent of my shows are for children. I also do some retirement homes. I charge $200–$250 per session. My shows run one hour.

The tips seem to run in streaks. I get tips 10% of the time. People don't know they are supposed to or allowed to tip. The average tip is an extra $20.

I also work at restaurants going table to table. I do magic and balloons. Sixty to seventy percent of the people at the tables will tip me. The average is $3–$4. Last week I got a $40 tip. I was with a man's kids for half an hour. The restaurant pays me $25–$50 an hour. I also get a good meal. Sometimes the tips are only $10 a night, but the average is $20.

For kids' parties, Americans tip the most while Indians (from India) don't seem to tip. Whites tip more than others. Spanish people rarely give more than a dollar.

Some entertainers wear tip buttons that say, "I accept tips." I don't think it looks good. Many people are not aware that they are supposed to tip or allowed to do so.

$ $ $

Lynn has been a clown in Seattle, Washington for 16 years. She also helps run a pre-school (essay not included). The following narrative details Lynn's experiences receiving tips for her work as a clown.

I love acting, and I love children. It is very rewarding to me to entertain people. I am very proud of myself when I can get even the adults to laugh. Ninety-nine percent of what I do is kids' parties. I also do some company picnics where I entertain the kids. I dress up like a clown and do balloons, magic, and games.

I sometimes work with a company that people can call and find a clown. I also help the company do training. When I work for the company, I get paid $50 an hour, and the owner bills me out at $110 an hour. I get paid more if clients explicitly ask for me. When I work for this company, they also pay for supplies such as makeup, balloons, and some mileage.

If someone calls me directly, I charge $165 for a 90-minute session. I book 80% of my work.

Male clowns get tipped more than female clowns. My male clown friends disagree, but it is the truth. I get a tip 25–30% of the time. Today, I got a $10 tip. I never get tips at the company picnics because there are other entertainers. The average tip when I get tipped is $20.

There is little pattern as to who tips the most. Koreans, Filipinos, and blacks are more likely to give me a lot of food to take home. It is usually about $20 worth of food. It is their form of tip. The tips don't seem to be based upon performance. It perplexes me as to why some people tip and others don't. Perhaps my tips are low because I charge so much.

$ $ $

Edward ran games working for Sea World in San Diego for a year and a half. His experience taking people to their cars at the San Diego Fair is discussed elsewhere in this book. This is Edward's experience with tips for his work as an entertainer.

The job was OK for a high school job. I definitely would not want to make it a career. The best part was seeing the expression on the kids' faces when they got toys. It was fun to see them laugh.

People would buy three balls for $5 and try to throw them into a barrel. Another game was three shots of a basketball for $10. People would win prizes. Thirty percent would legitimately win a prize. Even the biggest prize cost the company $2. The smaller toys cost 35 cents. If you tried to buy the bigger prizes, we would charge $100.

I earned $6.75 an hour. I also got a lot of tips. I would see about 60 families in an eight-hour shift. Half would give me a tip. The average tip was $3–$4, and I would average $100 a day in tips. Tips came from two sources. A person would buy $17 worth of chances, give me $20, and say keep the change, or I would get a lot of tips because I would make the kids happy. I would often give a kid a little toy even when they did not win or give them four balls instead of three balls.

We were not supposed to give the prizes away, but there was an unspoken rule that it was OK. The company wanted people to have a good time, and we would get good tips.

People with large families tipped the most. Asians tipped the least. My biggest tip was $50 from someone who said they liked my personality. On my best day, I made $235 in tips. I do well with tips because I am a people person, and I know how to play with kids.

$ $ $

Tammy is a party motivator in the Washington, D.C. area. She is also a part owner of the company. This is her story.

I've been doing this for ten years, and I love it. I am the MC at parties. I make announcements and introductions and try to get the kids to sing karaoke, play games, and dance together. We do Bar and Bat Mitzvahs, birthday parties, and corporate events. I love the effect I have on people. They have great big smiles, and I get a lot of positive reinforcement.

The price of the parties can range from $300 to $6,000. Some parties have DJs, an MC, and several dancers. There is also lighting and special effects. I can't tell you what our people get but the industry standard is for dancers and motivators to get between $50 and $250 a show, and the DJs are paid between $75 and $1,000 a show. Sometimes they get as much as $1,500. The business is all referral and word-of-mouth. If you are good and have a good reputation, you charge more.

We get more tips than other similar party developers. Seventy percent will give us tips. About half add it onto the bill, and the other half give tips to the individual performers. We probably average $20–$50 a person when tips are given. Sometimes the tips are not equal when the individual passes them out. They might give $20 to a dancer and $50 to a DJ. When they ask us to split the tips, everyone gets an equal share. You never know who will tip and who will not. There is no scale like in a restaurant. A tip shows that you are appreciated. Sometimes you do a great job and don't get a tip. And other times, it seems the party never got started, and you get a good tip. It seems that people in the service industry give more than lawyers. However, I really never know who will tip more. I am constantly surprised.

$ $ $

Doug has been a camp counselor at a fairly exclusive camp for boys in Pennsylvania for the last three years. Prior to the summer he started working at the camp for boys, he was a camper at this camp for four years. The following responses were provided by Doug regarding his experiences receiving tips as a camp counselor.

I love it. I would continue to go back there. Next year will be my last. I am studying to be a physical therapist, and the summer after next I have to do an internship over the summer.

I get paid $1,700 for the summer. I work there for eight weeks. We have kids who are there for two weeks, four weeks, six weeks, and eight weeks. Over the entire summer, I have about 18 kids in my cabin. There are two other counselors who also work with the cabin.

I got tips from about half of the parents. The average tip is $25–$30 per counselor. Ninety percent of the time the parents give the tip to each counselor, and 10% of the time they give it to one of us and ask us to distribute it. I have also been given soft pillows and t-shirts. I made about $200 last summer in tips.

If the parent does not give a tip to the CIT (counselor in training), I will give the CIT some of my tip.

Parents who tip the most have kids who I have connected with the most. They always give the tip at the end of the session. There is no difference in tips on whether the kids stay for two weeks or eight weeks.

Some counselors like the tips. The new ones get excited about it and may even brag about their tips. We are told not to expect tips or try to get a tip. We are told to try to give the tip back.

I think the parents have paid their money and there is no need to tip. I usually tell the parent it is not necessary. They always insist.

$ $ $

Danele works as a greeter for a cruise line in Ft. Lauderdale, Florida. She has been doing it for four and a half years. Her responses to the interview questions are reflected in the following narrative.

I like my job. I meet people. They are on vacation, and they are happy. It is not a difficult job. It is a good way to learn English. I am from the Basque region of Spain. I meet a lot of groups at the airport. There might be 40 people in a group, and I direct them to a bus that takes them either to their hotel or to the cruise ship. I work at night. In a typical night, I will greet 50–100 people.

I earn $11 an hour because I am a supervisor. Other greeters earn $8 an hour. I rarely get tips. One day I might get $2, and then I might not get a tip for two months.

$ $ $

Don was referred by Danele and works for the same cruise line that she does. This is Don's story.

I do two jobs for this cruise line. On weekends, I load luggage onto the bus, and during the week, I meet and greet people. I get paid $8 an hour.

I get few tips loading luggage onto the bus. I load luggage for 120 people a day. Maybe one person will tip me. I get $4–$5 on the weekend from tips. Senior citizens tip the most as they usually need help the most.

I actually get more tips from meeting and greeting people. People travel in groups of three or four. I get tips from five or so groups a night and average $20–$30 a night in tips.

Elderly people also tip the most as well as those in their twenties or thirties. Most of the younger people are on their first cruise and are expecting to spend money. I get more tips when I pay close attention to the people, keep them informed on what is happening, and talk to them.

I don't share my tips.

[Don refused the $10 payment for participation. During the interview, it was evident that he got a lot more in tips than Danele for meeting and greeting people. Because English is his native language, he was also more likely to strike up a conversation with people; although one can only speculate on the extent to which this affected the difference in their tips in this instance.]

$ $ $

Raphael has been a steward on cruise ships for the past 18 years. He was interviewed as he finished an Alaskan cruise. His responses to the interview questions are provided below.

I am from India, and this is my last cruise. I love being a steward. I've gotten to see the world. I've worked for the same cruise company, and we all get along. The crew comes from 67 different nations, and it is just like one big happy family.

My salary is about $50 a month. I make most of my money from tips. The tips are mostly given to the cruise company, and they give it to me every 15 days. The passengers are given guidelines about tipping. For a standard cabin, they are told that they should tip $3.50 per person per day ($4 per person per day for the concierge level), so for a typical seven day cruise, I should be getting $49 per couple for standard cabins.

On this cruise, 11 rooms pre-paid the tips, and 3 rooms gave me nothing. Unless they pre-pay, most people give me less than the standard rate; although a few pay me more. I usually get more from vacationers who know me more. Perhaps I've helped them in more than a customary manner, or perhaps we had more than the usual conversation. The people who don't tip me or give me less than expected are upset about some aspect of the cruise. This is usually not my fault. For example, one of the couples who did not tip me complained about smelling cigarette smoke, but there was nothing I could do about this. It wasn't fair for them not to tip me.

I share this with my assistant, who gets $1.20 per person per day. The waiters and busboys have their own system.

$ $ $

Stan was the captain and owner of a 46-foot sailboat in British Columbia that was for charter. This is his story.

I did this for eight years when I retired. I enjoyed it a lot.

People chartered the boat for a week, and that went for $2,000. I provided all the food, and it slept eight. My biggest tip was the booze. They provided the booze and often left quite a bit in booze.

I only occasionally got tips. After all, the boat cost a lot to charter. I probably got $2,000 a year in tips.

The only other person working on the boat was a cook who also made the bunks. I did not get involved in her tipping, but about two-thirds of clients gave her a tip. Her average tip was $50, sometimes $100. Germans were the most likely not to tip.

There is no need to send me $10.

$ $ $

Todd worked on a sailing boat, a schooner, out of Provincetown in Massachusetts. His work as a chambermaid and his work as restaurant server are discussed elsewhere. This is what Todd had to say about receiving tips for his work on a sail boat.

People would pay $15 for a two-hour sail. The boat was also chartered for weddings and other special occasions.

I got paid $300 per week and lived in the house of the captain for free. We sailed four–five days per week.

There was a very prominent tip jar. We averaged $1 or $2 per person. There was one other crew member. If 50 people were on the boat, we would split $75. I averaged $75 per day in tips. If we had a great day, we would give a tip out to the captain—perhaps $50.

Wedding parties and special charters paid the best. At one corporate function, we both got $100 bills.

It was a great job. I went sailing every day and watched the sunset. How much better could it be?

If people were seasick they did not tip well. They assumed they did not have to tip for a bad experience.

Just like the restaurant and the bed-and-breakfast that I worked at, lesbians tipped the least, and gay men tipped the most.

$ $ $

Zack worked on a parasail boat for a summer in Ocean City, Maryland. In another section, he discusses his job as a runner, busser, and short-order cook. The following narrative details Zack's experiences receiving tips for his work on a parasail boat.

It was a great job. It was awesome. I had a lot of fun and made a lot of money. Unfortunately, the boat was sold the next year, so I could not return to the job the next year.

I was paid $4–$5 per hour. We took six people out at a time. They paid $70 for the trip. We had a big sign stating the customary tip was 20%. About 80% of the clientele left a tip. The average tip was $10 per person. I split the tips with the driver of the boat. My job was to explain the process, strap them in, and take pictures with their cameras. On an average run, we would split $40. On an average day, I would get $100 in tips.

New Yorkers tipped the most. A big tip for us was $20. One guy gave us $80 in advance for his four kids. He said, "keep them alive."

Kids didn't tip.

$ $ $

Andrew is a hot air balloon pilot based in Connecticut. This is his story.

I have been giving rides for 32 years, and I love it. For many people, a balloon ride is their life-long dream, and I love to see happy expressions. I get to meet a lot of people.

I can take six people up at a time. I sometimes go to balloon festivals where there might be a hundred balloons. I am also hired to do promotions. With promotions, either we put a banner on the balloon and have people observe it during rush hour, or the balloon will be tethered near the store or event. I also get hired to give rides at events, parties, and annual outings. In these situations, we give tether rides that last for just a few minutes.

When we give full rides, we charge $225 per person. Between 30–40% of groups (which consist of a couple or a family) will give a tip. The average tip is between $20 and $100. The tips are equally split with my crew. The crew helps to tether the balloon, chase the balloon, and bring it back when it has landed.

About half the people who hire me for a party will give a tip. I charge $2,000 for parties and events, and the tips range between $100 and $300. Individuals who go up in the five-minute tether ride rarely provide a tip.

Men are the ones who usually give the tips. There are few teens or children who go up in the balloons. After the rides, I give everyone a flight certificate, and we have a champagne toast. If people are going to give a tip, they usually do so at this time. If someone refers an event to me, I usually give them 10% of the total proceeds as a referral fee.

$ $ $

Rachael is a naturalist on a wildlife watching boat in Alaska. This is her story.

Out of season, I am a substitute teacher. I would like to teach full-time, but times are hard right now; and there are not many openings. It is also very hard to live up here because of the cost of living.

I tell people what they see. I have been doing this for the last four months, and I love it. I love the outdoors. I love boats, and I love Alaska. It is the perfect job for me. It is much better than working in a store. The people I work for are great. They are family owned and keep a very safe boat.

Each tour takes about three hours. I put in another couple of hours getting the boat ready and later cleaning it. I am paid a little above minimum wage. There are typically 30–100 people on a tour with the average being 80. Almost all passengers come from the cruise ships.

We used to be able to ask people for tips, but that is not allowed anymore as it is deemed to be unprofessional. We do have a quart-size jar in which people can leave tips. Today, with 100 people on the boat, only $1 was put into the tip jar. In a typical week, I get $10 in tips. All tips are shared equally, and if someone hands me a tip, I put it into the jar.

I don't know why people tip so poorly. The tours are expensive. People buy t-shirts and burgers, so perhaps they don't have much money left over. I was told by some other people on our boat that the crews of the cruise boats discourage passengers from giving tips to us by saying that they don't have to tip us. The story is that if they tip us less, then more tips will be given to the crew of the cruise boat.

People from Australia and England are bad tippers. People from the high-end cruise ships tip more. Sometimes a person will make a prominent point of tipping, and that encourages other people to tip.

$ $ $

Shona is a tour guide at the Motown Historic Museum in Detroit, Michigan. She is a high school senior and has been working at the museum for 13 months. The following narrative details Shona's story in her own words.

I love working at the museum. I am a real fan of Motown. I get to talk about music all day.

I do five to ten tours on a Saturday over nine hours. During the week when I'm working it is slower, and I do two–three tours in four–five hours. Tour guides are paid between $6.50 and $8.00 an hour.

About 20% of the people will tip me. My average tip is $5. The biggest tip I ever got was $20. When I got that I said, yes! On my biggest Saturday I got $85. I average $60 on Saturdays and $20–$30 on weekdays. I get the tips at the end of a tour. People don't know they are allowed to tip. Sometimes when they see one person give a tip, others will follow. Once an older woman said very loudly, "Oh, can you take tips?" When I said yes, a lot of people in the tour tipped. I could have kissed her. I wish they had a sign saying that tips are allowed.

Teachers tip the most. They are very thankful that you are taking care of their kids. Teenagers tip the least.

Tipping is a wonderful thing.

I don't tip when I go to museums. If I had the money I would, but I'm a teenager.

$ $ $

Larry is a beach boy at a popular resort on the Delmarva Peninsula. This is what he had to say about receiving tips.

I've been doing this for 28 years. I rent out umbrellas and chairs. A chair goes for $5 a day, and an umbrella for $10. I bring the umbrella and chair to where they want to go and set them up.

I like my job. I am a teacher during the rest of the year, and this really helps supplement my income. I am outside, which I like. People are happy while they are on vacation, and I make good money. It got me through college, and my three kids get to live better.

I have 150–200 customers per day. It is a long day—ten hours. I make minimum wage. Ninety-five percent of the people will tip me. The average is $2–$3. Some will tip me $20 at the beginning or end of the week. I get around $200 per day in tips. I do much better than the other beach boys because I am opposite a fancy hotel, and my beach area is usually crowded. My best day ever was this Fourth of July. I got $500 in tips. My biggest tip ever was $100 for two umbrellas.

You never know who will give better tips. Some of the racial stereotypes are somewhat correct. Some foreigners and blacks will tip less. However, many will tip as much as other people. The amount of equipment has some effect but much smaller than you would think. Today, one person had one umbrella for $10 and gave me a $10 tip. Another person had four umbrellas and six chairs, and I got $3.

I also get a bonus at the end of the summer. I help the owner hire other beach boys and do the scheduling. My bonus is around $1,500, and it is not clear how that is determined. The boss takes care of me.

$ $ $

Vladamir is also a beach boy in the same town as Larry. He worked about a mile from the beach where Larry worked. The beach where Vladamir worked was far less crowded. He is from Russia, but his English is impeccable. He is also very personable. This is Vladamir's story.

I am from Russia and have been here for two months. I am in college in Russia. The job is nice because everyone is so relaxed. I get $6.15 an hour. I average putting out 30 umbrellas a day. The average tip is $2–$3. Eighty percent of people will tip me. On a busy day, I will make $50–$60 in tips. Today was slow. I only put out four umbrellas and got $11 in tips.

The better tippers are between the ages of 30 and 40. Mexicans and blacks don't tip very well.

It makes very little difference on how many umbrellas or chairs I put out. One guy yesterday gave me a $10 tip for a $10 umbrella. And for another guy, I put out four umbrellas and got $5.

I like the United States. Prices are strange. Bread costs three times what I pay in Russia, and cigarettes are very, very expensive. Electronic goods are cheap.

$ $ $

The narratives of those who provide family entertainment reflect a tremendous variety with respect to the kind of entertainment. However, there are a few patterns that emerge. Variation in base pay is one pattern that the stories told by family entertainers reveal. Most of those who provide family entertainment make at least minimum wage; although it appears that at least some positions on cruise lines pay below minimum wage. Some of the narratives indicate that a number of family entertainers make a base pay that is significantly more than minimum wage. The variation in salaries and wages before tips is unpredictable and not usually known by the customers. Customers are not likely to have much knowledge of the extent to which these workers rely on tips. In many cases, the tipping norms are reinforced by structural norms that inform the customers regarding the specific tipping standards. Some businesses post signs, allow entertainers to wear buttons requesting tips, or provide written materials that explain the standard tips for various workers. Yet, there are also a fair number of instances in which the customary practice remains unclear.

A few of the stories also indicate that people tend to follow the norms when they are explicitly discussed. For example, more people are described as likely to tip if at least one customer asks publicly about the custom. People are also described as more likely to follow the norm when the structural rules are made explicit in the form of signs, brochures, and other forms of information provided by the agency.

The stories told by the family entertainers interviewed seem to suggest that there is not a common pattern with respect to how those who receive tips interpret how or why they are tipped in the amount that they are tipped or why they may not be tipped. Tipping does not appear to be a clear signal with much potential to even affect quality. Some of the respondents explained the tipping behavior of their customers to be a function of the knowledge of the tipping norms. Others concluded that certain customer characteristics explain differences in tipping. None of the respondents reported any variation at all in their performance. Although some described the tip as an "appreciation" of their work, there was no explanation as to how the quality affected the tip or vice versa.

21

Adult Entertainment

Recently, adult entertainment has grown in popularity in the United States to the extent that adult entertainment is in many ways a dominant feature of American culture (Liepe-Levinson 2002). Adult entertainment is a broad term that includes work in casinos, cabaret, and sex work such as prostitution and exotic dance. In other words, entertainment that is exclusively for those old enough to consent and inappropriate for children.

Gambling is an industry that is rigidly regulated in most jurisdictions, and children are not allowed in casinos or on the gaming floor of any casino. Consequently, it is included in the analysis of adult entertainment. Casinos employ a huge variety of workers many of whom may receive tips, including but not limited to cashiers, bartenders, waiters and waitresses, roulette croupiers, blackjack dealers, valets, and so on. Generally, those in management positions within the casino are not tipped and do not share in the tip distribution system. Sex workers are not supposed to be employed by casinos, but it is commonly understood that sex workers may tip out casino workers to "work" the casino.

It is very difficult to estimate the number of sex workers in the United States. The narratives included in this analysis reflect a sample of sex workers over the age of 18. Weitzer (2005) reports that there are over 2,500 strip clubs in the United States and that 18% of American men said that at some point in their lives they had sex with a prostitute. He also points out that there are many different types of sex workers (prostitutes, strippers, phone sex operators, lap dancers, etc.), and analyses that lump them all together are not likely to describe the contextual and structural differences in the work experiences with a great deal of precision. One of the fundamental distinctions between the types of sex workers has to do with the extent to which there is agency or the freedom of the worker to enter into, exit, and negotiate their contract and work conditions. The degree of agency may also affect the tipping norms. Another distinction that Weitzer (2009) focuses on that might affect tipping is whether the sex work is indoor or street.

Tipping practices vary considerably across the numerous types of sex work, and the experiences of the sex workers who receive tips is often conditioned upon the processual orders (see, e.g.; Maines 2003; Bradley-Engen and Ulmer 2009) and structural organization (see, e.g.; Frank 2002; Chapkis 1997) of the work environment. Strauss (1993) outlines the processual orders[1] that affect tipping practices refer to the interaction of the following: (1) the practical, logistic organization of work; (2) the formal and informal norms associated with a work activity; and (3) the sentiment or emotions experienced during the interpersonal interactions between the participants. For example, the tips that a dancer at a club receives might be impacted by the interaction of the layout of the club which affects the flow of customers and workers throughout the club, the norms associated with tip outs to the DJ who determines access to the dance floor, and dancer's ability to "connect with" or "hustle" a customer. The formal rules and structure of the organization also regulate the tipping customs. For example, the business policies determine whether or not a prostitute in a legal brothel splits all the proceeds, including tips, with the house or if the tips belong exclusively to the prostitute.

There are some ways in which a cabaret performance may in some instances resemble an exotic dance or burlesque routine, but cabaret shows are considered a display of art and skill in cosmetics and entertainment. They do not strip, but revealing clothes are one way to demonstrate the skill of the performer at portraying a woman. It is the illusion of gender and allusion to sex that are considered the art of entertainment in this case. Cabaret performers are not sex workers. Although some cabaret performers may also do sex work, this could be true of virtually any job category. In fact, it was recently discovered that a professor at the University of Maryland was working for an escort service. In any case, it is the allusion to sex, the controversy over the manipulation of gender, and the "alternative lifestyle" that is represented that make it entertainment for adults.

$ $ $

Marissa has worked in casinos in Connecticut for 12 years. This is her story.

I do craps, roulette, blackjack, baccarat, and other "Asian" games (games that Asians play a lot). I do all the tables except for poker. It's a job. It pays the bills. It is not exciting anymore.

I get paid $6.50 an hour. At the craps tables, 45% will tip regardless of whether or not they win. The others will tip only if they win. Ninety percent of the tips come from people betting for you. If they bet $15 for themselves, they will put $1 down for you. If they are betting $50–$100, they will put $5 down for you. Ten percent will give you money.

People tip the most at craps and blackjack. You get the least at baccarat. You could go a whole night at baccarat, which is an Asian game, and not get a tip. People who play roulette don't tip as well as blackjack because the game is pure luck. People who know you tip more. People who are out to have fun tip the most. If people are trying to pay their bills, or they take the game too seriously, they don't tip very well. They will bang on the table and take the game personally.

In an eight-hour shift, I probably get $100 or $200 in tips. If you are dealing high-roller tables, you can sometimes get $100 here or $100 there.

All tips, without exception, are pooled. They are divided according to the number of hours worked. I average $12–$13 an hour in tips. My biggest tip was $500, but it made no difference because of the pooling. If you got a $10,000 tip you would probably see $1 of it. It is all cut-and-dry. Because you are not keeping your tips, it is not exciting. I think this is OK. Some nights you are playing baccarat and see no tips. It is fair that everything is split.

$ $ $

Rhoda is a blackjack dealer at a casino in Connecticut. The following narrative details her experiences receiving tips for this work.

I've been a dealer for high-stakes games for eight or nine years. I don't always like my job. Customers can be verbally abusive. I try to tune them out. The more money they have the more abusive they are.

I get a base salary of $6 an hour. I also get a toke rate. [The toke rate refers to the individual share of the tips divided among the staff.]

I average $14 an hour from the tips. All tips are placed in the toke and the entire shift shares them on a weekly basis pro-rated according to the number of hours that you work. We take no individual tips. Each week differs. Last week the toke rate was $17 per hour. Of course, I was on vacation!

I deal high stakes. The minimum bet is $200, and the average is between $200 and $1,000. I probably average $5 to $25 in tips per hand. There are three ways that I am given tips:

1. I get occasional tips throughout the person's play. If they win a hand, I am sometimes given a tip.
2. I get tips at the end of the person's session.
3. They often play a hand for me. It is not unusual for someone to play a $500 hand for me. If the hand wins, I win. If the hand loses, I get nothing.

People with the most money tip the most. However, sometimes a person will win $10,000 and give you a $5 tip.

Most of the time there is only one person at my table—sometimes two. High stakes players like to play by themselves. They have a lot of say on whom they will use as a dealer. There is one guy who is about 40 years old who will bet $20,000 in three hands. He won't use me as a dealer because I am a woman. He also talks to other dealers on how he doesn't like blacks. I am black.

Asians don't often tip but are not afraid to bet heavy. Young white males between 25 and 40 tip the most.

In a 40-hour week, I will deal for 20 people. Fifteen of them will give me a tip. The average tip is a couple of hundred dollars.

I don't feel resentment at dealers from the small stakes tables who are putting smaller tips into the common kitty. We really all put in the same. I get 15 tips a week, and they get many tips of $2.50 or $5 that mount up.

The waitresses here keep their own tips. One man tipped a guy waiter $10,000 for a drink! He got to keep it. On another day, this man lost $180,000. He is rude and chooses his own dealers.

I don't gamble myself. I see what it does to people.

$ $ $

Daniel worked as a cashier at a casino in Missouri for 18 months. The following narrative details Daniel's responses to questions about receiving tips for his work.

The job was just OK. There was one supervisor I did not like. In addition, it was very stressful when you counted down your balance. You started with $75,000 in cash, coins, and chips. A few times a month I did not balance. Once, I was off by $100 that could not be recovered, and I got a big lecture. Usually when

I was off balance, the money would be found in the bank deposit. I was once off by $2,000, but it was found.

I was paid $8 an hour. Five percent of regular players would tip me, and the average tip was $20. Among diamond players, 15–20% would give a tip, and the average tip was $50. When we got a tip, we would yell out "toke" and put the tip in a special container. This was split among all the cashiers when we got our paycheck. The average amount added to our paycheck was $20–$30.

People were more likely to tip if they won and if they were diamond players.

$ $ $

Deon is a cabaret performer in San Francisco. This is Deon's story.

I dress as a woman and lip sync songs at clubs. It is a hobby. I started doing it as a lark. I perform four or five times a year. I used to perform six or seven times a year, but since I adopted two kids, I have less time. I am pretty busy. My full-time job is working for a health care company as a project manager related to IT.

I get a cut of the door (usually around $50), and I get tips. If I am co-hosting the event, I get a bigger cut. During the number, people walk up to the stage to give me a tip, and I also walk among the people on the floor. About 50–70% will give me a tip. I am six feet tall and even taller in my high heels. People rarely put money in my clothes. They usually hand it to me. Sometimes a person might put it in his mouth, and I use my mouth to retrieve it.

The average tip is $2 to $3. People often give a single dollar or a five. On a good night, I get $60–$70 in tips. On a bad night, it might be $8–$10. I usually have good nights.

There is little difference on who tips. I lip sync traditional soul songs. People who recognize the song are more likely to tip, and those who come back for repeat performances are more likely to tip.

Eighty percent of the people in the audience are men. I perform in bar settings a lot and at charitable functions. Liquor is served at a bar but not at the charity functions. We usually don't share our tips. Drag queens[2] are not particularly honest. There are usually six or seven drag queens in a show.

It takes a couple of hours to get the makeup on and the costume right. I also pay a lot for the costumes and the makeup. I make no bones that I am there to make money. I will walk up to tables and put out my hand. I often work this into a number. Most people are pretty respectful. There is an informal agreement that I am there to perform, and you are there to give me money.

$ $ $

Rachael has been working as a legal prostitute in Nevada for the past year. This is her story.

I love this job because the money is real good. I am an independent contractor. I set my own prices as well as the dos and don'ts. I get checked every Thursday for STDs and once a month for HIV. We have ways to summon the sheriff quickly in case of a problem with a customer.

If the customer does not ask for someone by name, the brothel has a line-up where he picks the prostitute of his choice. We go up to the room and negotiate, usually over a cocktail. He tells me what he wants to do, and I tell him the price. Sometimes we haggle. Sometimes the date occurs outside of the brothel.

Prices really vary. They can range from $100 to $50,000. It depends on the guy, the gal, and what he wants to do. Typically, I charge $300 at the low end. I split half with the house. I also split the tips with the house and also pay them $20 a day for room and board. We have a full kitchen, but I pay for alcohol.

Half the customers give a tip. The average tip is $50. If I give a great time and make the person feel welcome, I get a bigger tip. My biggest tip was $700 on a date for which I charged $2,500. This date included champagne, use of the VIP room, and a massage. Married men are the most generous with tips.

Thirty percent of parties don't want sex. These people just want to hang out. A lot of guys are shy and don't know how to relate to women. They just want to relax and talk.

I am one of the few African-Americans in the house. I fulfill a lot of fantasies, and people pay for them. Twenty percent of my customers are married couples, and the tips can be real good when the wife is present. I also have a few lesbian clients.

Weekends are busier than weekdays. Seventy percent of my customers pay with a credit card, and the rest pay with cash. On an average night, after splitting with the house, I make between $500 and $2,000. About 25% of this is from tips. Most of us make over $100,000 a year.

$ $ $

Carolyn has been a stripper at a nightclub in Washington, D.C. for the past three months. She also provided some information about her work outside of the club as an escort. This is what Carolyn had to say about receiving tips for her work in adult entertainment.

I like what I do. I am an exhibitionist. I like to attract attention, and I like to dance. I work four nights a week at the club. I work 10–20 minutes every hour and usually work an eight-hour shift. There are eight to ten other dancers. I get paid $2.79 per hour. The club I work at has mostly Spanish girls. It has more of a working-class clientele. We don't have poles like the richer clubs. We just dance.

The audience can range from 10 people to 150 people. The fewer the people the more people tip. If it is not very full, 80% will tip. If it is a full house—40% will tip. The average tip is $1. Some people bring the tips to the stage, but most of the tips come from my walking around after my number. I do eight shifts in eight hours and probably get $30–$40 per shift. In a good night, I will make $500, and on a bad night, I will make $250. Most of the tips are put in my garter, and some of the tips are handed to me.

Part of this tipping also comes from me sitting with the customers as they buy me a drink. I negotiate the price in advance, but it is usually $20 for half an hour. About 30% of my tips come from this.

The people who tip the most are blacks and Latinos. They like big asses, and I have a big ass. Whites like skinny girls. Whites are more courteous.

I tip out every bartender and door person $1 per hour. On a Saturday night, the total is $25–$31. I give them the tip out directly.

I also get a commission on drinks that people buy when I am sitting with them. They get charged $17 a drink, and I get paid $4 per drink. I typically get ten drinks a night.

We are trying to extract as much from the customer as we can by using every trick in the book—within reason.

Some of the customers are schmucks. There are a few that only one or two girls will sit with. They are obnoxious and want to put their arm around you. They are boring and cannot hold an intelligent conversation.

There are very few women who come to the club. If they come with a guy the tips are OK. If they come alone or with another woman the tips are lousy. Lesbians don't tip well.

I have done some escort servicing—not much. I have not needed to expand my business much besides working the club.

The customer pays the escort service $200–$250 per hour. I keep 50% of that or with a better service I can keep 60%. I get to keep my tips. About 20% will give me a tip without being asked. My biggest tip was $400. A guy was just nice. I am trying to get as much out of the person as I can. If they want something besides normal intercourse [vaginal sex], I negotiate the additional price in advance. I get extra for kissing on the mouth or blow jobs, etc.

I get better tips from men who know what they want and smaller tips from those who are lonely, looking for company.

I tip out my driver $30. The tip out to the driver comes from the girl and not the escort service.

$ $ $

Betty is an actress, contemporary dancer and choreographer, and exotic dancer. The following narrative details her experiences receiving tips for her work as an adult entertainer.

I consider myself to be an entertainer. I do soap operas, plays, TV shows, and choreography. Most of my income is from exotic dancing. I've been dancing since high school. My mom danced on Broadway, and I went to college on a dance scholarship. I was born to dance and to entertain.

For my acting I get a regular check from ABC or whoever. I don't have an agent. I now work at a strip club in New Jersey. There is a seating area around the dance floor. If you are seated you are almost required to tip the girl. I do your basic Gypsy Rose Lee[3] routine. The club is a full nude club. Because it's a full nude club, we cannot serve liquor although customers can bring their own.

If you are stripping during the day, you receive $25 from the club. Otherwise, you pay $50–$75 to the club as a house fee. I also give $20 or more to the DJ. I will give the DJ more if he is helpful to me. In New York City, the fees are more expensive. The DJs get $40 plus. The house mom also gets $15. She helps me get dressed. The bouncer/VIP hostess gets 10% of any activity in the champagne rooms and so on. You can make $2,000 a night but pay $1,000 in tip outs.

In my regular club in New Jersey, I do three songs. People give me tips while I am on stage. It is rare to get tips after the dance routine. The average tip is a dollar. A really good tip is a couple of dollars. Five dollars is great.

Most of my money is made in the lap dance room. I charge $20 per song. I basically dry hump the guy for three–four minutes. I have my bottoms on, and he can't touch me. On a good night, I will do 25 plus lap dances a night. Maybe 10–20% of the customers will tip me. The average tip is $5. Some will give me a dollar. One Jewish guy once gave me $60. I think he tipped me so much because we talked for a long time before I did my lap dance. I am also Jewish.

I will earn $500 or more on a good night. Eighty to ninety percent of this comes from the lap dances. If I am doing a lot of lap dances, the DJ won't call me for a routine. That is how he gets his extra tip.

The club has a door fee of $20. For $8, you can get as much fruit juice and water as you want. The club also makes money by taking credit cards and giving funny money in return. For that funny money, the guy can buy lap dances and give tips. The club keeps 20% of the funny money that I turn in. I mostly get cash. And, I tell guys to give me cash, so I don't lose the 20%.

Businessmen are the most generous. They have the most money.

I also do private bachelor parties. I charge $300–$400 to show up. There is also a lot of tipping. I do a lot of fun things. I am a gymnast and will do pushups and sit-ups. I will raffle tickets and those with the most tickets can use toys on me. I will shower with guys for five minutes, but they have to keep their boxers on. I can get another $300–$400 from tips and these other charges.

Recently, I've been doing more crazy stuff. I am more confident. Since 9/11, people have been spending less money in the clubs. They prefer private time. Some still come to the club because it is like a reality show. They can see and feel real flesh. The internet has really hurt us. I used to get $1,000 a night. Men can get their porn on the internet and watch girls live who have camcorders. The media has made stripping more mainstream. We see movies with strip clubs. You can learn exotic dancing [in exercise videos and classes], and "The Sopranos" on HBO have glorified strip clubs.

We play the customer. It is a job. I am very honest. I only work two nights a week and make money from acting. I am different than the normal dancer. For me, dancing is more of a profession than a job. I don't hustle the guys. A lot of girls talk shit but don't deliver. They will say, "Give me money and you can touch my boobs," but when they go back to the rooms, they won't let him. Some will do what they can to make a buck. The closest I come to dishonesty is if a guy gives me 30 bucks for a $20 lap dance. I will say thank you and act as if he gave me a tip.

$ $ $

Judy works at a strip club in West Virginia. Her boyfriend also participated in this interview. The following narrative reflects the story told by Judy and her boyfriend.

The job is OK. I enjoy dancing, but I just like the money. I would rather be a bartender. Some days, especially the weekends, are OK because of the money.

I usually work a seven-hour shift. I go on stage with several other girls and dance to two songs. I get tips in my garter when I dance. I average $10–$20 per session in this type of tip.

I then go off stage and do private dancing. The private dance is like a lap dance. Some girls get more into it than I do. I charge $30 for a private dance, and the club gets $10 of it. I also do table dancing which is just dancing in front of their tables. I charge $10 for this and keep the entire $10. Probably about 20% give more than what is charged.

We also have shower rooms where two dancers give each other a shower. We charge $100 and keep $65 of that. In the champagne room there is more private time, and we get a minimum of $150 for 30 minutes. The club keeps $75. You can charge more than $150 and keep everything over $75. Some of the girls are pretty raunchy. I am not. We are actually a pretty clean club. I give the club $10 for every night that I dance. I don't make any money from selling alcohol because I am 19 years old. I get $1 for every Red Bull that someone buys me, but how much Red Bull can you drink?

On a weekend night, I average $300–$500 from all these sources. On a weekday night, I average $100–$200.

I don't like the champagne room because even with a camera and a bouncer, too much could be going on. In addition, if I get called for my dance and am busy, I will lose out on $50 being on stage. Some girls like the champagne room and are happy to earn $75 every half hour.

I tip out the bartender $10 a night. The DJ gets $5 on a weekday night and $10 on a weekend night. The bouncers are good. If they break up an incident, I will give them $10 or $20. Remember, there are hundreds of drunken guys around naked women.

Drug dealers and those in flashy cars are more generous. Older men are also more generous. I'm only 19 years old.

The breakdown of my income is 50% from table and private dancing, 40% from tips given to me when I am dancing, and 10% from private time in the champagne or shower room.

A lot of the girls are not to be trusted. If you owe a girl $10 and give her $100 you are not likely to get your change back. There are a lot of single moms and others who have problems who will do whatever they can to make a buck. There is a lot of twisted stuff going on in strip clubs. Most of the girls at our club won't go home with guys, as there is more money to be made from being in the club.

$ $ $

Sherry worked for an escort service in the Washington, D.C. area for three months. This is her story.

I did not "grow into" the job. I did not like the clientele. I had little choice about who my clients were. I was by myself and did not trust their response or why they wanted me. Some had prostitution in mind, and that is not what I did.

I had an agent who was an older lady. Customers would call her, and she would try to fix them up according to preferences based upon age, race, and other characteristics. I was one of the few minorities who worked for her. She would tell them the rate as well as what was expected, and she would call me. I would call the gentleman and find out what he wanted. My phone number was blocked as I did not want them to know how to contact me.

I charged between $120 and $250 per hour. There was a slight discount for more than one hour. When I first met them, the first thing I did was ask to see their driver's license, and I would phone this information to my agent. This is how I had some protection. Next, I received the payment, which was usually in cash but it could also be placed on a credit card. I would hide the money, so he would not know where it was. We then talked about plans for the evening. Twenty percent of the time we went to events, 20% to dinner, and 60% of the time we would go to his home or hotel room just to talk.

My agent would get half of the agreed upon price. If I stayed for extra hours, I kept 75% of the fee from the extra hours.

If he wanted sexual pleasure, I would say no and leave without returning the fee. My agent was supposed to tell him in advance that I was not a prostitute. However, she wanted me to get solicited, so I would leave with the money and could then go to another appointment. I did not trust her. She purposely did not tell them that I would leave if they asked for a sexual favor.

I was sometimes offered large sums for sexual favors. One guy offered me $1,000 if I would just take off my clothes while he masturbated. I knew not to do this.

I received a gratuity almost every time I was with someone. The average gratuity was $100. Most people I met had money. A few were scumbags who had a temporary source of money and were splurging for the weekend. A typical date was a general manager of a hotel in the Midwest who was in town and wanted to have someone to go to dinner with him.

I got scared a few times. One person was using a lot of cocaine and another person showed up with his friend. I did not trust my agent. I got frustrated with her screening process. I knew if I stayed in this job, I would eventually get into trouble. I now work for the Air Force.

$ $ $

The narratives of those in the various forms of adult entertainment sampled here perhaps reveal more differences than similarities. These differences reflect the diversity of the jobs that are included in the category of adult entertainment. The divergence in experiential evidence also likely reflects the processual and structural differences of the work environments, even within similar job categories. Future research may examine the interaction effects both within and across the job categories in sex work in particular and adult entertainment broadly.

While the interaction effects are difficult to capture through a single lens, these interviews do provide an understanding of varied experiences of tipped adult entertainers. The stories shared by the respondents demonstrate the ways in which the work environment contextualizes the experiences of the workers. At least from the perspective of the adult entertainers, the pragmatics of the workplace, the formal and informal norms, and the interpersonal relationships between the participants all impact the tipping practices as well as the structure of the organization. The effect of the organizational structure can be seen in examples of the formal organizational structure such as the tipping distribution system described by the casino workers and vary in accordance with informal organizational structures. For example, some of the narratives describe how tipping practices vary according to the location of the entertainment for practical reasons, such as a seat up-front at a strip club where tipping is "almost required" or how there is a limit to the number of people who can come to the stage to tip. The formal and informal norms are evidenced by policies that determine the tip outs and the reports of the common practices of tipping out more to a bouncer for breaking up a fight or a DJ who mixes the dance order to maximize a dancer's tips. The interpersonal relationships among the participants were described by many of the respondents. Perhaps the most memorable was the description of one of the escorts whose narrative revealed a considerable degree of mistrust of the clients and her agent, which affected her tips as well as her overall work experience. The narratives also make clear how the interaction of these factors regulate tipping norms.

Several of the narratives show how adult entertainers perceive their tips as a function of the complex interplay of the way they work the room, the formal and informal norms, and their relationships with other workers, clients, and management. For example, a cabaret performer describes how he regularly moves around the room to give people an opportunity to tip him. He "is there to make money, and you are there to give me money." He also reports that tips are not shared because according to Deon, "Drag queens are not particularly honest." Interestingly, this sort of distinguishing oneself from the competition is intrinsic to the industry. Describing one's own striptease as a burlesque show while talking about how other performers "play" clients or will "do anything to make a buck," is a marketing technique designed to generate social distance from other performers to establish value.

It is also interesting to note the extent to which race pervades the adult entertainment industry. Some of the escorts describe how agents determine the preferences of customers in terms of "age, race, and other characteristics." Some of the dancers describe the preferences of customers in terms of racial stereotypes. According to a dancer who is a black woman, "Blacks and Latinos like big asses" and "Whites like skinny girls." A prostitute in a legal brothel describes how being a black woman affects her business in that she "fulfills a lot of fantasies." Casino workers talk about how wealthy clients in particular would express their racial prejudices by excluding some dealers because of the race of the dealer. Again, people learn the values and attitudes of their identities as they interact with others. The strategies that people use to manage their emotional labor and to deal with the undercurrent of interpersonal conflict inherent in an unequal social structure are costly, and those who are required to do more emotional labor are likely to be undervalued and overburdened with emotional labor (see also, Hochschild 1983). These daily confrontations and the emotional work required to maintain civility reflect the payment and nonpayment of dues, and these debts fuel resistance (Kelley 1994).

Perhaps the only factor more prevalent than race in these narratives is gender. Although, the interpretation of the role gender plays in the experiences with the tipping norms in adult entertainment are not necessarily straightforward. When gender is considered independent from sex,[4] it is clear the women represent the majority of labor in adult entertainment; although they are not necessarily represented in large numbers in the management positions or positions of authority (see also, Farr 2004). There is also an implicit pattern whereby the women of the female sex may be less likely to receive tips when they do not behave in accordance with gender expectations. Future research may attempt to explore the experiences of males (perhaps with gender variations) in adult entertainment from both the customer and worker perspectives to better understand these gendered experiences.

NOTES

1. Processual orders refer to a perspective for making sense of an organization by modeling the social construction of status and control through a series of interactions. Dawson (2003) provides a useful description of the approach.

2. It is important to note that among cabaret performers and those who are a part of the gay community (even straight people) may refer to a cabaret performance as a "drag show" or a performer as a "drag queen" in an endearing manner that attempts to undermine the offensive nature of the reference. However, the words drag, queen, drag show, and drag queen are considered derogatory in most instances.

3. This is a reference to a famous American burlesque entertainer who was famous for her sometimes humorous, exaggerated striptease. In contemporary nomenclature, using the word burlesque to describe a striptease is a mechanism for defining the entertainment in a manner that affords greater dignity for the entertainer.

4. Sex is a biological term that denotes a chromosomal difference between males and females. Gender is a sociological term that attempts to reflect the norms and standards associated with being considered a woman or a man.

22

Musicians

The Census Bureau reports that there are 50,450 musicians, singers, and related workers in the United States earning an average of $43,000 per year. The musicians included in this sample work in bars and restaurants, perform on the streets, play at private parties and weddings, and provide music lessons. The experiences reported by the respondents included in this study imply that there may be a bimodal distribution affecting the average income of musicians counted in the Census; a few musicians with very high incomes and those with fairly low incomes. Obviously, this claim cannot be substantiated with the type of analysis in this study. However, it is evident that many of the musicians in our sample are not able to support themselves through musical performances alone.

In 2007, the Washington Post had Joshua Bell anonymously playing his multi-million dollar Stadivarius violin outside of a Metro stop in Washington, D.C. Over the course of 43 minutes, 1,097 people passed by. He received $32.17 in donations, and only one person recognized him. Her $20 donation is not counted in the $32.17.[1]

Most Americans have seen musicians who request tips with a tip jar in a bar or an open guitar case on the street; although they may not recognize their fame or talent. How many of us though have considered the extent to which musicians rely on tips. The tipping norms in the music business vary by venue and type of music, and conformity to the norms appears to be inversely related to the size of the crowd and the number of musicians. There are also a number of aspects of tipping musicians that seem vague. Are musicians who play in a bar, restaurant, or coffee house who have a tip jar also compensated by the owner? Do people tip when there is a cover charge? Is the tip an incentive, a form of appreciation, or a display of wealth and status?

$ $ $

Nolan plays piano and sings at a restaurant and bar in a beach resort on the Delmarva Peninsula. This is Nolan's story.

I play Broadway, old songs, news songs, jazz—everything but rap. I am paid $200 for a four hour shift. I've been working at this bar for a year and a half. On a really busy night, the manager might sometimes give me an extra $50 or $100.

About 25% of those who listen to me will leave a tip in the "big old tip jar." The average tip is $5. I get $115 a night during the off-season and $300 a night during the summer. I hope that 50% of my income comes from tips.

My biggest tip was $500. I do well because I am liked by dirty old men. Seriously, I am good at what I do. There is one guy who gives me $100 every time he comes in. I told him that was not necessary. He said you are very good at what you do, and I have a lot of money.

Sometimes the busiest nights are the worst for tips. It is too crowded and people cannot maneuver to the tip jar.

I do not share my tips.

I get the most tips from the regulars. They feel guilty if they don't tip. There is no cover. One guy once gave me 18 cents. I sometimes think I am a jukebox. You got two hours of music for 18 cents you asshole.

Demographically, there is no correct stereotype. It is said that Jews and lesbians don't tip very well. I don't find that.

I do occasional private parties. I charge $100 an hour. I am not expecting a tip, but 75% of the time they will add $50 or $100. If I don't get the tip, I don't feel bad. After all, I'm getting $100 an hour!

I sometimes play charity events for free. I am still usually tipped even though I asked not to receive pay. They probably feel guilty taking my time for free. I say no money but still get $50 or $100 in an envelope.

Once when I was in New York City, the bartender at a club had a huge cowbell that he rang every 30 minutes and said "time to tip the piano player." He then passed around the tip jar. The performer got $500 that night.

$ $ $

Raymond has been playing piano in Nevada for 21 years. His story is detailed in the following narrative.

I play in high-end hotels and resorts as well as at weddings and private parties. I play easy listening music—Gershwin, Broadway, New Age. I am the luckiest guy that I know. I play music and make a living with it.

I've been playing in the bar-restaurant of this high-end hotel for 20 years. They pay me $250–$350 a night for a four-hour shift. I have a tip jar and also sell CDs. In a typical night, five–ten people will give me a tip or buy a CD. The tips range from $1 to $5, a lot of $10s, and an occasional $20. I get $50–$100 a night in tips.

I get more from romantic-kissy couples. I know what songs they want me to play. Teachers and educators are the worst. They make a lot of requests and give no tips. I charge $250 an hour for private parties and weddings, and I have a two hour minimum. About half of my clients will give me a gratuity. The more affluent people understand that they should kick in an additional 20%. If I am there for three hours, I will get $750 plus $100 or $200. If they are really thankful and sincere, that overshadows any tip. However, the tips are delightful.

There is one very generous couple that I play for on New Years Eve. I charge triple because it is New Years, and there is a lot of demand. They pay me $750 an hour and give $500 or so in tips. They always say they can't do New Year's without me. Most people with hyper wealth are very generous and very nice.

I also play at an exclusive resort in Squaw Creek. This is in the hotel lobby. I am happy when people fall asleep listening to me after skiing. That means they are really relaxing. I get paid $250 a night. Tips are more variable. I might get $150 in tips one night and zero the next night. Younger people are more generous here. There are a lot of yuppies from the Bay area. People from the South are very generous. They like their vacations.

I also play at Catholic Mass on Sunday morning. I did not know I was supposed to be paid. I eventually told them to stop paying me, but if they wanted me, they would have to spend a couple of hundred thousand dollars on state-of-the-art sound equipment.[2]

Really savvy restaurant diners know to pay the bill with credit cards and to pay their tips in cash. Servers only have to declare 7% of their sales as tips for the IRS. I don't declare my tips.

I do well because I don't show up late, drink liquor on the job, or smoke. I am polite to everyone.

$ $ $

Todd is a singer-songwriter based in Washington, D.C. This is what he had to say about receiving tips for his work as a musician.

About a third of the shows that I do are tips only. This might be in bars or coffee houses. We (I have a partner) also sell CDs and t-shirts.

Every night is different. If a bucket is passed, about 75% of people will put something in it. With a tip jar or open guitar case, it might only be 10%. Most people put in paper bills. We don't often get change. Most people will put in a dollar or two. Sometimes someone will put in $5 or $10. The last two times I passed the bucket I got $11 and $60, respectively. I usually get $15 to $40 from the tip jar. I've never gotten over $100.

We also sell t-shirts and CDs. The t-shirts cost us $5 and we sell them for $15. The CDs cost us $2 and we sell them for $10. One night last week, we sold $350 in merchandise. On another night, we sold two CDs and one t-shirt. It really depends.

When I play with a band, we require a cover.

My partner likes the tip jars and passing the bucket. I don't like it. I'm a capitalist. I want to get paid for my work.

When we play at bars with guarantees (usually for $200) they are usually very smoky and loud. People also want to hear songs written by other people – songs that they know. They don't want to hear much of our own music.

When we go on tour, we usually do two–three shows on the way to a well-paying show. Each of the intermediate shows are for tips and don't pay well. When we get to the college show, we might get $400.

We also do house concerts. People invite us to their houses, and they invite 15 or so friends and provide food. They have a suggested donation of say—$10. It really varies. The last one was a bust when only eight people showed up. The food was good though. We also sold $40–$50 in CDs.

$ $ $

Reed plays in two different bands in the Baltimore area. He also acts as the manager for both bands. Reed shared the following story.

One of the bands is a rock-n-roll band, and the other is Caribbean. It is great work. I wish I could make enough money. I have to substitute teach. That is a lot like babysitting. I'm trying to bring some music education programs into the school system.

We do club gigs, private parties, and concerts. A club gig is working at a bar or restaurant. For a fancy restaurant, they usually pay us $800 for four hours. If we don't eat too much, they will pick up dinner. We don't leave a bucket out for these gigs and don't get many tips.

For weddings and private parties, we usually try to get $3,000. At the last wedding, I was given a couple hundred as a tip. I only split it with the drummer because we did all the set-up. About 25% of clients will give us extra as a tip. The average tip is a couple hundred dollars. Our biggest tip was $500. That was $100 for each of us. Occasionally, someone will ask for a special song and give us a tip for that. That does not happen often.

When I do the booking myself, I keep 15%. For lower paying jobs, we just split it up. We will often take the deposit and use it to fix the truck and for other expenses. If we use a booking agent, the agent keeps 15–20%. They will usually take a 50% deposit, and they take their commission from the deposit. We take the remainder at the event.

We don't promote our CDs at weddings. However, at public concerts we will sell our CDs for $10–$15. They cost us $2 to make.

I also play acoustic guitar at coffee houses. I used to put out a basket. I would get a couple of dollars. I've stopped putting out the bucket. I just love to play.

$ $ $

Bree both teaches and plays the cello in the D.C. area. She had this to say about receiving tips as a musician.

I love being a professional musician. There are three ways that I make money as a musician. My major source of income is teaching. I charge $40 for a 45 minute session. I have 23 students. I am always given the exact amount for these lessons, but around the holidays I get tips from about 15 of these students. I get either cash or gift cards. The amounts range from $20 to $50. I get a total of about $400 around the holidays.

I also play at private parties and weddings in three different quartets. We mostly do weddings. We charge $700 for two hours. We split the amount equally except if there was one person who did the booking. That person will usually take $50 before we split the rest.

About 25% of the time we get a tip. This is always in cash. It ranges from $25 to $100 extra per person. The average is $25–$30.

Those who are more opulent seem to give more. This seems to be true for both the lessons and the parties. We probably don't get as much tips at private parties. One perk is that we always get food.

I used to occasionally set up at parks or at the Metro with an open hat. I did this with one other person for a while at the Vienna Metro until they chased us away. We averaged $70–$80. We could go out and get a nice meal. Luckily, I don't have to do that anymore, but you never know.

$ $ $

Daryl used to be a full-time musician but currently characterizes himself as a semi-retired musician. He now works full-time as an occupational therapist and lives in the D.C. area. This is Daryl's story.

For the past ten years, I did a whole lot of weddings and private parties. We mostly played top 40 songs. I play sax and flute and prefer to play jazz. We were a 12-piece band, and we played almost every weekend.

Most people in the band received $300 per performance. The vocalist and the leader got $600. We charged around $5,000 to play. We rarely got tips. Less than 10% of clients tipped. We were too big to tip.

I also played in a jazz combo as either a trio or quartet. We would charge $400–$600 as a group. The leader who set it up would usually get an extra $25–$50. We would get tips maybe 20% of the time. The average tip was $20–$30 per person—sometimes $50.

We were more likely to get tips at private parties at someone's residence. We also were more likely to get a tip when we were contracted directly instead of going through an agency or caterer. This would make for a closer relationship. The smaller the event, the more likely we would get a tip.

The bigger the wedding or party, the less likely we were to get a tip. We would sort of get forgotten. If it was a sit-down dinner, we might not even get offered dinner.

[Daryl refused the $10 payment for participation.]

$ $ $

Collins has been playing and teaching jazz guitar for almost 50 years in the D.C. area. This is what Collins had to say about tips.

I love playing. It is a very spiritual thing to me. I tap into the artistic creative part of myself. My students feel it as well.

I play in restaurants, bars, concerts, private affairs, weddings, and dinner parties.

When I play at a restaurant or bar, I am paid between $50 and $150. I sometimes have an elaborate tip jar. It is a mesh pencil holder with a fan at the top made out of dollar bills: $1, $2, $3, $5, $10, a billion dollars. Some like looking at the fake bills. Five to twenty percent will put in a tip, and the average tip is a couple of bucks, sometimes $20. I keep records of all my tips. I average $20 a night in tips.

I don't know what type of people tip the most. I play solo or sometimes as a duo with a bass guitarist. We split the tips.

I charge $150–$300 to play private parties and weddings. Maybe 5% will pay extra. It is very surprising when they do, and it is usually $20 or $50 extra.

I once played for a movie opening at a fancy restaurant. They asked me to stay late, and many Greek musicians (the actor was Greek) played with me. They showered me with tips. I got $500 in tips that night. When they called me about the gig and asked me my price, they yelled at me and said, "I told you the name of the client and the name of the restaurant. You are charging too little. You jazz musicians are too stupid. The benefactor wants to support you. You got to charge more!" I doubled my quote.

I do concerts at the Kennedy Center and at the Corcoran. This can be solo or with a group. I get a union scale of $150 an hour, and there are no tips.

I have 17 students. My lessons are for two hours. I tell them the minimum charge is $40, but if they pay any more, it would be greatly appreciated. Some pay $50, $60, $80, and one pays $100. The average is $55. Those who are doctors and lawyers pay more. Only three–four pay the $40. For holidays, I got a total of maybe $500 in gift certificates and other gifts. I got a lot of personal gifts such as CDs.

$ $ $

Daniel has been playing classical guitar for many years in the Northeast. This is his story.

I am also a fireman. As a fireman, I refuse to take tips. My love is guitar. If I did not have a wife and kids, I would do it full-time. It is my retirement plan.

I sometimes go to Old Town Alexandria and play on street corners. The cops seem to know who is good and who is not. If you are bad, they will run you off. I have never been run off. I like playing on street corners. I get to practice. I get attention. I am appreciated, and I make some money. A dozen or so people will stop and listen. Some want to talk, but a few are quite rude.

I can leave with a couple of hundred dollars, and unlike playing in bars, I can repeat myself every 20 minutes. It is very ego-inflating. The amounts that people give me really vary. Sometimes I get a few cents. Once I got $50. The average is probably a buck. I don't know who gives the most because I am usually not paying attention.

There is sometimes competition. A flute player came up to me and asked when I was going to leave since this was his corner. I told him that there are four corners to the intersection. He tried to drown me out by revving up his amplifier. People were not happy with him.

One town close to where I live paid me $100 to play on the street corner. They wanted the town to look like Old Towne.

One restaurant where I sometimes play will guarantee me $50. The owner makes up the difference between my tips and $50. My usual minimum is $25 per hour. Watching me play is like watching someone knit. I am not very entertaining. The rednecks in the bar will ask for Lynrd Skynyrd. I will put out a tip jar if it is appropriate. Maybe half of the customers will put something in the jar. When I play at a coffee house, I get $15–$20 in the tip jar.

There is one restaurant that I play at where people look for me. I don't have a tip jar, but some people will come up and give me $20. I've gotten over $100 without the tip jar. People will shake hands to thank me and have the money in their fingers.

People want to pay the piper. The money is a token of esteem. It is nice to spend the money, and it is really nice to be appreciated.

[He refused the $10 payment for participation. Daniel said, "This one's on the house."]

$ $ $

Max and Irene have been married for many years. They live in Western Colorado, and play as a duo. Max plays guitar and banjo. Irene is also a facialist, and her experience receiving tips for her work in cosmetology is discussed elsewhere. The following narrative details the responses of Max and Irene regarding their experiences receiving tips for their work as musicians.

We play rock & roll, country, and jazz. A lot of what we play are our own songs. We play clubs, festivals, private parties, and weddings.

When we play at a club, we might play as a duo or with a band. On average, we get $100 per person.

If there is no cover, people expect to tip, and we will get a couple of hundred in the tip jar. About 60% of customers will put money in. If there is a cover, maybe 20% will put something in the tip jar, and the average is $30–$50.

We split the tips equally when we play with a band, and we don't know who is more likely to put money into the tip jar.

When we play festivals, the amount we get paid can really vary. Some festivals will pay us a hundred a person, and others will pay a couple of thousand. There are no tips at the festivals.

We get $200–$300 per person in the band for weddings and private parties. Fifty percent of the time we are given something extra. Usually, we get an extra $50 per person. Wealthy people are more likely to give us tips. We seem to get more when we play as a duo than with a band. It is probably easier to tip a duo. When we play in Aspen, we do well because it is part of their culture to tip well. Maybe it is just billionaires flaunting their wealth.

$ $ $

Aaron is a DJ. This is his story in his own words.

I love my job. I get a reaction from the crowd, and I am guided by the crowd. I get very good money. I mostly play clubs, and I get paid $300 for five hours of work. I play mostly hip-hop, R & B, Reggae, and Old-School such as Funk. People tip me for two reasons. Usually four–five people will make a request. About half will give me a dollar or two. I might get an extra $5 a night from requests. Usually older people will tip me. I also get tips for my performance. This really varies. A few people might give me $5 or $10. Every once in a while I will get a $20. I average $20–$30 a night from this type of tip.

I have also played a few engagement receptions. I get $300–$350 for these kinds of parties. They have always paid me the exact amount with nothing added.

$ $ $

The responses provided by the entertainers who receive tips for their musical talents reveal a few interesting trends. Most of the musicians report other sources of income, including selling merchandise during their performances. Several of the musicians provide musical lessons to supplement their incomes. Most of the tips reported for musical lessons came in the form of holiday gifts. However, there is a bit of variation. Some clients pay more than the quoted price for the lessons, but there is not much indication as to what might explain this variation.

For the most part, the musicians describe the tips as a form of appreciation rather than an incentive. Few of the musicians give much attention to who tips while they are playing. Most musicians may have some idea of the general crowd of people in a setting broadly, but they are concentrating on the music without much attention to the reward for their work. The tips do not seem to have any effect on the quality of the performance (at least according to the musicians' descriptions of the quality of their work). It is also interesting to note that wealthy people are perceived to tip more for "cultured" music.

Much like the experiences reported by strippers, musicians perceive fewer tips in bars when there are larger crowds. Also, band members receive fewer tips because they have to share them with more people, but it also seems as though people are less likely to tip when there are more band members. We didn't interview any "famous" musicians, but we did wonder about them. Has Bruce Springsteen ever received a tip since he became The Boss?

NOTES

1. See Gene Weingarten, "Pearls Before Breakfast," *The Washington Post Magazine*, April 8, 2007.

2. For an interesting analysis of the motivation of church organists, who appear to be more likely attracted by instrument quality rather than pay, refer to the following: Don J. Webber and Martin Freke. 2006. "Church Organists: Analyzing their Willingness to Play." *Journal of Socio-Economics* 35(5): 854–867.

23

Sports

Ski instructors are classified by the Census Bureau as lifeguards and other protective service workers. The 2000 Census reports 12,710 protective service workers, making an average of $28,000 annually. Golf and tennis pros fall under athletes, coaches, umpires, and related workers. There are 66,700 workers in this category, whose average annual earnings are estimated at $45,000. Fishing guides are classified as tour and travel guides. There are 9,900 tour and travel guides in the United States with earnings averaging an estimated $28,000 per year. Trainers fall within the category of recreation and fitness workers. There are an estimated 106,550 recreation and fitness workers earning on average $30,000 annually.

Sports instructors are another odd category as far as tipping is concerned. It is very unclear whether there is an expectation that the instructor is tipped by the customer and no clear standards regarding the tip amount if one is given. There are also differences in the expression of tipping norms across this context. Some of the variations include the number of people taking part in the sport or being instructed, the relative skill or difficulty of the job, social status, the type of interaction between the instructor and client(s), and the extent to which the client(s) are "entertained." There is also a degree of consistency across sports entertainment contexts. For example, tipping norms are predictably more likely to be followed when there is social pressure.

$ $ $

Martin has been teaching tennis at clubs in D.C. for 18 years. The following narrative details his experiences receiving tips for his work in sports entertainment.

I like it. I do it pretty well and get paid for it. I also run clubs. Seventy-five percent of running the club is administrative. I teach about 30 hours a week. A lot of the lessons are private, and a lot are group. I do both adults and kids. I charge $65 an hour for a private lesson, $25 each for groups of four, and $30 each for groups of three.

Members of the private club never pay more. They put their lesson on a chit, and I bill them twice a year. If the bill is for $1,023.87—they will write the check for the exact amount. An occasional non-member will give me extra. One guy who was very successful was billed $100 for his lesson but always gave $120. That was very rare.

I also taught tennis at Florida in resorts. They would pay inside the clubhouse and occasionally would come out and slip me $5 or $10. It was not very common—maybe one in twelve.

At the end of the season, the tennis teams will give me gifts: wine, tickets to the Redskins games, and gift certificates. Some people throughout the year would give an occasional bottle or wine or ticket to a sporting event. I was never given cash.

I have assistants who work under me. They might get more in tips. New assistants keep 50% of what they charge. Better assistants keep 70–75%. The rest all goes to me. I get a low salary from the club in return for getting all the proceeds from the tennis program.

At other clubs, the assistants keep 50% and 25% goes to the director and 25% to the club. At very big clubs, there is a $150,000 initiation fee for new members, and they will pay the director a bigger salary. He might get $120,000 in salary and $50,000–$70,000 of proceeds from the lessons. However, at smaller clubs that charge $3,000 to join, they can't pay the salary.

$ $ $

Arnold has been a golf pro for 15 years at a country club in the Washington, D.C. area. He was not particularly forthcoming during parts of the interview. The following narrative reflects Arnold's responses during the interview.

I am doing something I love; although the pay is not that great. I give lessons, manage the pro shop, oversee the driving range, do payroll, etc. I do not get any percentage from the pro shop. [He would not provide any details regarding his base salary.]

I give hour long lessons for which we charge $70–$80. We used to be able to keep 100% of that. However, they just reduced this down to 80% with the other 20% going to the country club. About half of the people will give me a tip. The average tip is $10. Someone once gave me a $1,500 tip. This is because he was able to do something very well after I taught him.

People are more likely to be generous when they are happy with their lesson. I used to do five lessons per day. I now only do five or so a week. I don't know why the number of lessons has decreased.

I also make money when I play tournaments.

[He refused the $10 payment for participation and requested that it be given to a charity.]

$ $ $

Becky has been a golf caddy in the Los Angeles area for several years. This is her story.

I love it. I love the game, and it is so much fun to be on the other side of the lines for tournaments.

When I play tournaments, I could not get paid because I want to maintain my amateur status. You cannot get paid as a caddy at major tournaments if you want to turn pro at some point. For those who are paid, they got 10–15% of what the person earns. I volunteer and receive tips. I did 12 or so tournaments—LPGA, PGA, and PGA seniors. Everyone tipped me. The average tip was $100 per day. Most of the volunteers worked one day out of a four day tournament. My biggest tip was $250 from someone I had caddied for before.

I also caddy at country clubs. I only carry one bag, and we go 18 holes. The people pay the pro shop, and I get paid $6.50 an hour. On average, it takes five hours to go 18 holes. Thirteen percent of people do not give me a tip. For those who give me a tip, the average tip is $50. My biggest tip was $80.

People tip better when they are playing really well. Serious golfers—those who get the early morning tee-time tip better. Those who play in the middle of the game and do a lot of goofing off do not tip well. Women are more likely than guys to use the golf carts. However, when they use a caddy, they do not tip well. People use a caddy when they want to walk or get advice.

There is no competition with the other caddies. We rotate. I've known the other caddies since I was seven. If someone needs money more than you do, you let them go ahead.

I also give informal lessons. This was when someone just wants advice. I've done this 60 or so times, and I do not charge. We do this over a bucket of balls. I only got tipped about 10–15% of the time, and the average tip is $20–$30.

I've caddied in a lot of intense conditions—116 degrees in the Arizona desert.

When you caddy you meet a lot of interesting people. I've met O.J. Simpson, Sylvester Stallone, and various deans at Harvard University.

[She would not accept the $10 payment for her participation.]

$ $ $

Thomas had a summer job as a caddy at a public golf course in Washington State. This is what Thomas had to say about his experiences receiving tips.

The job was awesome. I made my own schedule. I showed up when I wanted to. I was outside five hours a day, and I got good exercise by walking five–ten miles a day. I don't even play golf.

Although the course was public, it was expensive ($170 for green fees for 18 holes). They had no golf carts, and most people took their own clubs.

I was paid $35 per bag for 18 holes. Only occasionally did I double-up and take two bags. I went out once a day. The caddy master decided who would go out. It was a combination of seniority and how well you performed. Once they found out I did a good job, I went out all the time.

Everyone tipped. The average tip was double the $35. If you only got a $15 tip you would talk to the caddy master who would talk to the golfer. My biggest tip was $170. Old men tipped the best. People who drank also tipped a lot. Carrying several six-packs would be heavy. Old ladies would love to schmooze you, but they did not tip well.

Tournaments are the best. The typical tournament was sponsored by a local corporation or bank, and they would pre-pay the caddies $70. One day I received an extra $50, and the next time I received an extra $100.

If people carried their own bags, they might still tip you. Sometimes you would caddy for one person, and the other golfers would carry their own bags. If you raked for the other golfers and wiped down their golf balls, two-thirds would tip you $10–$20.

$ $ $

Leon works at a country club as a golf bag boy in upstate New York. He is a junior in high school, and this is his story.

This is my second year. I like it because I really like to play golf. I get paid $6.75 an hour. I clean golf clubs, carry bags, help clean up, and help out as a cashier. We don't charge for cleaning clubs, but about half the people will give you a tip. Most will give you a dollar or two. Every once in a while you might even get $10. On an average day, I get $15–$20 in tips.

Nicer people tip me the most. Old men tip well, and some women tip very well. Younger guys don't tip.

We don't have caddies. I did caddy once when I was asked to as a special favor. I charged $20 for nine holes, and I was given $40.

We don't work around the holidays, so I can't tell you about holiday tipping. We do very well around big tournaments. I will make $50 in two days. We have three or four bag boys during the tournaments, and we put all our tips in a jar. We trust each other. We divide the tips up at the end of the day based upon hours worked. We don't share during the week.

There is not real competition among the bag boys. We fool around. I'll say, "I know that guy will tip well" and run to him. We are just messing around.

$ $ $

Alassane is a foreign student from Africa who works as a locker room attendant at a country club.

I like what I do. I like the tips. The atmosphere is very relaxed, and they treat me all right. I can study when I am not busy. After the members play golf, I clean their shoes, replace the spikes, put the shoes back into the lockers, vacuum the locker room, clean the bathroom, replace lotions, and pass out towels. People who play tennis or go swimming also use the locker room.

I get paid $12 an hour. They do not have to tip me. However, 70% will give me a tip for cleaning their shoes. The average tip is $5 for cleaning shoes. I used to get $10 for fixing spikes. However, now the management charges for fixing spikes, and only about 20% will give me a tip above the $10 charge.

I only get tips for cleaning shoes. I rarely get tips for other reasons. On a busy weekend, I make $80–$100 a day on tips. On an average non-weekend day, the average is $25. My biggest tip was $60 from a guy who gave me three pairs of shoes to polish. It takes five–ten minutes to clean golf shoes. Some members are very picky and bring the shoes back if there is a spot left on the shoes. It is a very expensive country club. People pay over $50,000 to join and $1,000–$2,000 a month as their membership fee.

Whites tip the most. The few black members don't tip. Only one black member eventually gave me a tip of $5. People who are older are a bit more generous.

I do not share my tips with the other locker room attendant.

$ $ $

Jack has been a ski instructor for 30 years. He is also a realtor, and his experience with commissions is explored in another volume. The following narrative details Jack's experience receiving tips for his work as a ski instructor.

I was a building contractor in Vermont for years and I taught skiing at Stratton. I now teach skiing full-time at a Colorado resort. Skiing is my passion and there are a few dollars involved. I have been living in Colorado for four years. I love showing people my passion.

Most of those I teach are adults. The resort charges each person $80 for a group lesson that last about four hours. I mostly do group lessons because I have less seniority. My pay starts at $11.25 an hour. However, if they request me, I get $7 for that person. If they come back, I get $2. I also get $2 for each person in your group, and if they request me for a private lesson, I get 45% added on to my hourly rate. It adds up to $15–$18 an hour.

I also get a free lift ticket for myself and my wife and 10–12 complementary tickets that I can give my friends.

I get less tips from beginner lessons. About 30% will tip me and they usually do that on the last day. The average tip is $10–$20 for those who tip. You get much better tips from private lessons. Seventy-five percent will tip you then and the average tip is $20–$30. Last week I gave a private lesson to two kids and got a $140 tip.

People who do private lesson are more affluent. I also get better tips from those from the East Coast. Those who have been around and are more affluent tip the most. People from the UK used to not tip. Now, they are tipping as well as Americans. If you give a bad lesson, you don't get a good tip. If you work hard, a tip is a great gesture.

$ $ $

Ace works in the rental department of the ski shop at a ski resort in the Northeast. This is his story.

I've been working for the department for two years. I like the job because I get a lot of discounts, and I get to ski for free. We watch people's skis when they get lunch or want a break and don't want their skis stolen. We charge them $1 for a set of skis or a snowboard.

About 10% of people will give us a tip. People tip much more when it is really cold. Maybe 30% will tip. They feel sorry for you. The average tip is $1 or $2. I get about $5 an hour in tips. There are two of us working here. We alternate bringing people their skis, and we keep our own tips.

The busiest time is around lunch.

Older people tip the most, and males also tip well. Skiers tip more than snowboaders.

$ $ $

Alex teaches rock climbing in West Virginia and used to be a ski instructor. The following narrative reflects his experiences receiving tips.

I've been teaching rock climbing for six years. Rock climbing is a passion to me. It is a good way to make a living. You can make decent money.

A private guide costs $195 a day. I am paid by the person. I get $100 a day for the first person, $125 for two people, and $150 for three people. We have three or less people in a group. The work is very seasonal and depends upon the weather.

Some people don't know about tipping of guides. Seventy-five percent will give me a tip. The average tip is $20 a day per person. My biggest tip from one person was $200.

I get bigger tips from wealthier clients. The course is very expensive anyway. College kids tip less. People appreciate that you stress safety. Kids signed up by parents don't tip well. If I instruct for a family of three, I will get $20 in tips a day. If there are three unrelated people, I could get $60 a day.

It is weird. You work for tips and want the tips. I make sure to throw into the conversation that tips are allowed. For example, they might ask what I do in the off season, and I tell them that I go climbing in another country. They say, wow, that must be expensive, how can you afford it? I say tips were good last year.

I was a ski instructor for two years in college and one season in Colorado. Ninety-nine percent of my students tipped me in private lessons. People know about tipping in skiing. The average tip was $20. In group lessons about 50% tipped me and for the kids' programs—about 20% tipped me. Although the average size of the tip was higher in private lessons, I probably made more in tips from the group lessons. The ski resorts generally paid me 40% of the cost of the lesson.

$ $ $

Gene has been a trout fishing guide in Colorado for the past year. This is what Gene had to say about tipping norms in sports entertainment.

It is very rewarding to make people feel good when they catch fish. In the off-season, I am a student at a local university, and I help plow the roads. I teach fishing to groups, and I have one-on-one sessions.

The company I work for charges a lot. I don't know the exact amount, but it is a couple of hundred dollars. I'm paid between $90 and $150 for a trip. This is affected by how many people are in the group, whether I use a boat, and whether it is a half or full day.

Everyone has given me a tip. The average is $40, and my biggest tip was $100. Older rich guys are the most generous. Old ladies are the least generous. It makes a huge difference whether or not the customer catches fish.

I only split with another guide if there are two of us taking out a group.

$ $ $

Nick has been a white-water raft guide in Maryland and West Virginia for the past four years. He is also a ski instructor, and his experiences receiving tips for sports entertainment are discussed below.

I go down some pretty hairy rapids. It is a real treat. It is the best kind of work in the world. We charge $100 a day per person on most days and $120 on Saturdays. There are no more than three clients on a raft. The trip takes three to five hours, and I do one per day. I get paid $100 per trip—or about one-third of what is charged.

One-hundred percent will tip me. The boss gives a safety talk before the trip begins, and part of the talk is how we appreciate tips. There is also a sign about tipping. After the trip, there is a cookout, and they show videos of the trips. We also have a keg of beer. This is a good way to schmooze and get your tip. The average tip is $30–$40 in tips per raft trip.

My best tip was $140. I get bigger tips from those over 30 years of age. It is not always the doctors and lawyers who give the best tips. Usually, I get better tips from those who had a good experience. Families tip well.

We do not share our tips.

You can never guess for sure how tips will go. Tips are a big part of my job. It is like poker. When you leave the table, you feel good if you win and bad if you lose. If you did a great job and got a poor tip, you feel bad. Tips make a difference. It is hard skilled work, and we are not paid like a skilled worker. On the other hand, if I am thinking too much about tips I am not doing an effective job. I love my job, and I would almost do it for free.

You get better tips on pure enthusiasm rather than dropping hints. You got to be pure. If people ask me, I say the convention is $20 a day per person.

I am also a ski instructor at WISP resort in Western Maryland. I mostly do the children's programs with the better skiers. When parents pick up their kids at the end of the day, we give them a report card on how the kids did. Less than half will tip. I have a clip board where I always put $10 or $20 to try to initiate the tip.

On slow days, I only have one or two kids in my group. On busy days, there can be ten or so kids in a group. My total tips range from 0 to $60. Ten dollars is the average they give.

Return people tip the most. They know that tips are appreciated. Better skiers also tip more. Foreigners and non-whites tip less. We do not share our tips.

WISP pays me $7.25 an hour plus $1.50 per lesson. A lesson is a half-day, so if I have six kids all day, that is 12 lessons or $18 plus my hourly wage.

They start people out at minimum wage. We get free lift tickets. It is hard to get a job in Western Maryland. We are expendable.

$ $ $

Russ has been a rafting and kayak guide in Colorado for the past two years. This is his story.

In the off-season, I work construction. I love being a guide. It is a blast. I am paid to go down rivers. People have a good time, and it is not your typical nine to five job. There are six to seven people in a raft. These people row for the upper section of the river, and I get paid $40 per trip for this section. I row for the lower river, which is a scenic-flat tour, and I get paid $35 per trip for this. I typically do two trips per day. The customers are charged $45 per person for the upper section tour and $35 per person for the lower river scenic flat tour.

I am also a kayak guide. Customers are charged between $43 and $48 per person, and I get between $44 and $45 per trip. We try to have five customers per guide. Eighty percent of customers tip. The typical tip is $20 per group. A group is often a family. If there are smaller groups or individuals, I usually get $5–$10 from the smaller groups or individuals. I almost never get tips from organized groups such as church groups or wrestling clubs. I usually make $40–$60 per day in tips.

Families are more generous. College kids are far less likely to tip. People who tip are usually friendlier and more apt to engage in conversation. The tipping in rafting and kayaking are about the same.

We don't share tips except when there are groups of kayakers. For safety reasons, we have one guide per five kayakers. If we have more than one guide in a trip, we equally share the tips.

Tour guiding is different than restaurant tipping. It is not a flat 20%. It depends if they like you and if you did a good job. People are on vacation and ready to have a good time, and that helps with the tips.

$ $ $

Joel works as a personal trainer for a Gold's Gym in Ohio. He shared the following story about receiving tips for sports entertainment.

I hate working for them. They are a money hungry corporation. I'm more concerned with the well-being of the client, and they are more concerned with making money. Work-out sessions are half an hour in length. If you want to take more time taking measurements and talking to the client, they frown upon you.

Gold's charges $35 per half hour session. People can also buy packages at $20 per session. I get paid $7.50 per session. I am also expected to help around the gym when I am not with a client. I don't get paid for this. All my income is based on time with a paying client. The client pays the gym directly, and I get paid every two weeks. I am at the gym four to five hours per day. I make in the low 200s every two weeks.

I never get tips from clients. I once got a gift certificate for Christmas.

$ $ $

Belia is fitness trainer in a New Jersey suburb outside of New York City. She is originally from Czechoslovakia. This is Belia's story.

I have a degree in physical education and have been training for eight years. I love my job. I am an athlete, and this is my profession. I have my own studio. I charge $50 an hour and give 40 hours of training a week. Only two people give me more than what I charge. One person gives me $55 an hour and another gives me $60.

For holidays, everyone tips me and gives me cash. Most give me an hour's worth. A few give me two hours' worth. I occasionally get a gift certificate. I make double what I usually make for a week. No one ever asks what they should give. They know.

[Belia refused payment for her participation.]

$ $ $

These narratives demonstrate the pervasiveness of the tipping norm. Workers in sports entertainment may receive tips regardless of their base pay, which varies considerably. Base pay may vary quite a bit, but conformity to tipping norms in sports entertainment is very high, particularly when customers are lectured in advance, prompted, or socially pressured. People in sports entertainment consistently report that they love their work. They regularly describe their work as involving a high degree of skill. In fact, the stories told by the respondents in this section included much more information regarding their own performance; although the relationship between the quality of their performance and the tip remains unclear. The overwhelming perception is that people are more likely to tip when they are happy and have a good time. In addition, young people are often depicted as poor tippers, but there is not a clear indication as to whether this is because of a relative lack of resources or a difference in their knowledge or adherence to tipping norms.

24

Ushers and Sports Vendors

The Census Bureau reports that that 12,740 people have jobs as ushers, lobby attendants, and ticket takers. Their average annual earnings are $28,000. Vendors at sporting events are classified under door-to-door sales workers, news and street vendors, and related occupations (56,450; $31,000). We include ushers and sports vendors in the entertainment section because the primary functions of these occupations are to prevent disruption of the entertainment experience and to further enhance it. Even though some of the tasks of these workers may include handling food and beverages, their work serves to promote a seamless entertainment experience. Vendors bring food and beverages to patrons so that they do not have to leave their seats, and ushers help people find their seats in an efficient manner that minimizes the disruption to other spectators. In this book, there is a distinction between street vendors and sports vendors that is essentially related to the purpose of the work. Patrons of street vendors are generally trying to get food and drinks on the go; whereas sports vendors bring food and drinks to spectators who are not usually in a hurry and have the option of getting up to get the food and drinks themselves.[1]

Tipping norms related to ushers and sports vendors are unclear and sometimes arbitrary. For example, people may tip an usher at a sporting event but are far less likely to tip an usher at a charity event. A movie theatre usher may only be tipped if they provide a customer with a special service. Otherwise, they may be seen as responsible for ensuring that all the patrons in the theatre have tickets; a service for which people are not likely to tip. Vendors at sporting events might be tipped because they are providing a labor-intensive service that enhances the entertainment experience. At the same time, others may decide that the prices are exorbitant and choose not to tip vendors for that reason. Regardless of the logic that customers use to determine tipping practices, little is known about the experience of those receiving tips for these services. The narratives included in this chapter attempt to gain an understanding of the experiences that vendors and ushers have receiving tips for their work in entertainment settings.

$ $ $

Ian sells beer and food at sporting events in the D.C. area. This is his story.

I love working at sporting events. I started doing it for the money, but now I love it. It is a lot of fun. It is good exercise, and I meet a lot of interesting people. In the last year, I worked 75 baseball games, 15 football games, 35 basketball games, and three or four kiddie events. Several years ago we bought the beer or food from the arena. Now we work on commission. The arena fronts the product, and we turn in the money when we are done. The typical commission is between 12–15%.

I sell a beer for $7. That depends upon the venue. I sell between 5 and 12 cases of beer a night (24 bottles in a case). Fifty percent of people leave me a tip. The tips range from a buck or two up to ten bucks if someone is buying several beers at one time. The average for everyone is a buck.

I also sell ice cream and candy. The average tips are less, and the commission is the same. Cotton candy costs $3 and only 5–8% of people will leave a tip. On the other hand, the turnover is faster. At kiddie events I can also sell other merchandise, but the tips are crap. They are far and few between.

People who drink beer tip more. The more they drink, the more they tip. If the team is not doing well, people don't tip as well. Guys tip the best—especially those in their forties.

I love both my jobs. I'm a workaholic.

$ $ $

Roger is about to start his fourth season selling beer at Cincinnati Reds baseball games. He shared the following experiences receiving tips for his work as a stadium vendor.

I like selling beer because it is pretty good money and fun. However, drunk people can get a little annoying. It is good money for three hours of work. I get paid both commission and tips. I buy a case of beer for $144 and sell the beer for

$6 a piece. I get a 13% commission. I usually sell two or three cases a night and average making $50 a night. Half of that comes from the 13% commission, and the other half comes from tips.

The average tip is $1 a beer. My biggest tip was $40. A guy had a lot to drink and ordered $60 worth of beer, gave me a $100 bill, and said to keep the change.

Young people tip the most. Some older women also tip well—maybe because I am a young guy. People up high (in the cheap seats) don't tip a lot. They have less money. About 15% of people will not leave a tip at all.

You are also required to carry one other item—for example, water or peanuts. People don't tip well for those items. Beer is the best. People tip more later in the game. They have had more to drink and are looser with their money.

Tipping is better on Thursday, Friday, or Saturday night. People are there to party.

It is very cutthroat with other beer salesmen. If they see you walking toward a sale, they will try to cut you off. I have not had arguments over this, but other vendors have. They divide the stadium into ten areas. They are usually several beer salesmen in each area, and they can sell anywhere in that area.

$ $ $

Larry has been selling food from a concession stand at the Verizon Center for the past two years.

We sell food, beer, soda, and water. I love what I do. The hours are short, and the pay is great. The atmosphere is friendly. Management will support us when there is a customer dispute.

I was getting paid $10.50 an hour after six months. I now get $12.75 an hour. I also got an annual bonus of $80. In a typical night, I work four–five hours. I start work an hour before the gates open.

I average $60 a night in tips. We are not allowed to put out a tip cup, but people know to leave a tip on the register. We are not supposed to make them feel obligated to give a tip. As soon as they give the tip, we put it under the register.

There are five people working five registers. We do not share tips. However, we all help each other out getting food, and so on. The manager might help get the food, but we don't share our tips with him. He gets paid more.

In an average night, I serve 100 people. Thirty percent will leave me a tip. The average tip is $1 or $2. Sometimes I get $10. One lady gave me $20 for a soda after we had a pleasant conversation.

White men between 25 and 35 tip the most. People who buy drinks tip more. Kids don't tip. Urban African-Americans [respondent is black] are the worst tippers you will ever meet besides Asians and Indians [presumably this reference is to East Indians]. African-American women who are not urban are good tippers. Hispanics are good tippers.

People tip better at Caps [hockey] games compared the Wizards [basketball]. We do real well at Keith Urban concerts and Bruce Springsteen. Parents are tipping more at Hannah Montana now that we can sell drinks. The worst tippers are at Disney on Ice.

[Author's Note: Several vendors at the Verizon Center were spoken to informally when the first author went to events over the past few years. Some vendors appeared to not even know that they could take tips. Larry was extremely sociable and that probably affects his tips.]

$ $ $

Marjorie is an usher at a major league ballpark in the Midwest. She asked that the ballpark not be named. The following narrative details Marjorie's experiences receiving tips for her work as an usher in a sports venue.

I have been an usher for six years. I love it. I was born to be a fan of this team. I am their greatest fan. I used to live next to some of their players in the 1940s, and my dad used to play semi-pro ball. I am high up above home plate, and the view is great. I check tickets and take people to their seats if they ask. I sometimes have to help people when the seats get mixed up.

I get paid $8.95 an hour. I take 25–50 groups of people per game to their seats. About one-third are season ticket holders. On an average night, 10% will give me a tip. The average tip is a quarter per person, or $1 for four people. On an average night, I get $7 in tips. I am not in it for the tips. I don't care. I am there to watch the game. At the end of the season, season ticket holders don't give any extra tips. I wipe their seats when it rains and many still don't give a tip. Again, I am not there for the tips. I am there to have fun. When the game is going bad, the people are still fun.

I'm 70 years old. The best tippers are men 50–70 years old. Those under 30 don't tip. If there are four women, I might get a tip. I rarely get a tip from a single mom with kids.

$ $ $

USHERS AND SPORTS VENDORS

Kayin has been an usher at the Kennedy Center in Washington, D.C. for the last five months. This is his story.

I love it. I am a musician, so I get to listen to the NSO (National Symphony Orchestra). And, I get paid. I can't live on the salary, but it is money in my pocket.

I get paid $7.25 an hour. For a typical show, I take bring 20–300 people to their seats. It depends on the section in which I am working. About 3% will offer me a tip. We are not allowed to take tips, and I don't.

$ $ $

Shanique is an usher at Constitution Hall in Washington, D.C. This is her story in her own words.

It is a good part-time job. I've been there six months. I get paid $7 an hour, and my usual shift is four to five hours. My job is to take people to their seats. I also work as a door director. As a door director, I basically just tell people to go upstairs or downstairs.

I get tips from about 1% of the people. Last week, I took a few hundred people to their seats and did not get a tip. When I get a tip, it is usually $2. My biggest tip was for $6 from a middle-aged white guy at a Carly Simon concert.

When I started this job, I did not know that I could get tips. I never thought about it until I got my first tip. A tip is a courteous gesture. It comes out of a person's generosity. It is only required for waitresses.

$ $ $

Wayne has worked for the last six months at a movie theatre in Houston, Texas. This is what he had to say about receiving tips.

The job is pretty good. I get to interact with other people, and I get to see a lot of movies.

I clean up the theatre, serve food, and do some security. I get paid $5.30 an hour.

I get tips about three times a week. I get tips for helping people carry food and helping people find things they lost in the theatre. I will go in with my flashlight and help find things. I once found a wallet and was given $3. The average tip is about a dollar.

$ $ $

The stories provided by ushers and sports vendors seem to indicate that people are perceived to be more generous if they tip; although many of the narratives point out differences in peoples' ability to pay. According to those who receive tips for this line of work, people also appear to be more likely to tip if they believe that they are getting a special service. Vendors and ushers also describe people who seem to want to impress someone as tipping more. Many of the vendors and ushers sampled indicate that the work is its own reward or mention their love of the game as a primary motivating factor. A highly competitive work environment appears to be common in the sports arenas in particular, but the tips are not necessarily the factor that motivates the workers.

NOTE
1. Vendors who work the counters at sporting events often have tip jars.

Conclusions

Homo economicus is an individual attempting to maximize the tips received and minimize the tips disbursed. Interestingly, homo economicus seems to be as rare a find (and perhaps as controversial) as the missing link. Tipping is not a universal phenomenon. The social norms of tipping are confusing, sometimes controversial, and differ according to time, place, and context. In many ways, the practice that many contend originated as a means by which Europeans displayed class and superiority to servants has become an institution.

Segrave (1998) has written an excellent history of tipping. He traces tipping back to Tudor England where guests at masters' houses were expected to give "vails" to the servants if the service was appreciated. Controversy occurred in Tudor England about the cost of tipping and retaliation if the tips were not sufficient. Tipping made its way to the United States in the 1800s with similar debates. Tipping was so economically rewarding for coatroom checking that contractors bid against one another for the concession, and few of the tips actually went to the coat checker.

There have been attempts by different groups to eliminate tipping.[1] Some workers contend that tipping gave employers the rationale not to increase wages, and some believe that tipping was demeaning. They advocate for higher wages instead of tips. Some restaurants and hotels assert that tipping upsets the clientele. Many people who are supposed to give tips do not want to part with their money or are confused by the "etiquette" of tipping. Many have expressed the belief that tipping may lead to moral decay. Some states actually abolished tipping between 1909 and 1913. The laws were ignored.

Once tipping was established, it became very difficult to stop. Segrave (1998) provides an example of stopping any tipping before it takes root: The airline industry eradicated giving tips to flight attendants by banning it from the beginning and firing attendants who accepted tips. Today, most Americans believe tipping is a fair way to compensate for many types of services; although they also indicate that they hate the practice (albeit at lower rates—about 40% report resenting the convention).[2]

Tipping is not practiced in all countries. Lynn and Lynn (2004) find that the United States has the highest level of tipping compared to 45 other countries for restaurants and taxicabs. Lack of knowledge about the proper tip in most countries is so pervasive most travel guides have some discussion about the proper etiquette, and there are articles in the United States devoted to this issue.[3]

RANGE OF TIPPING

There is a range of tipping among different occupations. There is almost universal tipping (over 90%) of servers in restaurants, hair stylists (unless they own the salon), car valets, cab and limousine drivers, and people who rent umbrellas at the beach. The duties of service staff vary considerably with respect to the environment, wages, hours, working conditions, and the attitudes of the public and the employees. Yet, service staff and waitresses in particular tend to identify themselves as an occupational community (see also Cobble 1991). It is likely that this sort of solidarity helps maintain the practice.

However, there are several service-related jobs where the level of tipping is fairly rare: couriers, people who deliver flowers, tennis and golf instructors, and photographers, to name a few. It is not always apparent why this is the case although we offer some possible explanations below.

For a number of job categories there is great variability within. Some ski instructors reported getting tips half the time. Why not the other half? One raft guide received tips 100% of the time; while another got tips 75% of the time. One personal trainer never received a gratuity; while another got holiday presents from all of her clients. It is unclear whether these reported differences are a function of differences in the quality of the service, the strength of the tipping norm in the organizational context, or a perceptual error on the part of some respondents. The fact that several respondents seem to have some difficulty calculating percentages indicates that caution might be called for in the interpretation of tip estimates.

Is the fact that some blue-collar workers now receive gratuities the wave of the future? Changes in society and technology affect the tipping and commission practices. Several bellhops complained that wheels on suitcases have hurt their tips. Alternatively, the now ubiquitous tip jar at delis, coffee shops, and ice cream parlors would have been seen as distasteful ten years ago; though they may arguably be perceived as distasteful today as well.

Holiday tips are an anomaly. Nannies, housekeepers, and dog walkers get few tips during the year other than the holidays. A typical holiday present for these workers is up to a week's salary. So, if your dog walker gets $60 a week, $60 would be a fairly generous holiday present. Most postal workers also get few tips during the year but can get many small ($10–$20) tips for the holiday. Tips for postal workers are particularly interesting in the United States considering that any gift exchange offered to, solicited by, or accepted by or on the behalf of government workers is usually considered an illicit activity.

Other occupations such as servers and musicians get tips when service is rendered but only get occasional holiday tips. The exception is music teachers, who sometimes get a few tips during the year but often get thoughtful gifts for the holidays. People who do personal care such as hair stylists, dog groomers and massagers get tips when service is rendered and also get generous tips for the holidays. Doormen in apartments and condominiums get some tips during the year but get most of their tips around the holidays. Car valets get tips when service is rendered and some get holiday gifts from their regular customers. The standards for holiday tipping are especially discretionary and are transmitted primarily experientially.

FACTORS AFFECTING THE TIP

There are some interesting findings regarding how the activities of the recipients of the tips affect the size of the tip.

- The evidence regarding whether the quality of service affects the tip is inconsistent. Several respondents indicate that it makes no difference. People may come with a pre-set opinion of what to tip and tip that amount regardless of whether the service is good or bad. One pizza delivery driver says that it makes no difference whether he is on time or late. Scott, a server, says, "People come in expecting to tip a certain percent and will tip that amount regardless of good or bad service." Many others believe the level of service has a great effect. However, several restaurant servers also say that the quality of service is the most important factor affecting the tip. Some servers mention the need to play with the kids at the table, and car valets talk about helping put stuff into the cars. A home housekeeper indicates doing extra work such as a closet not normally cleaned, which might lead to extra compensation. A hotel chambermaid says people asking for extra towels are most likely to give a tip. A raft guide (essay not included) says his tips went up drastically in the second year, as he got better at avoiding the rocks and giving out information about the river, fauna, and animals. In any case, tips appear to be a weak signal of quality and are unlikely to serve a monitoring function.

- The amount of work tends to have less of an effect on the size of the tip than one might expect. The people renting umbrellas report that it makes little difference how many umbrellas they put up, and some of the camp counselors claim that it makes no difference whether kids stay for two weeks or eight weeks.
- Being able to "connect" with the person being served is consistently described as extremely important. During an interview, a cab driver mentions the need for the "gift of gab," and a doorman talks about how he tried to schmooze with people from the get-go. Many respondents speak of the need to have good people skills. One cab driver reports that you need to engage with the passenger, and if you are on your cell phone, you are not going to get a good tip. A chambermaid says she is tipped more by people she sees on a daily basis.
- The language ability of the service worker has an important effect and is somewhat related to the point above. Respondents whose English is not "up to standards" receive lower tips. There are several situations in which a native-born American and a foreign national with a heavy accent had identical jobs and very different experiences with tips. We suspect the level of service is identical (i.e.; quickly retrieving a car from the parking lot or taking someone to a bus), but people tip more if the recipient of the tip is more "engaging" and "enthusiastic." Expressing enthusiasm requires a command of the English language. Part of this difference is racial, but we believe it is strongly affected by whether or not one could "establish a bond" with the person. Several people receiving tips who were not native English speakers but who spoke impeccable English and had excellent people skills, do not appear to have any disadvantage regarding receiving tips. People with difficulty communicating in English are

often ignored or treated as though speaking English is part of the quality of the service.
- Numerous respondents came across as "go-getters," "live-wires." The upbeat, high energy, and positive attitude that they successfully exude seems to communicate something that people appreciate as quality in service provision. Usually, when asked what affects their tips, these people mention the quality of service and being able to connect. They also report higher tips. Perhaps their positive attitude coincides with an overestimation of quality and tipping, but it is at least equally likely that these people are interpreted as approachable and likeable. They are effectively conveying qualities that people are more likely to reward.
- A variety of people ask for tips. The strippers interviewed as well as the cabaret performer are unabashed about walking (or dancing) up to people and soliciting (even expecting) tips. Further, the bellhop who brings luggage to your room is likely to have a number of very pointed reminders that you are supposed to tip.

There are a variety of situational factors that also affect the tip.

- Weekends are usually busier for restaurants than weekdays. Similarly, the total bill is usually higher for dinner than for lunch, when people tend to order less alcohol.
- Some settings call for tips, and others do not. A musician is far more likely to be tipped at a bar if there is no cover charge at the door or if someone working in the bar literally calls for tips. A clown is more likely to get tipped at a children's party than at a corporate function. There is some evidence to suggest that it is not simply professionalization that inhibits tipping norms. The corporate environment appears to censor tipping.
- Sometimes there are too many bussers, servers, and hosts. Consequently, the individual tip out amount is smaller. It is important to note that managers have an interest in scheduling more labor than necessary for a shift because the cost per hour for the owner is low relative to the perceived efficiency payoff. However, managers also need to consider how these decisions are likely to affect the motivation of tipped employees. In effect, this strategy may not produce the expected efficiency gain if workers calculate this as a personal cost. In addition, workers within the distribution system are likely to be less generous in the tip out as people are not likely to be perceived as having to "hustle." In

essence, management has the capacity to impact employee motivation as well as facilitate a cooperative work environment if the appropriate number of staff are scheduled. Likewise, too many musicians can inhibit tipping. Musicians in large bands rarely get tipped at all because people perceive there to be too many for the tip to be impactful, or not perceived as an insult.

- Teachers are far more likely to get gratuities if the kids are younger and if the school district is more affluent.
- Tips appear to be higher on the East Coast and the West Coast.[4] Servers seem to get 18–20% on the coasts and 14–15% in other areas. One masseuse who moved from Indiana to Washington, D.C. reports being pleasantly surprised that her tip percentage increased.
- The percentage tip is higher at an upscale hair salon or restaurant. However, this does not translate into "upscale" people being perceived as more generous, which we discuss in more detail below. Patrons of upscale establishments might be perceived as more generous for personal service. However, for other types of services, they might be considered less generous (e.g.; delivery and parking).

Another factor affecting the tip is the perception of the type (as distinct from quality) of service. People who deliver pizza are almost always tipped, while couriers are rarely tipped. Couriers are often assumed to be business-related, similar to the copier repairman, and appear to rarely receive tips. Most car valets and cab drivers are tipped, but the person who transports you to your house from the car dealership is only sometimes tipped. Alternatively, the person from Enterprise Rent-a-Car who drops you off at the repair shop is never tipped. Similarly, massage therapists are usually tipped when the massage is perceived as a personal service and rarely tipped if the massage is medically advised. The closer the service is to a "personal" service the greater the likelihood of a tip and the more personable the tipped employee is expected to be when engaging customers. The consequence of this is that the more personal the service, the more emotional labor is involved in the provision of the service.

Factors that do not seem to affect the tip are also interesting. The participants in this study report very little relationship between the work effort and the tip. For example, baggage handlers regularly report that the number of bags that they handle, the weight, or the difficulty of the job is not obviously associated with the tip size. People in the restaurant industry often describe customer characteristics when explaining their perspective on conformity to tipping norms but rarely discuss the quality of the service they provide. The point of interest here is that if the economic conceptualization of tipping norms applies, the relationship between the work effort and quality must be apparent to the worker. This is rarely the case.

WHO ARE THE BIG TIPPERS?

So, who tips the most and who tips the least? With some exceptions, there is surprisingly little consensus on this question.

- Foreigners, particularly Asians and Europeans, have a bad reputation for tipping among the American workers interviewed across job categories. Many respondents stated that it is not in the culture of Europeans or Asians to tip. Many servers report tips in the single percentages from Asians and Europeans. However, a few servers in upscale restaurants say that tipping by foreigners seems to have improved over the last couple of years.
- People who drink alcohol with the meal are perceived as more likely to tip. This finding is consistent with Lynn's (1988) analysis demonstrating a positive relationship between alcohol consumption and tip size. In restaurants, this is due to the fact that restaurants serving liquor are usually a little more upscale, the total bill is higher, and people who are "feeling good" are a bit freer with their money. Concession workers at sporting events also report that people tip more for beer than for non-alcoholic items, and beer drinkers tip more as the night progresses.
- Kids and teenagers are, virtually without exception, seen as bad tippers. This is often blamed on the fact that teens do not have the money. As Shona says, "If I had the money, I would, but I'm a teenager." Some claim that teens are not properly taught how to tip or are simply too selfish. We should point out that Shona reports making fairly good tips. It is likely that the contention that teens do not have the money is based on the notion that they are still establishing themselves, but we generally have lower expectations of teenagers too.
- Senior citizens are usually seen as bad tippers. Some respondents say the cause of this is the limited income of some senior citizens. Many are thought to be unaware of the proper etiquette of tipping, and some senior citizens come across to tipped employees as if it is their right to get free service.
- Among those who mention black-white differences, some say the stereotype that blacks are bad tippers is false.[5] However, of the 17 people who mention race, 12 say that blacks are worse tippers compared to others. Somewhat surprising is the

fact that two-thirds of those who say that blacks are bad tippers are themselves African-American. One possible explanation for this has to do with the extent of racial/ethnic segregation that persists in the United States (see e.g.; Massey and Denton 1993; Rocha and Espino 2008). Employees and customers of the same race are more likely to encounter one another in these settings. However, whether or not perception and reality are accurate indicators of conformity to tipping norms is debatable. It should be noted that the black share of America's wealth has only increased by 0.05% since the end of slavery (see Bowles, Gintis, and Groves 2005). Despite the potential difference in the ability to pay and the widely noted differences in the quality of service provided to black people in the United States, the expectation that black people conform to tipping norms that essentially result in a higher charge for lower quality service (or no likely service at all in the case of taxis) persists. A few of the respondents who mention race in this study confirm that lower quality service is regularly provided to black customers, but these same respondents fail to account for this in the evaluation of tipping practices.

- Some respondents view Hispanics as bad tippers while others say they are the best tippers.
- The most disagreement among respondents is on the role of class. Many respondents say the wealthy are most likely to tip. This seems to be particularly true in upscale restaurants and hair salons. In addition, several servers say that businessmen are more likely to be good tippers. For many other activities, the middle class or "normal" people are characterized as most likely to tip. This is particularly true for delivery services, loading of cars, and blue-collar services. The vehemence of some of the comments is fairly striking. According to one cab driver, "She didn't get rich by giving it away!"
- For the several people who mention sexual orientation—gays, particularly gay men, are seen as good tippers. One respondent explains this by saying gays have more disposable income and are more likely to work in the service industry; hence, understand the need for tipping. Some respondents claim that lesbians are bad tippers. It is unknown whether or not our sample includes responses from lesbians, and only those who made mention of their own status as gay men are known. More importantly, we have no real information as to how workers draw conclusions about the sexual orientation of customers. Even in settings that are "gay clubs" or "lesbian bars" there is usually a fair number of people who would describe themselves as straight. One conclusion that can be reached from this data is that employees make some assumptions

about customers based on some general social cues, and this is likely to affect the type of service that people receive.
- Some servers say that families are better tippers; while others point to families as worse tippers.
- A number of servers say people on dates appear to tip well.
- There is no consistent pattern with respect to gender. It seems that men tip more if a "cute" waitress serves them. It is not clear whether women are more likely to tip depending upon the gender of the server.
- People with previous experience in the service industry are often expected to be good tippers. Many servers say that they themselves tip more after working in the industry. They claim to now realize the difficulty of the job and that servers rely upon tips to survive. Several servers refer to an "ethic" of servers giving outrageously good tips to other servers. This "ethic" may also be a norm of reciprocity. It is not uncommon for servers providing service, particularly in bars and restaurants, to provide free products to other servers that they know with the expectation of a higher tip.

Even though foreigners, kids, and senior citizens are seen as being the worst tippers, and other groups are often seen as better tippers, remember that we are dealing with estimated averages. Not all foreigners, kids, and senior citizens are seen as bad tippers. Many respondents say it really makes no difference, including when it comes to race and ethnicity. The common phrase repeated by many is that the "stereotypes don't work" or as Sabrina says, "You never know who will tip more." Even most of those who characterized certain groups as bad tippers, know that there are many exceptions to what they think of as the rule.

In some ways, the most fascinating aspects of these narratives are the perceptual errors themselves. In the cognitive sciences, it is common knowledge that people seek out information that supports what they already believe and discount information that contradicts their pre-existing beliefs. The anti-Semitic remarks illustrate this point pretty clearly. Take for example, Marissa's statement that "[s]ome Jewish ladies try to get breaks on the price." The greatest likelihood is that these sorts of anti-Semitic stereotypes lead people to take note of interactions that support their stereotype and do not take note of instances that are not a part of the belief system. When the ethnicity of the client is unknown or when people who are not Jewish attempt to barter, it less likely to be stored in memory because it does not fit the stereotype. Moreover, the behavior of different people is classified and judged disparately. When some people barter, they are deemed miserly or shrewd, but when servers expect reciprocity (free drinks for example) from other servers for higher tips, it is an "ethic."

TIP OUTS
There are four different models of tip outs in restaurants.

- The tip out system requiring the most trust is a pool. All tips are pooled and then pro-rated by the hour and perhaps by the job (server, busser, runner, etc.). This occurs in some restaurants, all tip jars, some parking valet services, and some hotel cleaning services. The restaurants using this system are family restaurants where the staff tend to have long-standing relationships. With pooling, everyone helps each other at their job and could thus be more efficient. However, it requires a certain level of trust, and if someone does not carry their weight, this creates resentment that undermines both efficiency and effectiveness.
- An intermediate level of trust occurs when the tip out is a percentage of the server's tip. The servers have to be trusted to honestly report their tips. For the most part, few bussers, runners, bartenders, or hosts complain about dishonesty among the servers.
- The system that leaves nothing to chance is when the tip is based on a percentage of sales (more likely found in chain restaurants where there is probably more anonymity). Usually a computerized statement at the end of each shift tells the server how much to include in the tip outs. This creates resentment among some servers because it is believed that some bussers/runners/bartenders may not adequately earn their tip out. The system is far more impersonal. As Denise puts it, "I do not like the system because not everyone is working hard. If I don't receive good tips I get screwed. I should tip out of my tips. The problem with that would be that people would have to trust me."
- Sometimes the tip out is voluntary. In some situations, the server is supposed to tip out, but the amount is not specified. It is not unusual for servers, bartenders, and hair stylists to give more than what is required by the distribution system or to give when nothing at all is required. Servers describe themselves as giving more in order to say thank you for good service and to ensure good service in the future. Servers might also give something to the host, which is not required, in order to say thank you for seating people in their section. People have surprisingly strong opinions about the voluntary tip outs. Some hair stylists say that the shampoo person is exploited, often overlooked by the

customer in getting a tip, and should always get a little extra from the stylist. Others say they received a "real" wage and are responsible for their own tips. Surprisingly, there is little-to-no mention of the extent to which tipping in these cases might be conditioned upon the voluntary nature of the service. In some cases, customers may not be aware of the tipping etiquette because it may seem from the client's perspective that the stylist chose to have the assistant wash hair. In other cases, the same stylist washes, cuts, and styles the customer's hair. Since this is not the customer's choice, the customer may assume that the organizational rules regarding the tip out are a matter for the staff, as is the case in restaurant tips for bussers and runners. Without direct communication clients have no way of knowing the pay scale and whose responsibility it is to tip out other workers in the salon. However, shampoo assistants may be more likely than bussers or runners to receive tips directly from customers because shampoo assistants have more direct client contact.

There is a lot of variation in the tip out. Who is included, and what percentages are given? Some restaurants have runners and not bussers and vice versa. Similarly, some restaurants have hosts and/or bartenders, and others do not. When they are present, bussers, runners, and bartenders are usually included in the tip out. However, some bussers, runners, and hosts have "real" salaries and may not be included. Similarly, cooks also have "real" salaries and are rarely included in the tip out.

Bartenders usually have two sources of tips: (1) directly from the bar and (2) from the tip out from the servers. The logic of the server tip out is that since the bartenders are making drinks for the servers, they deserve a tip out. However, bartenders often make at least the standard minimum wage, and servers rarely make the standard minimum wage. In some cases, their percentage is based upon liquor sales, sometimes upon total sales, and in a few situations, it is voluntary. Bartenders sometimes provide their own tip out to their helpers—a barback, for example, if one is working. This is usually based upon a percentage of the bartender's own tips. Hair stylists sometimes also have assistants performing shampooing and sweeping. They are rarely included in a formal tip out but are sometimes included in a voluntary tip out.

Some tip outs are close to bribes. This occurs in some airports where cab drivers often give tip outs to the dispatcher. Some airports have explicit policies that prohibit this practice; although some of the respondents indicate that such rules may not be followed. In addition, there are other airports that allow tip outs to dispatchers. In other settings, tipping postal workers and publicly employed sanitation workers is akin to bribery; particularly when government employees sabotage service to those citizens who do not tip. Scott referred to other postal employees who really hustle bringing in the garbage cans of postal recipients, etc. and are able to get $2,000 in holiday tips.

FAIRNESS AND HONESTY
There is a surprising amount of fairness and honesty conveyed in these stories. Tips are almost always pro-rated according to hours worked for people who share the proceeds of a tip jar or when chambermaids pool their tips. There seems to be little attempt for people to try to get more than an hourly pro-rated share by stating their job is more skilled or more labor intensive. Managers are usually excluded from the proceeds of this sharing unless they also do some of the same tasks as line employees. There are also some cases in which the owners and managers take the tips of employees as if the tips are business income. For example, the owner of the limousine company that Omar works for takes half of his tips. The justification for this policy is unclear, but treating the tip as company profit potentially undermines any possible performance-enhancing effect of tips. It is also likely that if customers knew that half the tips went to the owner, many would not tip.

Tips are rarely stolen. Most servers report that they never have a problem with tips disappearing from a table. In most of the situations where tips are pocketed, the offender is caught and fired. There is more gray area in the sharing of tips. When the server tips out based upon a percentage of his or her tips it is pretty easy for the server to understate the nightly tip. A few servers say they purposely do this when the busser, bartender, or runner is not working really hard. However, most runners, bussers, and bartenders report that honesty is not a serious problem. If a server under-tipped one night, they often make it up the next night. Several people who report getting ripped off claim to not be upset by it: "I guess the person really needed the money."

There may be several reasons for depictions of fairness and honesty within the tipping system. First, people are generally honest; particularly when they have to work with the same person over time. Second, the servers want good service from the staff. If they under-tip, this is likely to eventually result in bad service and affect their bottom line. Remember, many servers claim to over-tip. If they are supposed to give $8, they say that they give $10 or $12 to say thank you and to encourage good work in the future. Third, it is harder to cheat than it might appear. Servers and runners know the tip out amount to be expected. A few go to the manager when this appears too low. Fourth, the perception that an individual is not contributing also affects one's reputation, which can be costly.

KNOWLEDGE OF COMPENSATION STRUCTURE
A lack of knowledge is evident among some of those who received tips. Individual tip percentage estimates sometimes have large ranges (e.g., 10–18%), and average estimated dollar amounts reported vary by large margins. It is likely that some respondents may feel uncomfortable talking about money to an interviewer. However, it also became apparent that many simply do not know, and in some situations, the math they report is simply impossible.

JOB SATISFACTION
The focus of this book is on tips. However, the first question asked is whether or not they like their job and why. This question serves two purposes. First, it puts people at ease. Most people do not like to talk about their compensation. They are more willing to talk about their pay after they talk about what they do for work and what they think about it.

Second, what people think about their work is fascinating. Asking about tips, commissions, and bonuses frames the discussion of what they think about their jobs. Similarly, respondents often talk about their compensation structure in terms of whether it contributes to a positive or negative work experience. Questions about whether they like their job, what they do at their job, and how they receive their compensation are integral to understanding the organizational context in which tipping norms operate and workers live their experiences.

Approximately 90% of respondents express satisfaction with their job.[6] Factors that affect this include: relating to people such as coworkers, managers, and customers; the pay; the compensation structure; the conditions of the work; and the nature of the work. Respondents often point to people that they relate to as reasons for liking or disliking their jobs. This type of reason is the most common basis for evaluating work. The following are select quotes that highlight this:

- I did not really care if I was tipped because the restaurant was so much fun. I loved working there and thought the owner was a great guy. [Steve who worked at a Crab House as a busser]
- I like the work because I like my boss. We have a lot of fun. [Carrie, who worked at a restaurant, essay not included]

- The environment is nice and the managers and the staff make the job fun. [Wanda at Clyde's]
- The manager is cool. I have some good friends. [Roberto at T.G.I. Friday's]
- The bosses are great. They are awesome. [Sabrina at IHOP]
- It has a good social atmosphere and is very relaxed. I am mostly with people my age. [Thomas, the Hookah preparer]
- I absolutely loved working there. The owner was very flexible, and he was very loyal to the employees. He helped us a lot. [Jonathan, who worked at a restaurant in Seattle]
- I loved it. The people were good, it was a lot of fun, and I looked forward to going to work. [Torrie at a Mexican restaurant]
- I loved it. The people who owned it were family friends. It was very laid back, fun, and busy. [Betsy at a family restaurant]
- I love the restaurant. It is not corporate. It is individually owned, and I can wear whatever I want. [Todd at an upscale restaurant in Rehoboth]
- I like it a lot because I interact with people. I am a big talker as you can tell. [Mary at a fancy hotel restaurant]
- I love working at Starbuck's. It is very busy. People want their coffee immediately. I like the people who work there. [Daniel]
- The job was fun. I was with my friends. [Nancy at an ice cream parlor, essay not included]

Similarly, Larry likes the people he parked cars for at the ski resort. Margaret likes meeting people while she drives a limo. Mercedes became great friends with her customers after over 15 years of giving manicures. Alejandro loves being a doorman because he is a people person (essay not included). Quincy likes being a doorman at a hotel because the owner is good to the employees. Miles loves being a busboy because the staff is so nice, and several bartenders and servers said they love their jobs because they could talk with the customers or that they are "people persons."

Some of the respondents dislike their jobs because of the people that they have to relate to at their job. The following are some quotes from people who dislike their jobs because of the people with whom they work:

- I hated this job. No one respected me. The servers, hostess, and manager would yell at me. There was no "please." They did not take the time to get to know you. [Zack at an Outback restaurant]

- I had real problems with the manager. The first manager only wanted black people as servers, and the second manager was very inappropriate in his dealings with women, both in his touching and in his comments. [Mary at Uno's]
- I eventually disliked the job because people talked down to you. The customers did not respect you. I got written up a lot because when they were rude to me, I was rude back to them. [Samuel at an upscale restaurant in D.C.]
- I hated working there. I had to get dressed up and wear a nice white shirt. People make the job. I did not like the manager. I liked the Mexican cooks better. The customers had a lot of money and a sense of entitlement. They would order you around. [Nathan at a fancy Italian restaurant at a Colorado ski resort]
- No one liked the job because the owner was a jerk. [Daniel at a deli]

Similarly, Rhoda was not happy as a dealer in a casino because many customers were verbally abusive, and Scott hated his job at T.G.I. Friday's because the customers were all rich, spoiled yuppies who didn't tip. Nathan says it best, "People make the job." The definitive difference between those who like their job and those who do not is the experience with people, particularly management. Every person who interacts with the public encounters people who are rude or disrespectful, the critical lesson for management is that the emotional costs of these interactions can be mitigated by managers who extend trust and support to employees.

AMOUNT OF COMPENSATION

Although pay is another issue mentioned by some of the respondents, it is somewhat surprising that so few raise the issue. Carla loves working as a nanny but had to quit that job because of the low pay. Luke complains about earning minimum wage at Kroger (essay not included). Carter objects to the low wages he makes delivering pizza for Domino's. Randy protests that she made too little and never understood how the tip out worked as a busser, and Kelen, a hostess, says, "They don't pay enough. They should have a decent base pay (essay not included). A lot of hostesses have left lately." On the other hand, Fred at Friendly's states, "I did not like my boss, but I liked the money that I made"; Kwame, who was a redcap and appeared to be making close to minimum wage, reports, "I like my job. I am able to pay my bills and take care of my family."

COMPENSATION STRUCTURE (VARIABLE INCOME)

Having variable income (which is the focus of this book) often came up as a reason for liking or disliking one's job. A lot of people thrive on the competition and a variable reward system. The following are some select quotes:

- I have control over how much money I make. My tips depend upon the quality of my work. [Cam, a server at a restaurant]
- The harder you work the better your reward. [Jack, who parked cars]

In a similar vein, some of the narratives indicate that a few tipped employees like being independent and feeling they have a lot of control over their own income. Others indicate that they simply like to "hustle." There are several respondents who have had a number of jobs over the years involving tips. They seem to gravitate toward positions that provide them certain rewards. They thrive on the competition with others and within themselves. Yet, there are those who do not care for work that had variable income. A number of respondents note feeling vulnerable because of the extent to which they rely on certain shifts to ensure that their bills are paid. These feelings of vulnerability reflect an insecurity, self-consciousness, or awareness of the desire of some tippers to display a degree of superiority.

WORKING CONDITIONS

The conditions of the workplace often affected what people thought of their jobs. Many people want a low-stress, fun job that is not boring. Some of the more memorable statements include the following:

- I am the luckiest guy that I know. I play music and make a living with it. [Raymond, a musician]
- It is actually more fun than I thought it would be. It is not repetitive or boring, and I have a friend who works there. [Riley at Uno's, essay not included]

Also instructive are the comments of several pizza-delivery drivers who say that they like to listen to music when they drive and that no one bothers them. Carolyn likes being a stripper because she describes herself as an exhibitionist. Becky loves being a caddy because she loves golf. Jack loves being a ski instructor because skiing is his passion. Zack's job on a parasail boat is "awesome." Russ' job as a rafting guide is "a blast." Bob likes keeping in shape delivering furniture.

Tammy likes delivering mail because it is an outside job, and most of the sports instructors report that they like being outside. A lot of the nannies state that they love children.

However, some report poor work conditions from their perspective. Cory does not like parking cars in the winter. John does not like driving a charter bus when the weather is bad. Jean-Pierre does not like driving a cab because it is dangerous.[7] Scott has a lot of complaints about safety issues while delivering mail. Wilma does not like being a hair stylist because the work is too tiring, and Kayla a former employee of IHOP says, "The bad side was that the work got boring" (essay not included).

Many divulge that they like or dislike their job based on the flexibility in the schedule. The more people have control over or can at least affect their schedule, the happier they are in their jobs. People are in school, have other jobs, family responsibilities, or desires for extracurricular activities such as sports, art, or other hobbies.

THE NATURE OF THE WORK
Some people simply like the work. Eileen loves grooming horses because she loves horses. Steve loves dogs and loves grooming them as well. Josh loves working on cars and also likes washing them. Many of the teachers report a great deal of gratification when the students learn. The clowns love acting. Many of those selling items at sporting events say they love the sport. Several hair stylists say they love their job because they enjoy using their creativity to help clients look their best.

WHO REFUSED PAYMENT FOR PARTICIPATION
It is interesting that about a quarter of the respondents refuse the $10 payment for participation, despite exceptional efforts to encourage the acceptance of payment.[8] There are four groups who tended to refuse.

- People within one degree of separation from the interviewer often refuse the $10 payment for participation and the referral fee.
- Some respondents seem to find the research very interesting, and several report being thankful for the opportunity to vent.
- People with a lot of money tend to refuse payment. About two-thirds of those whose income is reportedly very high refuse to take the money for participation.

- Some people who are very poor refuse the $10 payment for participation. A variety of cab drivers, car valets, pizza delivery workers, and others refuse payment. In a number of these cases, they indicate that they feel that they had not done anything that would merit payment.

All in all, the following lessons are evident. Interestingly, tips do not appear to increase in accordance with inequality, and tips do not alleviate the discomfort of inequality from the perspective of the tipped employee when they are given to demonstrate status over another. Tips may in some cases serve a redistributive function, but they are not consistent with regard to social status. And, conformity to tipping norms is likewise inconsistent across work contexts. One of the principal mechanisms for fostering conformity lies within the organizational hierarchy. Management plays a critical role in establishing or virtually eliminating tipping within the work environment through policy. For example, policy determines the norm within the work context when management permits or prohibits tip jars. Innovation initiated by management or corporate policy can also affect tipping norms. For example, establishing cart corrals practically (though not entirely) eliminates the practice of tipping in the loading and carting services at some grocery and retail stores.

The evidence in this study also indicates that tips are a weak signal of quality and are not likely to serve as an effective monitoring mechanism. People appear to conform to tipping norms for social and emotional rather than strictly rational reasons. People tip to demonstrate status and for economic redistribution, and people conform to tipping norms for many of the same reasons that people conform to norms in general—because of the feelings evoked by compliance. This is best illustrated by the narratives that reveal how customers respond when confronted about inconsistencies in tipping. When confronted about a low tip or no tip, customers may argue with one another, show embarrassment, and expound on a list of complaints (that servers rarely attribute to service quality), but ultimately—this direct confrontation tends to compel conformity. Interestingly, those who are likely to gain the least from prevailing social norms that also tend to impose higher costs may resist tipping norms or are sometimes perceived as noncompliant. These narratives reveal a general trend in the experiences of tipped employees regarding demographic differences in conformity to tipping norms. The trend is that tipped employees take more note of demographic differences among clients than they notice differences in service quality. However, future research is necessary to determine the extent to which this is a perceptual error on the part of the worker or a form of resistance by those who are marginalized by stereotypes.

The factor consistently shown to facilitate reciprocity is trust. People who are extended trust are more trusting. The absence of trust in the workplace contributes to a work environment that imposes additional, unnecessary costs on employees and likely affects the experiences of customers. Establishing trust requires that those with power in the organization build trust, primarily by responsibly extending trust to subordinates (see Miller 1993). Consequently, management is enhanced when consequences are consistently applied and workers are afforded a degree of control over their work environment. Management strategies that overuse authority are likely to be resisted, and providing employees with effective training and support is more likely to facilitate a work environment that compensates for the emotional cost of their labor. Management should also consider the value added by confronting stereotypes that impact job performance. Growing a business starts with investing in employees, and those employees also have to recognize the potential in every opportunity.

NOTES

1. For the modern argument to abolish tipping, see Margalioth (2006).

2. A June 2002 telephone survey conducted for Associated Press asks, "In this country the practice of tipping for various kinds of services is widespread—for waiters in restaurants, for hairdressers and barbers, for taxis and so on. How do you feel about the practice of tipping—that it is a fair way to compensate people who perform various services, or that it's unfair to customers to expect them to pay extra for services they already paid for?" Seventy-three percent of respondents conclude it is fair.

3. For example, see Ruth J. Katz, "Tip Sheet: What to Give the Super, What to Slip the Handyman, and other Gratuitous Advice for the Holiday Season," *New York*, December 18, 1989; and Cindy Loose, "Tipping Points," *Washington Post*, April 16, 2006, p.1.

4. Lynn (2006) finds in a national telephone survey that knowledge about what is the proper tip for waiters and waitresses varies by region.

5. Lynn (2004) using a national telephone survey finds that blacks tip less than whites and are more likely to give a fixed amount and argues that blacks tip less than whites because they have less knowledge about the social norms of tipping. He suggests addressing this through educational campaigns. However, given the consistent findings that blacks are less likely to be tipped in virtually every circumstance, perhaps it is rational behavior not to participate in a norm that imposes undue costs. It might be more effectual to invest in educational campaigns aimed at reducing discrimination.

6. The National Opinion Research Center–General Social Survey shows that 57% of Americans were completely or very satisfied with their jobs, and 30% were fairly satisfied with their jobs in 2006.

7. Some of the cab drivers are studies in contrast. Some indicate that the tips are not that important to them; while others cite how hard they worked for tips. A few report that they enjoy hanging out at the airport or hotel waiting in line listening to music and talking to other drivers. They seem to work very long hours but contend that they are happy to be in situations in which they are not earning any money at all (the down time).

8. The last question of the interview when conducted by telephone is as follows: "What address should I use to send the $10 as a thank you for your participation?" If a person says no, two follow-up attempts to get participants to accept the $10 payment are made by the interviewer.

References

Altman, Morris. 2006. *Handbook of Contemporary Behavioral Economics: Foundations and Developments*. New York: M.E. Sharpe.

Aronson, Elliot. 2003. *The Social Animal*. Ninth Edition. New York: Worth Publishers.

Asch, Solomon. 1955. "Opinions and Social Pressure." *Scientific American* 193: 31–35.

Ayres, Ian, Fredrick Vars, and Nasser Zakariya. Forthcoming. "To Insure Prejudice: Racial Disparities in Taxicab Tipping." Yale Law School, Public Law Working Paper No. 50; and Yale Law & Economics research Paper No. 276. Avaliable at SSRN: http://papers.ssrn.com/sol3/papers.cfm?abstract_id=401201. Site last visited on February 2, 2010.

Azar, Ofer. 2004. "What Sustains Social Norms and How They Evolve? The Case of Tipping." *Journal of Economic Behavior and Organization* 54(1): 49–64.

Azar, Ofer. 2005. "Who Do We Tip and Why? An Empirical Investigation." *Applied Economics* 37(16): 1871–1879.

Azar, Ofer. 2007a. "Why Pay Extra? Tipping and the Importance of Social Norms and Feelings in Economic Theory." *Journal of Socio-Economics* 36(2): 250–265.

Azar, Ofer. 2007b. "The Social Norm of Tipping: A Review." *Journal of Applied Social Psychology* 37(2): 380–402.

Azar, Ofer. 2008. "The Impact of Tipping on Firm Strategy and Market Outcomes." *Journal of Strategic Management Education* 4.

Bearman, Peter. 2005. *Doormen*. Chicago: University of Chicago Press.

Ben-Ner, Avner and Louis Putterman. 1998. *Economics, Values, and Organization*. Cambridge: Cambridge University Press.

Ben-Zion, U. and E. Karni. 1977. "Tip Payments and the Quality of Service." In O.C. Ashenfelter and W.E. Oates (Eds.) *Essays in Labor Market Analysis*. New York: Wiley.

Berkowitz, A. 2004. "An Overview of the Social Norms Approach." In Lederman et al. (Eds.) *Changing the Culture of College Drinking.* Westport: Greenwood Press.

Bicchieri, Christina. 2006. *The Grammar of Society: The Nature and Dynamics of Social Norms.* New York: Cambridge University Press.

Billing, Yvonne Due, and Mats Alvesson. 1994. *Gender, Managers, and Organizations.* New York: Walker de Gruyter & Co.

Binmore, Ken. 2005. *Natural Justice.* Oxford: Oxford University Press.

Bodvarsson, Orn B. and William A. Gibson. 1997. "Economics and Restaurant Gratuities: Determining Tip Rates." *American Journal of Economics and Sociology* 56: 187–203.

Borsari, B. and K. Carey. 2003. "Descriptive and Injunctive Norms in College Drinking: A Meta-Analytical Integration." *Journal of Studies on Alcohol* 64(3): 331.

Bowles, Samuel, Herbert Gintis, and Melissa Osborne Groves. 2005. *Unequal Chances.* Princeton: Princeton University Press.

Bradley-Engen, Mindy S., and Jeffery T. Ulmer. 2009. "Social Worlds of Stripping: The Processual Orders of Exotic Dance." *The Sociological Quarterly* 50: 29–60.

Brenner, M. 2001. *Tipping for Success: Secrets for How to Get in and Get Great Service.* Sherman Oaks, CA: Brenmark House.

Butler, Suellen and James K. Skipper, Jr. 1981. "Working for Tips: an Examination of Trust and Reciprocity in a Secondary Relationship of the Restaurant Organization." *The Sociological Quarterly* 22(1): 15–27.

Chapkis, Wendy. 1997. *Live Sex Acts: Women Performing Erotic Labor.* New York: Routledge.

Cialdini, R., R. Reno, and C. Kallgren. 1990. "A Focus Theory of Normative Conduct: Recycling the Concepts of Norms to Reduce Littering in Public Places." *Journal of Personality and Social Psychology* 58: 1015–1026.

Cobble, Dorothy Sue. 1991. *Dishing it Out: Waitresses and Their Unions in the Twentieth Century.* Chicago: University of Chicago Press.

Coleman, James S. 1990. *Foundations of Social Theory.* Cambridge MA: Harvard University Press.

Conlin, M., T. O'Donoghue, and M. Lynn. 2003. "The Norm of Restaurant Tipping." *Journal of Economic Behavior and Organization* 52: 297–321.

Dawson, Patrick. 2003. *Reshaping Change: A Processual Approach.* New York: Routledge.

Ehrenreich, Barbara (2002). *Nickel and Dimed: On (Not) Getting By in America.* New York: MacMillan.

Ellickson, Robert C. 1991. *Order Without Law: How Neighbors Settle Disputes.* Cambridge MA: Harvard University Press.

Farnham, Brian. 2000. "Tipping Points: If It's True that Money Talks, What are Your Tips Saying About You?" *New York.* August 14, 2000.

Farr, Kathryn. 2004. *Sex Trafficking: The Global Market in Women and Children.* New York: Worth.

REFERENCES

Fehr, Ernst, Urs Fischbacher, and Simon Gächter. 2002. "Strong Reciprocity, Human Cooperation, and the Enforcement of Social Norms." *Human Nature* 13: 1–25.

Frank, Katherine. 2002. *G-Strings and Sympathy: Strip Club Regulars and Male Desire*. Durham, NC: Duke University Press.

Gerson, J. and K. Peiss. 1985. "Boundaries, Negotiation, Consciousness: Reconceptualizing Gender Relations." *Social Problems* 32(4): 317–331.

Groer, Annie. 2006. "For Tipping at Home, There are no Givens." *Washington Post*. September 18. Page H1.

Gutek, Barbara. 1985. *Sex and the Workplace*. San Francisco: Jossey-Bass.

Hemenway, D. 1993. *Prices and Choices: Microeconomic Vignettes*. Lanham: University Press of America.

Henrich, Joe, Robert Boyd, Samuel Bowles, Ernst Fehr, and Herbert Gintis, eds. 2004. *Foundations of Human Sociality: Economic Experiments and Ethnographic Evidence in 15 Small-Scale Societies*. Oxford: Oxford University Press.

Hochschild, Arlie Russell. 1983. *The Managed Heart: Commercialization of Human Feeling*. Berkeley: University of California Press.

Honey, M. 1987. "The Interview as Text: Hermeneutics Considered as a Model for Analyzing the Clinically Informed Research Interview." *Human Development* 30: 69–82.

Hume, [1739]. 1978. *A Treatise of Human Nature*. Oxford: Oxford University Press.

Jacob, Nancy L. and Alfred L. Page. 1980. "Production, Information Costs, and Economic Organization: The Buyer Monitoring Case." *American Economic Review* 76(4): 728–741.

Kandori, Michihiro, George Mailath, and Rafael Rob. 1993. "Learning, Mutation, and Long-Run Equilibria in Games." *Econometrica* 61: 29–56.

Kelley, Robin. 1994. *Race Rebels: Culture, Politics, and the Black Working Class*. New York: Free Press.

LaPointe, Eleanor. 1992. "Relationships with Waitresses: Gendered Social Distance in Restaurant Hierarchies." *Qualitative Sociology* 15(4): 377–393.

Leodoro, Gina and Michael Lynn. 2007. "The Effect of Server Posture on the Tips of Whites and Blacks." *Journal of Applied Social Psychology* 37: 201–209.

Lewis, David. 1969. *Convention: A Philosophical Study*. Cambridge MA: Harvard University Press.

Liepe-Levinson, Katherine. 2002. *Strip Show: Performances of Gender and Desire*. New York: Routledge.

Loe, Meika. 1996. "Working for Men: At the Intersection of Power, Gender, and Sexuality." *Sociological Inquiry* 66(4): 399–421.

Lynn, Michael. 1988. "The Effects of Alcohol Consumption on Tipping." *Personality and Social Psychology Bulletin* 14(1): 87–91.

Lynn, Michael. 2004. "Black-White Differences in Tipping Various Service Providers." *Journal of Applied Social Psychology* 34(11): 2261–2271.

Lynn, Michael. 2006. "Geodemographic Differences in Knowledge About the Restaurant Tipping Norm." *Journal of Applied Social Psychology* 36(3): 740–750.

Lynn, Michael and Ann Lynn. 2004. "National Values and Tipping Customs: A Replication and Extension." *Hospitality and Tourism Research* 28(3): 356–364.

Lynn, Michael and Michael McCall. 2000. "Gratitude and Gratuity: A Meta-Analysis of Research on the Service-Tipping Relationship." *Journal of Socio-Economics* 29: 203–214.

Lynn, Michael and Tony Simons. 2000. "Predictors of Male and Female Servers' Average Tip Earnings." *Journal of Applied Social Psychology* 30: 241–252.

Macdonald, Cameron Lynne, and Carmen Sirianni. 1996. *Working in the Service Society*. Philadelphia: Temple University Press.

Maines, David R. 2003. "Interactionism's Place." *Symbolic Interaction* 26: 5–18.

Mann, Leon. 1969. "Queue Culture: The Waiting Line as a Social System." *American Journal of Sociology* 75(3): 340.

Margalioth, Yoram. 2006. "The Case Against Tipping." Paper presented at the International Conference on Labor Issues. Eilat, Israel.

Massey, Douglas S., and Nancy A. Denton. *American Apartheid: Segregation and the Making of the Underclass*. Cambridge, MA: Harvard University Press.

Merton, Robert. 1949. *Social Theory and Social Structure*. Glencoe: Free Press.

Milgram, Stanley. 1965. "Some Conditions of Obedience and Disobedience to Authority." *Human Relations* 18: 57–75.

Miller, Gary. 1993. *Managerial Dilemmas: The Political Economy of Hierarchy*. Cambridge: Cambridge University Press.

Perkins, H. 2003. *The Social Norms Approach to Preventing School and College Age Substance Abuse*. San Francisco: Jossey-Bass.

Rind, Bruce, and Prashant Bordia. 1995. "Effects of Server's 'Thank You' and Personalizing on Restaurant Tipping." *Journal of Applied Social Psychology* 25: 745–751.

Rocha, Rene R., and Rodolfo Espino. 2008. "Racial Threat, Residential Segregation, and the Policy Attitudes of Anglos." *Political Research Quarterly* 62(2): 415–426.

Rose-Ackerman, Susan. 1998. "Bribes and Gifts." In *Economics, Values, and Organization*, pp. 296–328. Edited by Avner Ben-Ner and Louis Putterman. Cambridge, MA: Cambridge University Press.

Roth, Alvin E. 1985. *Toward a Focal Point Theory of Bargaining in Game-Theoretic Models of Bargaining*. New York: Cambridge University Press.

Samuelson, Larry. 1997. *Evolutionary Games and Equilibrium Selection*. Cambridge MA: MIT Press.

Schram, Sanford, and Brian Caterino. 2006. *Making Political Science Matter: Debating Knowledge, Research, and Method*. New York: NYU Press.

Schwartz, Zvi. 1997. "The Economics of Tipping: Tips, Profits, and the Market's Demand-Supply Equilibrium." *Tourism Economics* 3(3): 265–279.

Segrave, K. 1998. *Tipping: An American Social History of Gratuities*. Jefferson, NC: McFarland.

Seiter, John. S., and Robert H. Gass. 2005. "The Effect of Patriotic Messages on Restaurant Tipping." *Journal of Applied Social Psychology* 35: 1197–1205.

Seltzer, R. 2005. Nonresponse in Telephone Surveys: The Reporting of Outcome Measures. American Statistical Association, *2005 ASA Proceedings*.

Shannon, Claude E. 1949. *A Mathematical Theory of Communication*. Urbana: University of Illinois Press.

Shapiro, Thomas. 2004. *The Hidden Cost of Being African American*. Oxford: Oxford University Press.

Shea, Shawn. 1998. *Psychiatric Interviewing: The Art of Understanding*. New York: Saunders.

Sherif, M. 1935. "An Experimental Study of Stereotypes." *Journal of Abnormal and Social Psychology* 29(4).

Sisk, David E. and Edward C. Gallick. 1985. "Tips and Commissions: A Study in Economic Contracting." Federal Trade Commission Bureau of Economics Working Paper #125.

Spradley, James P., and Brenda J. Mann. 1975. *The Cocktail Waitress: Woman's Work in a Man's World*. New York: Wiley.

Star, N. 1988. *The International Guide to Tipping*. New York: Berkeley.

Strauss, Anselm. 1993. *Continual Permutations of Action*. New York: Aldine de Gruyter.

Wärneryd, Karl. 1994. "Transaction Cost, Institutions, and Evolution." *Journal of Economic Behavior and Organization* 25: 219–239.

Webster, Murray. 1975. *Actions and Actors: Principles of Social Psychology*. Cambridge: Winthrop Press.

West, C. and D. Zimmerman. 1987. "Doing Gender." *Gender and Society* 1(2): 125–151.

Weitzer, Ronald. 2005. "The Growing Moral Panic Over Prostitution and Sex Trafficking." *The Criminologist* 30(5): 1–4.

Weitzer, Ronald. 2009. "Sociology of Sex Work." *Annual Review of Sociology* 35: 213–234.

Young, H. Peyton. 1998. "Conventional Contracts." *Review of Economic Studies* 65: 773–792.

Zimbardo, P.G. and Lieppe, M.R. 1991. *The Psychology of Attitude Change And Social Influence*. Philadelphia: Temple University Press.

Index

adult entertainment, 194, 207, 214, 218, 219
agency. *See* contractual agency

baksheesh, viii
bar-back, 39, 40, 42, 44, 46, 47, 52, 53, 62. *See also* bar porter
barista, 81
bartender, viii, xv, xxiii, xxx, 2, 6–8, 10–11, 13, 19–23, 26–31, 34–47, 51–68, 75–76, 81, 92, 207, 213, 215–216, 222, 258–260
Bell, Joshua, 221
bellhop, 89–90, 131, 251, 253
blue collar, 169, 251
burlesque, 208, 219–220
busser, viii, 2, 8–10, 14, 22, 27–28, 31, 33–36, 46–47, 49, 51–52, 55–57, 60–63, 67–68, 70, 75, 93, 101, 202, 253–261, 258, 263

cabaret, 206, 208, 218, 220, 253
chain restaurants, 5, 11–12, 15, 17, 24, 258

cocktail waitress, 39, 44, 46–47, 69
compensation structure, 261, 264
contractual agency, 208, 267
cosmetology, 149, 151, 154, 161, 228

doorman, 46, 90, 103, 135, 252, 262

emotional labor, 15, 24, 32, 103, 119, 219, 254, 267
equity, xv–xvi, xix, xx, 103, 266
etiquette, 88, 105, 126–127, 143, 249–250, 255, 259

fairness, xxiv, 8, 18, 28, 30, 36–37, 70–71, 76, 135–136, 140, 151, 172, 201, 209, 250, 261–261, 267
family eateries, 18, 20
family entertainment, 195, 206
food runner, viii, xxix, 2, 6–9, 11, 13, 20–23, 26–28, 30–31, 33–36, 51, 53–56, 59, 65–67, 76, 130, 202, 258–261

gratuity, xv, xvi–xix, xx–xxi, xxv, 79, 183, 187, 191, 241, 249–250

275

hookah, 73, 78, 107, 262

incentive, xx, 53, 222, 229, 254–255
inducement (bribe), xv, 14, 87, 257
institutionalization, xvi, xxii, xxvi, 117, 249

lobby attendant, 89–91, 94, 103, 193, 243

management, xxi, xxiv, 6, 13–17, 24, 66–67, 69, 86, 89, 91, 117, 119, 124, 207, 218–219, 235, 245, 254, 263, 266–267

norms, xxi; attitudinal, xxi, xxvi, 178, 250; behavioral, xxi, 206; conformity, xxi–xxii, 36, 79, 119, 206, 221, 231, 241, 254, 266; contextual, xxvi, 103, 191, 208, 218; economic, xxiii–xxiv, 2, 14, 178; enforcement, xxii–xxiii, 36, 88, 117, 119, 179; internalization, xxiii; professional, 81, 161, 167, 181, 183, 187, 253; structural, 116–117, 119, 150, 179, 183, 185, 195, 196, 206, 208, 218. *See also* social norms; social regulatory regime

officiant, 179, 181
organizational structure, 69–71, 117, 208, 218

porter: airport (skycap or redcap), 120, 121; bar, 39; hotel, 90. *See also* bellhop; lobby attendant
processual order, 208, 218–220

reciprocity, xxiv, 14–15, 257–258, 267

sample, xxx–xxi; convenience, xxi; random, xxx–xxi; snowball, xxi
semi-structured interview, xxvi–xxxii; advantages, xxxii; limitations, xxxii
social norm (social code), xv, xxi, 36, 117, 185, 196, 249
social pressure, xx, 24, 231, 241,
social regulatory regime, xxii, 88, 117, 119, 218, 249
socialization, xxiii, 17, 46, 46–47, 69, 90, 161, 241, 250
sommelier (wine steward), 73
Springsteen, Bruce, 230

tipping, xv; customs, xvi–xix; durability, xxv, 79, 183, 187, 191, 241, 249–250; opposition, xx, 249; proponents, xx–xi. *See also* gratuity
tip out (distribution system), viii, ix, 6–15, 17, 19–23, 26–27, 29, 31, 34–36, 45, 47, 50–54, 56, 58–60, 63–64, 66–68, 70, 74, 76, 149, 152, 202, 207–208, 213–214, 216, 218, 253, 258–260
transaction cost, xxiii
trust, xxi–xxiv, 6, 14, 20, 24, 35–37, 40, 46, 50, 55, 76, 98, 129–130, 144, 216–218, 235, 258, 263, 267

vail, xxiv, 249

white collar, 169

About the Authors

Richard Seltzer is professor of political science at Howard University. His most recent books with The Rowman & Litttlefield Publishing Group are *Experiencing Racism: Exploring Discrimination through the Eyes of College Students* (with Nicole Johnson) and *Contemporary Controversies and the American Racial Divide* (with Robert Smith).

Holona LeAnne Ochs is assistant professor of political science at Lehigh University. She received her doctorate in political science from the University of Kansas, her master's degree in clinical marriage and family therapy, and bachelor's degree in psychology from Kansas State University. She was awarded the Howard Baumgartel Peace and Justice Award in 2007 and has published her research on social justice and governance in journals including *Justice Research and Policy Journal of Public Affairs Education, Policy Studies Journal, Social Science Quarterly,* and *American Politics Research.*